INDONESIA

SUMATRA, JAVA, BALI, LOMBOK, SULAWESI

Authors:
David E. F. Henley, James J. Fox, Putu Davies,
Anthony J. S. Reid, Yohanni Johns, Robyn Maxwell,
G. Adrian Horridge, Colin P. Groves, Berthold Schwarz

An Up-to-date travel guide
with 118 color photos
and 24 maps

Dear Reader: Being up-to-date is the main goal of the Nelles series. Our correspondents help keep us abreast of the latest developments in the travel scene, while our cartographers see to it that maps are also kept completely current. However, as the travel world is constantly changing, we cannot guarantee that all the information contained in our books is always valid. Should you come across a discrepancy, please contact us at: Nelles Verlag, Schleissheimer Str. 371 b, 80935 Munich, Germany, tel. (089) 3571940, fax. (089) 35719430, e-mail: Nelles.Verlag@T-Online.de

Note: Distances and measurements, including temperatures, used in this guide are metric. For conversion information, please see the *Guidelines* section of this book.

LEGEND

▨ Public or Significant Building	Lebak	Place Mentioned in Text	▬ National Border
■ Hotel	✳	Place of Interest	— Administrativ Border
● Restaurant	◤	International Airport	═ Expressway
▨ ○ Shopping Center, Market	◄	Airfield	═ Principal Highway
♨ Buddhist Temple	♣	National Park	═ Main Road
☙ Hindu Temple	☀	Beach	═ Provincial Road
✚ Church	⑥	Route Number	— Track
☾ Mosque	Mt. Gede 2958	Mountain Summit (Height in Meters)	Railway
			\ 18 / Distance in Kilometers

INDONESIA
Sumatra, Java, Bali, Lombok, Sulawesi
© Nelles Verlag GmbH, 80935 München
    All rights reserved

Third Revised Edition 2000
ISBN 3-88618-085-9
Printed in Slovenia

Publisher:	Günter Nelles	**Cartography:**	Nelles Verlag GmbH
Managing Editor:	Berthold Schwarz	**Color**	
Project Editor:	David Henley	**Separation:**	Priegnitz, Munich
Editor:	Rebekah Rollo	**Printed by:**	Gorenjski Tisk

- T06 -

TABLE OF CONTENTS

FEATURES

GUIDELINES

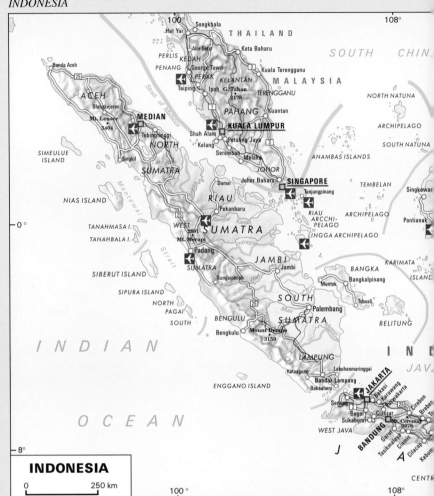

INDONESIA

0 _____ 250 km

LIST OF MAPS

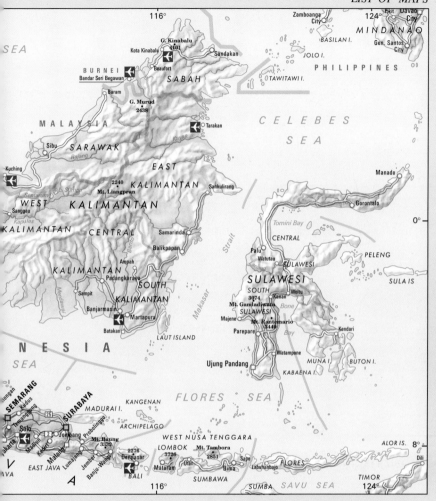

INDONESIA

AND THE WORLD

Indonesia is a strange blank in the modern world's imagination. Other Asian nations – Japan, China, India, Pakistan – have widespread popular stereotypes. But is there a stereotypical Indonesian? What does he or she look like? A barefoot peasant in a coolie hat? A tatooed tribesman with blowpipe and jungle knife? A poised dancer in batik and gold? A braided general? The images are too many, too disparate and too vague. The landscapes which could stand for Indonesia are just as ambiguous. On a postcard, the fabled beaches of Bali look indistinguishable from those of Jamaica or Tahiti, while temples, rice paddies and rain forests seem to the layman to blur with the backdrops of tropical Asia as a whole.

Why is it that foreign images of this great and beautiful archipelago are so confused? After all, Indonesia is a major nation by any standards. Its 13,600 islands span fully one-eighth of the circumference of the earth and in 2000 its 209 million citizens made it the world's fourth most populous country. Indonesia also has an impressive and surprising history; parts of it have been civilized longer than Europe. As early as the 16th century Portugal, Spain and Holland were fighting for control of the country's spice trade and Indonesia was the very first Asian country to free itself, in 1945, from colonial rule through a national revolution.

Yet some of the major reasons for the country's present obscurity are also historical. Indonesia was not part of the great global empires of Portugal, Spain,

Preceding pages: The magic and mystery of Borobudur. A traditional Kecak dance on Bali. Left: A detail from Borobudur.

Britain and France, but the sole substantial jewel in the colonial crown of the tiny Netherlands. Between the 17th century and the Second World War, it was remote from the mainstream of world history, a strange remnant both of old Asia and of Dutch overseas power, contributing little to the world except the sugar, coffee, rubber and other tropical crops upon which the diet and industry of Europe and America came to depend. The Japanese occupation (1942-45) released a tide of revolution which swept away the placid, old Dutch East Indies and proclaimed in their place a volatile new nation calling itself Indonesia, a term then familiar only to a few oriental scholars. For two brief decades, the infant state projected itself into the international spotlight, confronting the superpowers and posturing as the leader of world anti-colonialism. Then in 1965, the assertive order fell victim to the tension and chaos which its own romantic radicalism had produced at home. A military regime picked up the pieces and ruled until 1998; stability and economic development always placed above either personal freedoms or human rights. For the last quarter of a century, Indonesia has once more been waiting in the wings of history, a distant presence remembered only in fleeting press reports of reconstruction and repression. Of the developed countries, only Australia, the southern neighbor, retains a slightly more complete picture of the enigmatic archipelago.

There are other, equally important reasons why single images and stereotypes of Indonesia refuse to come into sharp focus. One is the country's vast and profound complexity. Of all of the countries that exist today, only India and perhaps China can match Indonesia in either the number of cultural influences which it has been exposed to throughout the centuries or in the diversity of distinct traditions still present in its various regions. Every one of the major world religions,

for example, has found its way here, and each is still represented by living communities as well as monuments to the dead. Throughout its history every ideology and every political system, from the nation-state to the Islamic state, has had its Indonesian exponents.

The final difficulty of trying to find universal symbols for Indonesia is that many of those symbols which mean most to Indonesians themselves are impenetrable to outsiders. At first encounter, some seem so alien as to defy memory itself. Few untrained Westerners, for instance, can recall a passage of the aimless, haunting music of the Javanese *gamelan* orchestra. Its rippling gongs run scales to which Western minds are not attuned, its interlocking rhythms find no echo in Western hearts. In the same vein, to someone familiar neither with the Indian gods and heroes nor with their In-

Above: Traveling by bemo – a popular means of transportation. Right: Women replanting seedlings in a Lombok rice paddy.

donesian mutations, the filigreed, double-jointed shadow-puppets of the *wayang kulit* epic, good and evil alike, may be too strange to evoke any reaction other than curiosity. Even when the outsider has learned to love such things for reasons other than their mystery, they retain an elusive quality which makes them difficult to recall or appreciate outside their native Indonesian context.

Pinned to the wall of a European living room, the shadow puppet is an absurdity; reduced to a deathless cassette and activated at the touch of a button, the *gamelan* loses all its life. But put them together in the hot Javanese night, with the buzz of the audience and the rich, sharp smell of clove cigarettes, and they generate the kind of magic which all travel guides celebrate but none can begin to evoke. A startling number of visitors agree that Indonesia, more than any other land, is an experience which cannot be wrapped up and taken home. This sensual, transient quality, this powerful and obscure spirit of place, is absolutely intrinsic to Indone-

sia, and can best be understood by experiencing it in person. It is perhaps the strongest reason for going there.

A Pattern of Islands

On a map, Indonesia's composite geography seems to mirror its cultural complexity. The pattern of contorted islands is as intricate and strange as a shadow puppet. Some of the island names – Java, Sumatra, Ambon, Timor – are half-familiar from yellowed textbooks, vague notes on the margins of European history, the stuff of forgotten trade disputes and diplomatic wrangles. Others, victims of the nationalist passion for renaming, no longer carry any international associations. Squat Kalimantan, the largest member of the archipelago, is what Joseph Conrad and Somerset Maugham knew as Borneo. Spidery Sulawesi, in the center, was the melodious Celebes. Nusa Tenggara was the Lesser Sundas, the small islands east of Bali that stretch from Lombok to Timor. Maluku was the Moluccas, the legendary spice islands. Irian Jaya is the western half of remote New Guinea, where Melanesia and the Pacific begin; Britain and Holland divided New Guinea between them by a gentleman's agreement, with the result that while the east is now independent as Papua New Guinea, the west is part of Jakarta's Dutch inheritance. The full extent of that inheritance, as every Indonesian schoolchild knows, stretches "from Sabang to Merauke," from the northern tip of Sumatra to the Papuan border, a span much greater than America's "sea to shining sea." Superimposed upon Europe, Indonesia would reach from Ireland to the Caspian Sea. Indonesians call their country *tanah air*, "earth and water," and most of its vastness – more than three million square kilometers – is sea. However, even the dry land amounts to some 1.9 million square kilometers, an area larger than Tibet or Mexico.

The most striking regular feature of the archipelago is the graceful curve of its southern margin, a smooth and almost

15

continuous arc formed by Sumatra, Java and Nusa Tenggara. This barrier marks a geological battleground upon which two vast continental plates converge. Away to the northwest, a different section of the same front has thrown up the mighty Himalayas; its continuation can be seen sweeping down from Tibet, to Sumatra and through Burma and the Andaman Islands. At the margin of the Indian ocean the granite raft upon which both India and Australia float is forced downwards, beneath the stronger Asian plate of which most of Indonesia is a half-drowned extension. The edge of Asia folds and buckles into the mountain range which is the backbone of both Sumatra and Java; beneath it, the sunken edge of Indo-Australia melts in the burning depths, spewing up magma to feed dozens of great volcanoes. The volcanic highlands of Indonesia's southwestern rim stand like a giant dyke, shielding the gentle, shallow

Above: Trying to stay dry in the heavy monsoon rainfall in Java.

16

seas around Malaysia and Kalimantan from the storms of the Indian Ocean, which stretches deep and empty from the equator to Antarctica. East of Java, the archipelago crumbles gradually away into a confetti pattern of tiny islands.

Sun and Rain

Nature has generally smiled upon Indonesia, though not everywhere with equal sweetness. Straddling the equator, the archipelago is perpetually hot and reliably wet; except for Timor and adjacent parts of Nusa Tenggara, which suffer through very dry summers. Everywhere there are two fairly distinct seasons. Between November and April, cold, heavy winter air spilling out of the distant Asian steppes sets up a wind system which brings a wet monsoon sweeping down across the South China Sea. Veering west to blow from the northwest as it crosses the equator, the monsoon unleashes drenching rain wherever it touches land. The rest of the year is hotter and drier, but west of Bali an entire month without rain is a rarity even in the so-called dry season. The seasonal distinction increases from west to east and from north to south. However, local factors like topography and altitude often have as much influence on the weather, if not more, as the seasons. At sea level, temperatures seldom stray outside a range of 22-32°C, day or night, year round. This is actually not as hot as, say, an Australian summer; but because air humidity never falls below 50 percent and often approaches total saturation, it feels much hotter. However, the heat eases rapidly with altitude, and Indonesia has plenty of mountains. On a windswept pass in the highlands of Java, the temperature may fall almost to freezing point in the early hours, while the summits of Irian Jaya are cold enough to cradle the only permanent icecap in the eastern tropics.

Heavy rainfall means heavy cloud cover. In many areas, the average day follows a predictable weather cycle. After a bright start, clouds build up steadily all morning, only to empty themselves in an ineluctable afternoon downpour.

Especially in highland areas, the typical Indonesian skyscape is not the luminous blue which newcomers may expect, but an overcast sky more menacing than ever glowered upon Manchester or Boston, under which the vivid tropical colors shine with a dark, suppressed intensity. At night electrical storms often light up the horizon for hours at a time. It is the weather that is largely responsible for the unexpectedly dark, almost gothic, aspect of Indonesia's beauty.

Man and Nature

Of the hundreds of volcanoes in Indonesia, 61 are still officially listed as active. When the infamous island-mountain of Krakatau exploded in the Sunda Strait in 1883, it destroyed 165 villages and killed more than 36,000 people. But the volcanoes are bringers of life as well as death. Their ash and lava often supply vital minerals which can make the soil almost permanently fertile, even in the face of 3000 mm of rainfall per year. This is why the greatest concentrations of population in Indonesia cluster at the very feet of the deadly mountains.

In its virgin state, virtually all of Indonesia looks fertile enough. In most areas the natural vegetation is, or would be, lush, tropical rain forest towering 40 meters above the ground. Though it shrinks daily, Indonesia's rain forest area amounts to one-tenth of the world total. The presence of rain forest, however, reflects only heat and rainfall, never the suitability of the underlying land for sustained agriculture.

Often these "green cathedrals" are founded upon an acidic wreck of a soil, and survive only by their highly evolved ability to recycle nutrients before they can be washed down into the lifeless earth. Over vast tracts of Sumatra, Kalimantan and the eastern islands, agriculture has traditionally been possible only by the technique based on the *ladang*. A *ladang* is a crude clearing slashed and burned out of the forest. It can be planted with subsistence crops, but within two or three years the unprotected soil is depleted of nutrients and the farmer must open a new *ladang* elsewhere. The Dutch called this *roofbouw*, or "robber-farming." Constrained by the forest's own ability to regenerate itself after the nutrient theft, it could ultimately only support a sparse population.

The fertile volcanic soils of Java and Bali, on the other hand, as well as an ideal geographic position between the droughts of Nusa Tenggara and the perpetual rain of the equatorial islands, made possible not only much longer cultivation periods on dry fields, but also a completely different and much more intensive agricultural technique: the *sawah* or irrigated rice paddy. This ecological con-

trast is the foundation for the classic distinction which has been drawn between "Inner Indonesia" – Java and Bali – and the "Outer Islands" – the rest of the archipelago. The dichotomy is far from perfect, as there are many ancient outposts of irrigated farming in the Outer Islands; however, it does identify a crucial bifurcation in Indonesian history. Java and Bali have become teeming agrarian islands, more densely populated than Holland or Japan but incomparably poorer; on the other hand Sumatra and Kalimantan have remained rich, empty frontiers for the planter, the logger and the miner. To examine just how this division occurre, one must switch from natural history to human history.

There have probably been people in Indonesia for as long as there have been people at all. More than 1.8 million years

Above: An impressive volcanic eruption on Krakatau. Right: Taking a shower. Far right: The unmistakable Melanesian physical traits.

ago, members of the near-human species *Homo erectus*, which ranged from Africa to China, lived in Java. The discovery of their skulls in 1891 threw Indonesia into the center of the then bitter debate over human evolution and the "missing link."

We still do not know whether the Javanese *Homo erectus* contributed any of his genes to *Homo sapiens*, of whom the first Indonesian evidence dates from some 40,000 years ago. The earliest *Homo sapiens* populations were small hunter-gatherer communities sparsely scattered across the forests and beaches of islands which fused and parted as the sea level oscillated to the slow rhythm of the Ice Age. These people were probably small, dark-skinned and fuzzy-haired, and remnants of their race survive as the "Negrito" populations of remote parts of the Philippines and the Malay peninsula. But in Indonesia proper, except for Irian Jaya and the far eastern islands, all previous populations have been obliterated by newcomers, whom scholars call Austronesians.

The Austronesian Story

As a physical type, the Austronesian group is characterized by the faces which we associate with Malaysians, Filipinos and Polynesians: brown skin, thick black hair, round eyes. They must have originated on the mainland of China, but there is no trace of them there now; they have become an archipelagic race. Their great odyssey probably began around 7000 years ago – a very short time by the standards of prehistory – with the colonization of Taiwan. Until recently it was believed that the immigrants entered Indonesia from the Malay peninsula, but now it seems that their progress was seaborne from the beginning: from China via Taiwan to the Philippines and beyond. Over the millennia, ever-improving sailcraft dispersed them across the warm oceans like floating mangrove seeds, and by about A.D. 1000 Austronesian colonists had occupied tropical islands and coasts over more than half the circumference of the earth, from Madagascar to Easter Island. Indonesia lay at the center of this vast distribution.

Besides their nautical skills, the Austronesian migrants had another secret of success: agriculture. The peoples which they displaced were slaves to nature; the newcomers understood and could predict, and therefore control and modify the effects of nature. It used to be thought that the immigrants were dry *ladang* farmers, and that they had no rice at first. Recent research, however, suggests that the Austronesians not only brought rice with them, but also grew it in wet fields, perhaps on the naturally irrigated flood plains of major rivers – not true *sawah*, but certainly its ancestor. The need to seek out such special environments may help explain the extraordinary speed of the expansion. If this is so, then today's *ladang* is not an ancient relic, but a recent adaptation.

What kind of people were these distant ancestors of the modern Indonesians? Their societies were of the sort usually described as "tribal." They had no or-

19

ganized states, and lived in small communities held together by custom rather than law. They were very conscious of individual status, but took charisma and achievement as well as descent and kinship into account when according it; purely hereditary offices were rare. Slavery was then universally practiced, though of a milder type than was practiced in Europe. The position of women was relatively fortunate; in particular, women were often credited with magical and religious authority. Untouched by the great religions, the Austronesians adhered to a complex variety of beliefs based upon the souls of living and dead people, plants and objects, upon the stages of life and agricultural cycles, and upon such paired concepts as male-female, old-young, and earth-sky, interpreted as cosmic dichotomies. Life was heavily spiced with ritual. Some rituals demanded human sacrifice and led to internecine war. Another very Austronesian ritual practice was the "second funeral" in which the ashes or decomposed corpse of a long-dead person was exhumed and reinterred in order to insure the soul's proper "send-off" into the Hereafter.

The Austronesians generally fashioned their clothes, their homes and many of their tools from plant material: wood, bamboo, rattan, palm leaves, pounded bark, cotton and hemp. Even their shrines and temples were usually wooden, although monolithic monuments were occasionally carved in stone. The material culture had a throw-away quality: since even houses were relatively cheaply built and easily replaced, people tended to spend more time decorating their own bodies – tattooing, tooth filing – than beautifying their environment. However, many Austronesian groups became accomplished weavers, producing superb

textiles for use in ritual and trade. Metalwork was introduced around the time of Christ, and skilled blacksmiths were soon found in the remotest villages; however, Indonesia is not rich in ore deposits and the high price of iron restricted its use to essentials. For recreation, the ancestral Indonesians gambled on cockfights, chewed a mild stimulant based upon the betel-nut, and played music on metal gongs. "Gong" is in fact an Austronesian word, which later entered English.

This, then, was the cultural basis upon which subsequent influences would build. But it was far from being a uniform foundation. Beyond Sulawesi in the east, the Austronesian expansion had mysteriously halted on the threshold of New Guinea, the few pioneers there intermarrying with black-skinned Melanesians to produce strange hybrid races and cultures. Even in the purely Austronesian areas west of the archipelago, the diversity was, and is, huge. Nowhere is this more clear than in the field of languages. During the long expansion of the Austronesians, their lost ancestral tongue splintered into a Babel of more than 700 related but mutually unintelligible languages, of which about 200 are spoken in Indonesia. Parallel to the linguistic divisions ran countless other local differences. There were patrilineal societies and matrilineal ones, warrior-leaders and matriarchs, mountain farmers and boat-dwelling sea-gypsies, gold miners and palm tappers.

Some of the detail of this diversity was to be softened in later centuries, as groups of previously independent communities were brought under the influence of single states, single religions, single trading systems. On a larger scale, however, different chunks of the archipelago would be pulled in different social and economic directions, creating broad divisions which had not existed before. One such division to emerge was that between Inner and Outer Indonesia. An-

Right: Monks celebrating the Buddist New Year in Candi Mendut, Java.

other, less decisive but, almost as pronounced division, separated a historically crucial western segment – Sumatra, Java, Bali and to some extent Lombok – from the eastern islands and Borneo, which participated only fitfully in major historical developments. After the coming of the Austronesians, almost all of the important external influences brought to Indonesia were to come from the west – from India, from the Middle East, from Europe. Most strongly and uniformly affected were always Sumatra, the immediate window to the west, and Inner Indonesia, almost as accessible and with its natural fecundity a perennial magnet for traders, missionaries and conquerors.

The Spirit of India

The first important foreign influences came in from India, on a cultural current that washed the shores of all of Southeast Asia, from the beginning of the Christian era until the European Renaissance. From Burma to Bali and from Vietnam to Sumatra, so many Hindu and Buddhist kingdoms appeared during these centuries that Indian nationalists would later talk of a "Greater India" in the far east.

In Hinduism, the accumulated wisdom of the Sanskrit-speaking Aryan people, India had a world-view more philosophically and aesthetically advanced than the magical and animistic religions of Southeast Asia. Hinduism boasted a plethora of striking gods and goddesses, of which the central triad were Brahma, the creator, Vishnu, the preserver, and Shiva, the destroyer. This baroque pantheon must have appealed strongly to existing Indonesian sensibilities. However, it was also combined with elegant doctrines of moral law, the immortality of the soul, ultimate liberation from earthly suffering, and an absolute reality behind the phenomenal world. Buddhism, founded by a prince of Hindu India in the fifth century B.C., took the philosophical tendency of Hinduism still further, doubting even the existence of gods. The first of the universal salvation religions, Buddhism identi-

21

fied desire itself, rather than frustration of desire, as the source of human sorrow, and proposed a set of techniques to free the individual from both desire and sorrow. India also had more down-to-earth cultural goods to offer. One was the useful skill of writing, then unknown in Southeast Asia; others included new architectural techniques, new artistic styles, and new agricultural advances.

Some hearts and minds were won over more quickly and completely than others. The upper social strata were most strongly affected by Indianization; indeed, they may have owed their existence to it. Just as caste, kingship, royal ritual, scribes and bureaucracy had helped the nomadic, warring tribes of northern India become the great Asokan empire, so Indian influence in Indonesia made chiefs and strongmen into *raja*, warriors into *ksatria* knights, and tribal federations into theocratic kingdoms. According to the Indian political model, the *raja* was an incarnation of one of the gods, and his kingdom a miniature of the universe with the capital at its navel.

The early Hindu-Buddhist period in Southeast Asia is known only from fragmentary inscriptions and from sparse, cryptic references in Chinese travelogues and diplomatic sources. There was an Indianized polity in Indochina in the second century A.D., but the earliest sure evidence for Indonesia is from the early fifth century, by which time there were Hindu rulers in West Java, where the state was called Tarumanegara, and at a now obscure place called Muara Kaman on the Mahakam river in East Kalimantan. Over the following centuries, Indian cultural influence in Kalimantan gradually faded into insignificance and the area of intense Indianization in the archipelago became restricted to western Indonesia. Today, Indian culture in In-

Right: Wayang kulit (shadow puppets) from the Ramayana epic.

donesia is most strongly associated with Bali and Lombok, where a form of Hinduism is still practiced, and with Java, where the most spectacular Hindu and Buddhist monuments are found. It was Sumatra, however, which produced the archipelago's first really important Indianized state. This was Srivijaya, a maritime power which rose in the seventh century and dominated the western seas of Indonesia for more than 400 years. Apparently based upon oceanic trade, Srivijaya comprised a number of dispersed harbor cities of which the most important was probably Palembang. Its elite was Buddhist, and its capital a major center for Buddhist learning.

In Java, meanwhile, the focus of activity moved from the west to the center. The first temples of the eerie Hindu sanctuary on the Dieng Plateau date from the end of the seventh century. The eighth and ninth centuries saw, in Central Java, a spate of monument-building unparalleled in Indonesian history. The widely celebrated Borobudur, the largest Buddhist stupa in the world, dates from this period, as does the matchless Hindu temple complex of Prambanan.

In the first half of the tenth century, Java's political center of gravity shifted abruptly eastwards again, coming to rest in the valleys around the Arjuna-Kawi-Kelud mountain group in East Java. The eastern period of Javanese history is characterized by the blending of the two Indian religions with each other and with indigenous beliefs, and by great political flux. After a long period of division, East Java was reunited in the thirteenth century by the ruthless Singosari dynasty. In 1294, Singosari's successor Majapahit, the last and greatest of the Indianized states, was founded on the Brantas delta, upstream of Surabaya. Majapahit combined a bountiful rice-producing hinterland with the maritime power which Srivijaya had now lost. Under King Hayam Wuruk and his vizier Gajah Mada, it was

able, in its fourteenth-century heyday, to become a Southeast Asian superpower, claiming tribute from the coastal kingdoms throughout the archipelago and beyond. After 1389, however, Majapahit fell victim to internal decay and external competition, declining until it was finally overrun by Muslim enemies in about 1527. Much of its elite is said to have fled to Bali, bringing new cultural life and prestige to an island which, like Java, had already been at least partly Hindu for more than six centuries.

Indian culture not only inspired the builders of Indonesia's beutiful temples, but also influenced many other areas of the arts. The beloved shadow-plays, for instance, originated in the south of India. And much of Indonesia's classical repertoire, like the raw material for most of the country's of traditional literature, comes from the *Ramayana* and *Mahabharata* Sanskrit epics.

Without the Indian period, the cultural heritage of western Indonesia would be very different and much poorer. How-

ever, what happened was no simple transfusion of Indian ideas and styles in their original forms. The Indonesian temples, for instance, combine Indian motifs from different periods in novel ways, and blend them with entirely indigenous elements. And through the Indonesian distorting lens, the statues and puppets of India became subtler, lither and weirder. The Indian influence is perhaps best understood as an inspirational spirit, infusing Indonesia as the spirit of Greece once infused Europe. The classic judgement on the result of this mixing and adapting of Indian styles and periods is that of the Indian poet Rabindranath Tagore, who traveled to Java in 1927 and observed, "I see India everywhere, but I do not recognize it."

New Forces: Islam and Europe

Whether it was Indians or Indonesians, priests or traders who introduced the archipelago to the cultural wealth of India, they did so by sea. One reason that

23

Above: Colorfully veiled Muslim women from Sumbawa.

long-distance shipping was already well established was the material wealth of Indonesia – gold, aromatics and spices. Even if Indonesia had not produced any valuable commodities of its own, the western islands would still have become major foci of commerce, for they lie at the meeting place of the two Asian monsoons. Each year, wind blows from the west for just long enough to take sailing vessels from India to Indonesia, or from Indonesia to China, before it reverses, blowing the sailors back home.

Moreover, all ships sailing through the archipelago, unless they are following some wildly circuitous route, must pass through one of two narrow straits: the Sunda Strait, between Java and Sumatra, or the Malacca Strait, between Sumatra and the Malay peninsula. At the beginning of the fifteenth century, a new gatekeeper state, Malacca, appeared on the peninsular side of the strait which still

bears its name. The new city quickly became so central to the global trade in spices and oriental luxuries that it was said that whoever controlled Malacca had "his hand on the throat of Venice." Malacca lies in present-day Malaysia, but has played an important role in the history of western Indonesia as a focus of the two portentous changes which spelled the end of the Hindu-Buddhist period: the coming of Islam and the arrival of the Europeans.

The youngest and most dynamic of the great religions, Islam was founded in Arabia by Mohammed, six centuries after Christ. Within a century of the Prophet's death in A.D. 632, Islamic caliphs had conquered a huge arid swathe of the Old World from Spain to the threshold of India. From the mid-13th century onwards, Islam began to dominate the cosmopolitan culture of the trading system between India and China, and it was possibly with business in mind that the far-sighted ruler of Malacca decided, around 1436, to become a follower of

Mohammed. However, Malacca was not the first outpost of Islam in the area: the kingdoms of Perlak and Samudra on the coast of present-day Aceh in northern Sumatra were apparently Muslim as early as the 1290s, and even in Java there are a few Islamic tombstones from the fourteenth century. But the conversion of the greatest trading port in Southeast Asia gave Islam a powerful new core from which it radiated to the numerous Indonesian port kingdoms now freeing themselves from the slackening grip of Majapahit and other residual Hindu-Buddhist powers. The most important of the new states was Demak, which conquered and Islamized the whole north coast of Java between 1505 and 1546, administering the final death-blow to Majapahit in the process.

Islam in Indonesia was spread partly by economic calculation, partly by the sword. Enduring conversion, however, is seldom a simple matter of greed or fear, and many have speculated on what intrinsic aspects of the religion may have attracted Indonesians.

Islam in its purest form – austere, demanding, egalitarian and uncompromisingly monotheistic – seems so discordant with the tenor of the existing culture that some have seen its acceptance as a symptom of social revolution, accompanying the rise of a new merchant class. Most of the sparse evidence, however, suggests that the first converts were made among the old Hindu-Buddhist aristocracy itself. Another possibility is that Islam arrived in an unorthodox mystical form which made it more digestible for Indonesians. In either case, the early impact of the new religion upon the popular consciousness was very uneven. In some areas, including Aceh, it put down strong roots which would deepen with the centuries. Elsewhere it lay dormant: selected Islamic rituals were incorporated into existing lifestyles, but there would be little sense of Islam as a self-contained world-view, nor as a redeeming faith, until the nineteenth or twentieth centuries. A few areas, including the mountains of north-central Sumatra, were simply untouched. Nevertheless, in the long run Islam has proven by far the most successful religion in Indonesia. Today it claims 87 percent of the population as adherents, giving Indonesia, on paper at least, the largest Islamic population of any country on earth.

The rise of Islam in Indonesia heralded no great artistic revival like that experienced in India under the Mughals. Many temples, particularly in Sumatra, were vandalized, yet in their place came mosques differing little from Hindu shrines, later giving way in turn to simple copies of Arab designs. The Islamic taboo on representation of human and animal forms cramped the visual arts, although it possibly contributed to the unique stylistic motifs of some textile designs. Music was only slightly affected, for instance by the adoption of the two-string Middle Eastern lute or *rebab*. The Arabic alphabet, however, supplanted older Sanskrit-based scripts in many Islamized areas and remained a common method of writing Indonesian languages until superseded by Roman characters in the present century.

It was not by a wide margin that Islam outran Europe to Indonesia. In 1509, when much of Sumatra and most of Java were still under Hindu-Buddhist kings, the first ships of distant Portugal appeared in the Strait of Malacca. The world's greatest states, industries and even technologies were still in Asia, but the tiny kingdoms of Europe had already begun to cast giant shadows across the globe. Unable to break into the close-knit Islamic trading network, the Portuguese quickly resorted to violence. In 1511, about 1200 ragged soldiers, their greed matched only by their fanatical courage and faith in a merciless God, successfully stormed Malacca, the most important

port in Southeast Asia. The sultan retired to the hills, expecting the marauders to plunder the city and leave, as a local enemy would have done. Instead, the Portuguese rebuilt the defenses and settled in for a 130-year stay. From Malacca they quickly reached Maluku, where the most valuable spices, clove and nutmeg, were grown and where, a decade later, they came face to face with the first of their Spanish rivals to accomplish the almost incredible feat of sailing to the East Indies the long way, via Cape Horn and the vast Pacific. Europe had encompassed the world.

In Indonesia, however, it was not immediately apparent that a new age had begun. Unable to sustain the momentum of their initial expansion, the Portuguese gradually became a peculiar but perennial fixture of the Indonesian trading world, while the Spaniards restricted their activities to Maluku and Sulawesi,

Above: A remnant from the VOC era. Right: A painting of Christ on a WWII bunker.

and ultimately retreated to the present-day Philippines. A pidgin Portuguese was established for a time as a lingua franca of the archipelago, and Jesuit missionaries founded some Christian communities in eastern Indonesia, but there were no substantial territorial conquests. After its capture by the infidel, Malacca prospered as a waystation for Portuguese ships sailing to and from China, Japan and Maluku, but lost much of its former native trade to Johor, at the tip of the Malay peninsula, and to Aceh, which became one of the most powerful states in Southeast Asia. By the middle of the seventeenth century the only remnants of Portuguese power were a few outposts in the Lesser Sundas.

In the Shadow of the VOC

Malacca itself was lost in 1641, not to an Asian monarchy, nor to a European one, but to a commercial consortium – the Dutch *Vereenigde Oost-Indische Compagnie* or United East India Company. The VOC, as it was mercifully known, was formed in 1602 to pool the resources of several Dutch ports for the great venture of displacing Portugal in the Indonesian spice trade. A pioneer Dutch expedition in 1596 had already proved that, with the aid of leaked Portuguese maps, the voyage was possible. The VOC was a major development in the history of capitalism, for it was one of the first global corporations. In Asia it was also a state in its own right, minting money, fighting wars and concluding treaties. It formed the thread linking Indonesian history for almost two centuries, and laid the foundations of the colonial Dutch East Indies which followed.

Like their Portuguese predecessors, the Dutch were only interested in profit, not in conquest for its own sake. But the greater resources and organizational skills of the VOC did make it capable of succeeding where the Portuguese had

failed: in enforcing monopoly trading conditions, at least for certain zones and commodities. In Maluku, it went so far as to organize annual naval expeditions to locate and burn all unauthorized clove plantations. Even in Java, where its influence was more tenuous, the constant endeavour to determine the very conditions of trade led to ever-deepening political involvements which eventually made the VOC a territorial power.

The rise of the VOC was a more critical turning point in Indonesian history than the arrival of the Portuguese. In the sixteenth century, most of the wealthy commerce of Indonesia was still in indigenous hands. With vast tracts of forest still uninhabited, it is even possible that there were more Indonesians in the cities than in the countryside; certainly the archipelago was more urban, in relation to its total population, than Europe. The Javanese, hardly known today as a seafaring race, were then great shipbuilders; the name of one of their traditional vessels, the *jong*, is misapplied in English

to the Chinese "junk." By 1700, however, almost all Javanese trade was controlled by the Dutch. And when in need of middlemen, the VOC promoted the growth of Chinese enclaves, creating a pariah business class which survives to this day. Marginalized in the towns, indigenous Indonesians turned back to the fields, where they were encouraged, or forced, to produce cash crops like coffee and tobacco which were in high demand in European markets. The new Indonesian was to be neither tribesman nor urbanite, but peasant. These changes were most pronounced in Java, where the VOC had its Asian capital, Batavia (now Jakarta), and where Dutch commercial operations came to be concentrated. In Sumatra, where VOC interest was intermittent, more of the old order survived, although trade suffered badly because of Dutch competition.

Indigenous states could resist Dutch pressure only by imitating the armaments, the organization, the discipline and the grim rationality of the intruders.

27

The one power which came closest to defeating the VOC was the Javanese kingdom of Mataram, which flourished in the late sixteenth century near the modern city of Yogakarta in Central Java. Under the rule of Sultan Agung (1613-46), Mataram became a powerful centralized state. Agung conquered almost the whole of Java and almost captured Batavia. However, the pace of change proved too much for Java's political traditions; Agung's son Amangkurat eventually lost control of his vassals and was deposed. Turning this to their advantage, the VOC regained the initiative by backing Amangkurat's son in the ensuing civil war. The VOC-Amangkurat victory brought Mataram effectively under Dutch suzereinty. However, internal problems continued, due in part to ambiguous Javanese conceptions about royal succession and legitimacy, and the empire finally disintegrated in 1755.

Above: Detail from a painting in the Palace of Justice in Klungkung, Bali.

The Imperial Indies

Constant involvement in Javanese wars ultimately weakened the company finances, while rampant corruption and a shift in European demand away from spices and coffee towards Chinese tea and Indian textiles made the effort less and less worthwhile. In 1799, the VOC collapsed into bankruptcy and its Asian possessions passed to the Dutch state. The truly colonial phase of Indonesian history had begun. Holland, however, was now caught up in the Napoleonic wars, thus bringing confusion to the new colony.

A French-backed regime in the occupied Netherlands dispatched a soldier, Herman Willem Daendals, to fortify Java against British attack; his most lasting achievement was the island's first arterial highway, the Great Post Road, of which the British made grateful use when they took Java anyway in 1811. The legendary Thomas Stamford Raffles – naturalist, linguist, diplomat and visionary – now took over the reins of government at the age of 30, promulgating so many enlightened reforms that the short-term result was administrative chaos. Raffles had planned for an Indonesia permanently under the Union Jack, but five years later the dream was shattered by the news that the peace settlement in Europe left no room for a British Batavia. Java was returned to the Dutch, Raffles consoled himself by founding Singapore, and in 1824 remaining British outposts in Sumatra were swapped for Dutch Malacca, fixing what has now become the Malaysia-Indonesia border. The turmoil of the period had deeply disturbed the Indonesian status quo, and in 1825 large parts of Java erupted in rebellion under a disaffected aristocrat, Diponegoro. It took five years for the Dutch to bring this Java War to an end, by which time they were determined to extract a profit from Indonesia at last.

The Dutch dubbed their method of extortion *cultuurstelsel*, the "cultivation system." Every village had to reserve one-fifth of its land for the cultivation of exportable goods – sugar cane, coffee, tea, indigo, tobacco, pepper – and their harvest was calculated as a part of their taxes. This system was hugely successful as a source of finance for Holland, but in Java it caused misery and hardship. Assessed crop values were unrealistically low, profit over and above the tax rate was not repaid, abuses and excesses among officials were commonplace.

The iniquities of the system are the subject of the classic Dutch novel *Max Havelaar,* published by a disillusioned colonial official in 1860. As much because of changed economic conditions as for ethical reasons, the *cultuurstelsel* was ultimately dismantled in a series of piecemeal reforms beginning in 1870. The new strategy was to open Indonesia to private investment; once more, it was to prove more advantageous to Dutchmen than to Indonesians.

Ironically, it was during the privations of the *cultuurstelsel* period that Java's population boom got underway. In 1815 there were perhaps four million people on the island, but by 1870 the figure had almost quadrupled. By 1930 it would reach 41 million. The full range of factors behind this explosion is not understood, but Dutch innoculation and irrigation programs must have played a part, as must the deep peace which settled over Java from 1830 until 1942. Demography crystallized the divergence between Inner and Outer Indonesia: 62 percent of today's 209 million Indonesians live in Java or Bali, which together make up only nine percent of the country's land area.

The Indonesian Dream

Modernity came suddenly to Indonesia. In 1900 Java was still in the grip of a sort of supercharged feudalism in which the barons had become bureaucrats but the peasants showed no sign of becoming citizens. Sumatra was a patchwork of tribal anachronisms, antique Muslim ports and sultanates, and plantations worked by opium-enslaved coolies. Immersed in Hinduism, Bali was virtually unknown to Europeans. Few Indonesians lived in cities of any size, and almost none had enjoyed a secular education.

Moreover, there was still no sense of solidarity or shared identity among the culturally diverse peoples of Indonesia. Those who had resisted the expansion of Dutch power over the years had fought for many things – gods, kings, pride, honor, wealth, renown, even perhaps loyalty to an ethnic people – but nationalism was not among their motives. It is a myth that Dutch rule was founded upon a principle of "divide and rule." Until the very last years, there was nothing to divide: the archipelago had not known any sort of political unity since Majapahit, and perhaps not even then.

The year 1908 saw both the death of the old idiom of anti-colonial resistance and the birth of the new. In Bali, the last defiant Hindu dynasty committed mass suicide before Dutch rifles at Klungkung; in Batavia, the first modern nationalist organization, Budi Utomo, was formed. Budi Utomo was novel in that it was a voluntary, secular association devoted primarily to the very Western ideal of "progress" – not only for its members, but for the Javanese people as a whole. In the coming years, the leadership of Budi Utomo would add two more ideals to complete its triad of nationalist aspirations: progress, unity and freedom.

There were many strands in the emerging nationalist movement, many of which were never satisfactorily spun together. Some drew their inspiration from the great current of Islamic renewal that was flowing from Cairo and Istanbul, others from the Communism of the Russian Revolution. However, by 1927, when the Indonesian National Party was founded under the charismatic leadership of a Javanese engineer called Sukarno, there was at least a minimal consensus: "progress" was economic and mental; "unity" was that of all the peoples of Indonesia; and "freedom" meant to be rid of colonial rule.

Two factors that contributed most to the rise of nationalism were Western education and the press. The former was initially a gift of the new "ethical" colonial policy proclaimed by the young Queen Wilhelmina in 1901; later it was widely imitated by the Indonesian-run schools, Islamic as well as secular. Directly or indirectly, Western schooling taught criticism both of traditional Indonesian society and of the iniquities of the colonial situation.

The growing native press, meanwhile, sustained a new sense of national community. Its medium was Malay, the language of the Malacca Strait, long a lingua franca in the trading ports of the archipelago and the official language of the lower colonial administration. Few spoke it as a mother tongue, but it was a good leveller: renamed Indonesian, it was adopted in 1928 as the "national language" – a hopeful gesture at the time, but a momentous reality today. Although an authentic Austronesian language, Indonesian has incorporated huge numbers of words borrowed from Sanskrit, Arabic, Portuguese, Dutch and English, making it a veritable guidebook to the archipelago's history.

At first, the Dutch were inclined to look indulgently upon the Indonesian political awakening as proof of the success of their own "civilizing mission." A degree of limited democracy was introduced in 1916 in the form of a *Volksraad* or People's Council. Then an abortive communist uprising in 1926 shocked the authorities into a harder line. Radical leaders were exiled to remote islands and a mild form of police state created to deny urban nationalism access to the rural masses. The principle of independence was not really conceded even as a long-term target.

The Price of Freedom

The Dutch would certainly have been there for a lot longer if the catastrophe of the Pacific War had not intervened. The speed with which the Dutch East Indies fell to the Japanese invaders in the first weeks of 1942 was a shock and a revelation to all Indonesians. Like the Dutch, the Japanese were determined to rule Indonesia to their own advantage, but their methods were quite new: spectacle, indoctrination, mass mobilization, arbitrary violence. While their former masters starved in prison camps, Indonesians were drilled, marched, worked, robbed and lectured to by the nation which styled

Right: A street poster commemorating Independence Day, in Jakarta.

itself as the "Light of Asia." The only consistent message was hatred of the West. Where the Indonesian nationalists could help, they were used by the Japanese, who gave them the mass audiences and radio broadcasts they had always been denied by the Dutch. Only a brave few refused to collaborate, but many nevertheless kept their heads, realizing that the Japanese were losing the war and that their chance to be more than tools would soon come. On August 17, 1945, two days after the surrender of Japan, but with Japanese forces still in occupation, Sukarno and Mohammed Hatta proclaimed national independence "in the name of the people of Indonesia." The Indonesian revolution had begun.

The revolution was a time of extreme disorder, in which Indonesians fought their own countrymen as often as foreign troops. Aristocrats too slow to move with the times were swept away; ideological, religious and personal factions among the revolutionaries battled with each other. Nevertheless, in the end enough Indonesians did rally to the red and white national banner to make the dream of independence a reality. It was achieved by a strange combination of bitter military struggle and cool-headed international diplomacy. Thousands of armed youths, mostly trained in Japanese militias, provided the former; a handful of Dutch-educated politicians were responsible for the latter. During the revolution Holland was able physically to reconquer much of its former colony, but, not understanding why so many Indonesians valued a chaotic freedom above the colonial *rust en orde* ("peace and order"), the Dutch won back few hearts. World opinion, too, turned against them. The decisive moment came when the United States, greatly impressed by the ability of the young Indonesian Republic to put down the communist uprising on its own territory in 1948, threatened to cut reconstruction aid to the war torn Netherlands. In December 1949, the Dutch finally recognized the independence of Indonesia except West New Guinea (Irian Jaya).

31

The first 15 years of independence produced just two areas of significant achievement: education, where the expansion of primary schooling more than kept pace with renewed population growth, and nation-building in the mental sense, where the magical oratory of President Sukarno strengthened the patriotism and national pride forged during the revolution. The physical nation, on the other hand, came close to breakdown, and the parliamentary democracy introduced during the revolution collapsed.

After a short boom during the Korean War, the economy went into decline; the Dutch had developed what was in some respects a model colonial economy, but they had done it by themselves, with some Chinese help: Indonesians had not been trained for management and were ill-prepared for the huge task of development. Yet politicians placed the blame for economic failure at the feet of the re-

Above: Former President Suharto and his wife at a ceremony in Bali.

maining foreign businesses, almost the only ones still operating efficiently. The nationalization of all Dutch enterprises at the end of 1957 heralded a spiral of hyperinflation and chaos. The machinery of government also began to break down.

The formation of political parties sharpened old ethnic, religious and economic rivalries and created new ideological ones. The most ominous tensions were set up by the success of the Indonesian Communist Party, reconstructed after the failed revolt of 1948, in winning support among the underdogs of rural Java and Bali. Communist cadres and development programs gave self-respect and ambition to the landless and powerless of the villages, destroying the symmetry of old hierarchies and generating simmering hatreds. The anger of devout Muslims and Hindus at the atheism of the Left heightened the danger of an explosion. In parliament, meanwhile, no party or stable coalition could hold power for long enough to pursue policies instead of tactics. The election of 1955, the first free election in Indonesia's history, gave seats to 28 parties, none with more than a quarter of the total vote. The president and the army grew sick of the bickering ineffectiveness of the civilian politicians. A series of regional rebellions gave Sukarno an excuse to declare martial law in 1957 and introduce "guided democracy," a nebulous concept according to which the elected parliament was replaced by an appointed council deemed to represent social groups – youth, peasants, workers, women, regions, religions and so on – rather than political parties. In 1958, the most serious regional challenge, a rebel government called PRRI in West Sumatra, was firmly suppressed by troops loyal to Sukarno.

A New Order

As the 1960s began, Sukarno became progressively less realistic, commissioning ever more grandiose prestige projects and monuments, governing by slogans, flinging insults at the superpowers, and embarking upon military adventures against "neo-colonial" Malaysia and Dutch New Guinea. In 1962, the USA pressured Holland into surrendering the last remnant of its empire and in 1963 Irian Jaya fell under Indonesian administration. In the meantime, prices were rising by 30-50 percent a month, Indonesia had a foreign debt of $2.5 billion, blackouts darkened the cities and Sukarno had moved the Greenwich meridian to Jakarta.

On September 30, 1965, a bungled coup attempt was blamed upon the communists, with whom Sukarno had become very close in the last years. The army gave the signal for a purge of communists, which quickly snowballed into a horrific communal massacre as pent-up tensions erupted in the villages. Half a million people or more are thought to have died, mostly in Java and Bali. Sukarno, father of the nation, was dis-

credited; over the next two years he was discreetly eased out of power. General Suharto, the army officer who had thwarted the coup, became president on March 12, 1967 and, with support from the military, established a regime he called the New Order.

It cannot be argued that the New Order did not bring improvements. Suharto was able to bring inflation under control and, with the generous support of the West, countless development programs were successfully initiated. The infrastructure was noticeably improved, and export business boomed. At the same time, overall living conditions for the Indonesian population, which grows by approximately three million people per year, also improved. People soon began speaking of the Indonesian economic miracle. Food production was up 50 percent. Whereas Indonesia was the world's largest impoter of rice in the 1960s, by 1985 it grew enough rice to cover its own needs. The per capita income as well as the average life expectancy increased.

Large-scale family planning programs were also a great success. A 1970s growth rate of 2.4 percent was lowered to 1.8 percent by thc 1980s; over 100,000 new schools were also built.

However, the New Order was not without disadvantages. Suharto and his governing party, Golkar, ran a dictatorship with help from the army and police. Critics and members of the opposition were either jailed or placed under house arrest; the press, radio and TV stations were under the control of the government. The "elections" that were held every five years were a farce; the results were always manipulated and the outcome was known far in advance. Besides the ruling Golkar, only two other parties were tolerated: the PPP, the Islam-oriented United Development Party (Party Persatuan Pembangunan), and the PDI, the Democratic Party (Party Demokrasi Indonesia). Neither party's candidates, however, were ever given a fair chance.

Many of the economic improvements tended to benefit only a privileged minority, which meant that the rich became even richer and the poor became poorer. This was also true for Indonesia's different regions, especially rural areas like Java, which saw an increase in poverty. Corruption was rampant throughout the entire administration, from the lowest bureaucrat all the way to the President. In addition to that, Suharto's nepotism began to take on increasingly large dimensions. He extended privileges and power, and supplied particularly lucrative monopolies to his close friends and especially his sons and daughters.

For more than 30 years Suharto, who liked to be recognized as *Bapak Pembangunan*, the Father of Development, held the reins of power; he ensured that he was elected to six five-year presidential terms. After the March 10, 1998 election Suharto named B. J. Habibie, former Minister for Research and Technology, as his Vice-President. Previous elections in May 1997 had shown that Golkar, as expected, won with 75 percent of the vote, followed by the PPP with 22 percent and the PDI with three percent of the vote.

Crisis and New Elections

Despite facing growing criticism in the 1990s, Suharto most likely would have remained President for a few more years if Indonesia hadn't been hit by the growing financial and economic crisis that started in Thailand in August 1997. Within months the value of the Indonesian Rupiah dropped dramatically. In July 1997 $1 bought Rp 2400, by the spring of 1998 $1 bought Rp 9000 and had, earlier in the year, climbed as high as Rp 15,000.

Right: Modern transportation in North Bali.

As the value of the Rupiah fell, the cost of import goods rose, which led to a 100-200 percent increase in the price of domestic goods. Despite increases in the cost of living, salaries remained low. In just a short time the Indonesian per capita income fell by 75 percent. Several private banks and the airline company Sempati were forced to shut down resulting in even higher levels of unemployment.

Violent disturbances bloodied much of Indonesia. In April and May 1998 student protests calling for the removal of President Suharto were held in Jakarta, Medan, Yogyakatta and Solo. Furious about and panicked by the price increases, Indonesians rioted and plundered supermarkets, shopping centers and other businesses. Most victims of these attacks were successful *orang cina*, the disliked Chinese minority. Racist attacks against the Chinese spread to other areas of the country and lead to even more ethnic- and religious-based confrontations. In West Kalimantan the local Christian Dayak attacked the immigrant Islamic Maduresen. Additional Christian-Muslim confrontations took place in Kupang, West Timor, and in Ambon, Banda and Tanimbar on the Moluccan Islands. In addition to the violence, underground independence movements in Aceh and East Timor were revived.

Attempts by the International Monetary Fund (IMF) to help get the financial crisis under control were unsuccessful because they made fundamental economic reform a condition of their subsidies. Suharto could neither ensure such reforms, nor did he want to.

As the disturbances reached their climax in May 1998 – in Jakarta alone over 6000 buildings were damanged or destroyed and up to 1200 people were killed – Suharto finally accepted the inevitable. On May 21, 1998, he resigned from the office of President and appointed Vice-President Habibie as the new President of Indonesia.

As a technocrat and ardent follower of Suharto, the Indonesians trusted Habibie almost as little as they'd trusted his predecessor. It was obvious that he was viewed as just a temporary solution. Even though Habibie immediately released a few political prisoners and promised reforms and new elections he failed to bring the crisis under control. His promised reforms never took place and the new elections were continuously postponed. Then, in November 1998, just as in the previous May, there were calls for *Reformasi* and *Demokrasi*. There were also new and bloody clashes between demonstrating students and the military.

After a date, June 7, 1999, was finally set for new elections, the beginning of 1999 was relatively quiet. This time over 50 parties participated and the PDI, with 34 percent of the vote, came out ahead of Golkar, who captured 22 percent.

Shortly after the June elections, violence broke out in East Timor which had, with Habibie's permission, held a referendum and voted for the territory's independence. The election of a President was delayed and, after losing an East Timor-related confidence vote in the People's Consultative Assembly (MPR) in October 1999, Habibie withdrew as a candidate. Many expected Megawati Sukarnoputri (PDI), long-time opposition leader, daughter of former-President Sukarno and the people's popular choice, to be elected. However, in a country whose political scene is full of surprises, the MPR elected Muslim leader Abdurrahman Wahid (PPP), who is nearly blind and wracked by health problems to the post of President, with Sukarnoputri as his Vice-President.

It remains to be seen if this new era of political openness can begin to unify the archipelago's diverse cultures, ease racial, ethnic and religions tensions, and channel the energies that have recently been expended on violence into reaching long-term stability and a lasting solution to Indonesia's worst ever economic crisis.

THE CULTURE
OF JAVA

Before he was named Susuhunan Paku Buwana V, Crown Prince Adipati Anom of the court of Surakarta commissioned court poets to compile a compendium of all that was known of Java. He sent each poet on a journey – one to East Java, one to West Java and the third to Mecca because Java's history was, by that time, inextricably connected with Islam.

Upon their return, these poets composed a twelve-volume encyclopedia of Javanese culture and history known as the *Seluk Tambanglaras* or *Serat Centhini*. The literary device that was used to convey all that was considered worth recording was a series of interconnected journeys taken by different characters in search of knowledge. Visiting the important places on Java involved a string of adventures. Every location had its tales and some local figure was always called upon to reveal something new. Thus, in recounting a history of Java, the *Serat Centhini* covers everything from the significance of the shape of the Javanese *kris* (ceremonial sword) to the many ways of making love, and ranges from the highest forms of religious knowledge to the basest techniques of thievery.

The *Serat Centhini* is a marvelous source of knowledge about Java, but unfortunately the entire work includes some 6000 manuscript pages, all written in Javanese verse. Although it could still be used as a traveler's guide, it would never fit in a backpack and one would hardly wish to recommend all of its adventures. The modern traveler needs something a little more accessible, perhaps somewhat less detailed and certainly more contem-

Left: A court official at the kraton (royal palace) in Yogyakarta.

porary. It is best therefore, to begin with some of the basic features that make Java one of the most remarkable and fascinating islands on earth.

Java is the site of the oldest and most important fossil remains of early man. Various sites – such as Trinil, Ngandong, and Sangiran – located along the Solo river as it extends into East Java, have yielded a large collection of prehistoric human remains. These remarkable fossil finds and their association with various artifacts suggest continual habitation for over 800,000 years, with the early development of populations over this period. That these populations lived in small nomadic bands, that they were hunters and gatherers and that they sheltered in caves and exploited the rich shellfish resources of Java, can be deduced from the evidence they left behind. Beyond this, one can only speculate on the nature of their social and cultural life.

The Austronesian Heritage

The beginnings of the Neolithic era on Java are generally associated with the arrival of Austronesian-speaking populations. To have spread as they did in so short a period, the early Austronesians must have been rather skillful sailors. They relied not just on hunting, fishing and gathering, but had begun to cultivate rice, millet, and certain tree crops. They also brought with them domesticated chickens and pigs. Early Austronesian sites reveal the use of pottery and suggest the beginnings of weaving and the use of cloth made from bark. More important still, the presence of related and relatively mobile island populations led to a more rapid diffusion of cultural ideas and goods.

Five Austronesian-related languages are important to a hisotical understanding of Java. The first of these is Javanese itself – the language of the majority of the Central and East Javan population. The

majority of people in West Java speak Sundanese, the second of these languages. There is no rigid border dividing speakers of Sundanese and Javanese, and in the adjoining areas between West and Central Java, people speak both languages in a fashion that shows the strong influences they have had on each other. A dialect of Javanese is also spoken in two historically important former court centers, Banten and Cirebon, on the north coast of West Java.

The third language of importance on Java is Madurese. This is the language of the peopleliving on the north coast of the eastern end of Java. The island of Madura has for centuries been part of the cultural sphere of Java and the Madurese have played a critical role in Java's history, moving in large numbers from their island to Java. Now over 20 percent of East Javans speak Madurese as their first language. In large parts of Pasuruan, Probo-

Above: Plowing a rice paddy in Central Java.

linggo and Jember, in East Java, the majority of the people speak Madurese.

The fourth language of historical importance is Malay, which forms the basis of modern Bahasa Indonesi, the national language of Indonesia. Today all Javan schoolchildren learn Indonesian. It is the only language of education in elementary schools from third grade onwards. However, the use of Malay on Java is not just a recent phenomenon. One of the oldest inscriptions found on Java, dating from A.D. 832, is written in a form of old Malay. For a long time it was the *lingua franca* for trade throughout the Indonesian archipelago and was vital in the northern coastal cities of Java.

The fifth Austronesian language of importance on Java is Balinese. Java's culture has exerted a strong influence on Bali, but the cultural exchange has not been exclusively one-way. As Java was transformed by Islam, Balinese rulers sent military expeditions to support the the Hindu rulers at the far eastern end of Java. As a result of this assistance, the populations at the easternmost end of Java have often been oriented more to Bali than to the rulers of central Java.

Non-Austronesian Languages

Four other languages have figured prominently in Java's history. The first of these is Sanskrit, which was introduced by traders from India, and was used as a religious and literary language by the rulers of Java.

The first inscriptions in Sanskrit are those by a ruler using the Sanskrit name Purnavarman, from a kingdom called Taruma in the western part of West Java. In Sanskrit, Java was known as the great *Yawadwipa*, a designation that is used on an inscription, found in Central Java, from the early 8th century, and again on a later inscription from the 11th century, which was found in East Java. The 8th to 15th centuries saw a great flowering of Hindu and Buddhist culture on Java and the building of some of the most remarkable temple complexes in the world. The central idea behind virtually all of these edifices was to create a dwelling place for the gods. In the course of this Hindu-Buddhist period, the use of Old Javanese gradually began to replace Sanskrit in texts and inscriptions and even the Indian-style of temples began to show an increasingly distinctive Javanese style.

With the coming of Islam, Arabic began to exert a profound influence on Java. From the 13th century onward, this influence was notable and has continued to the present day. The chief institution of Islamic learning on Java has been the *pesantren*. The *pesantren* is based on a relationship between a learned teacher who is respectfully referred to as a *kyai* and a group of pupils called *santri*, who support themselves and their *kyai* while they learn.

The foundation of Islam on Java is now popularly associated with nine saints known as the *Wali Songo* whose tombs,

scattered along the north coast of Java, are places of special reverence. The mystic powers of these saints suggest a strong Sufi background to the establishment of Islam and the *pesantren* have maintained this tradition in teaching *tasawwuf*, mystic knowledge, as the highest form of Islamic learning. The most important of the Islamic *tarekat* orders ("Muslim brotherhoods," which on Java are not confined to men) have strong links to the *pesantren* and *Nahdatul Ulama* (Indonesia's most important Islamic organization) as well, and these organizations foster Sufi religious practices. All of this makes Islam a complex and potent force that has penetrated all aspects of Javanese life.

Dutch is yet another language that has had an important influence on Java. Initially, at the beginning of the 17th century, its use was confined to merchants and officials of the Dutch East India Company. Malay was used as the common language, even in many of the early Dutch settlements, including Batavia — the center of the Company's trading network in Asia. Portuguese was, for a long time, a more important and common language than Dutch. As a result, Dutch had to be promoted, but always remained the language of a small elite. When, in the 19th century, Java's nobility were admitted to this elite and were given access to a Dutch education, the language began to exert considerable influence. Many leaders of the 20th century's Nationalist movement spoke Dutch. The previous Sultan of Yogyakarta, Hamengku Buwono IX, was summoned back from Holland in 1939 to replace his father and went on to become one of Indonesia's most respected Nationalist leaders.

After the struggle for independence from the Netherlands, English replaced Dutch as Indonesia's preferred foreign language in the national education system. English is now taught widely in schools throughout the country; three English-language newspapers are pub-

lished in Jakarta, and various English-language programs are regularly broadcast on television.

Social Geography of Java

The Javanese classify the different areas of Java in terms of historical and linguistic criteria. At the far western end of Java is Banten; moving eastward is the large area known as Sunda, whose mountain heartland is referred to as Priangan; the north coast from Cirebon to Gresik (near Surabaya) is called the Pasisir. The rest of Java takes its orientation from the court centers of Central Java – Surakarta (Solo) and Yogyakarta (Yogya). The territory surrounding these centers, which once formed the main area of jurisdiction of the kingdom of Mataram, is known as the Negara Agung. To the west are the areas of Bagelen and Banyumas; to the east, as far as Malang, is the Mancane-

Above: An ornate Javanese kris (ceremonial sword). Right: Dieng Plateau landscape.

gara. This area came under the strong, but less direct cultural influence of the courts. The eastern land beyond this area of influence is described as the Tanah Sebarang Wetan, and at the far eastern end of Java is Blambangan. Jakarta, was founded in 1619 by the Dutch East India Company, as its trading center. Batavia, and Surabaya, which have long and often independent histories, are generally considered as separate entities in this native geography. This social geography embodies a Mataram-centered view of Java, so the history of Mataram provides a key to an understanding of Java.

The Rise of Mataram

Sultan Agung reigned from 1613 to 1646, and is accorded a pre-eminent role in the creation of the kingdom of Mataram. His grandfather, Senopati, had already advanced the dynasty and overthrown the kingdom of Pajang to which Mataram had been subordinate. His father had ruled for 12 years. Despite this, it is Sultan Agung, not Senopati nor his father, Panembahan Seda Ing Krapyak, who is considered as the symbolic pinnacle of the kingdom of Mataram.

From the 14th century onward, the ports of Java's north coast, the Pasisir, adopted and developed distinct Islamic traditions while remaining open to Chinese and, later, European influences. Complex and cosmopolitan, the Pasisir opened gateways to the rest of Java. By contrast, although occupying an area of previous Hindu-Buddhist culture, Mataram was then a backwater, better known for its military organization than for its art and learning. It was during the reign of Sultan Agung that Mataram began the task of making itself not just the political center of Java but also the center of Javanese culture and refinement.

Sultan Agung's efforts involved incorporation and synthesis. After his conquest of the north coast, he brought the Crown Prince of the royal house of Surabaya, Raden Mas Pekik, to his court so that he could pass the arts and literature of the Surabayan court onto the people of Mataram. At the time, Surabaya was a center of culture and Islamic learning, and Raden Mas Pekik claimed descent from one of the most important Islamic saints in the Javanese tradition. Later Sultan Agung gave his sister in marriage to Raden Mas Pekik and some years later arranged for his son to marry the daughter of Raden Mas Pekik, thus binding the dynasty of Surabaya to that of Mataram.

Austronesian languages, such as Balinese and Sundanese, and even the language of Tonga, in the Pacific, recognize different speech levels, but no Austronesian language has elaborated them to the extent that Javanese has. These levels, reffered to as *unggah-ungguhing*, form the basis of social politeness. It is clear that the Mataram court, in its quest for refinement, gave impetus to the development of ever-increasing forms of linguis-

tic elaboration. There are distinct speech levels in Javanese marking social strata: *ngoko* (low), *madya* (middle) and *krama* (high), with a number of special vocabularies to bridge such cases as when a person of high status addresses an elder of lower status.

As well as developing linguistic etiquette, Sultan Agung helped preserve some of Java's ancient traditions. Like his grandfather before him, the Sultan was believed to be capable of consorting with the powerful Queen of the Seas. This relationship has always provided one of the traditional underpinnings of the Mataram dynasty and to this day is still commemorated in various court rituals. One of the most important of these is called *Labuan,* in which an offering representing the ruler is carried in procession to the shores of the south coast and then cast into the sea.

At the height of his power, although recognized as a Muslim ruler, Sultan Agung had not yet reconciled his reign with the forces of Islam. By one account,

this reconciliation came in a dream, while Agung was in Blambangan in East Java.

Sultan Agung's Dream

In this dream, the figure of an old man, resplendent as the moon, appeared to Sultan Agung and identified himself as the lord of an important burial site at a place known as Tembayat, or simply Bayat, in the center of Mataram's territory. The tomb is said to be the resting place of an Islamic saint known as Ki Pandhan Arang who originally came from Semarang, on the north coast of Java. Popular folk tradition, however, which still survives today, identifies Ki Pandhan Arang as the last Hindu ruler of the kingdom of Majapahit who disappeared from his palace rather than face a struggle with his Muslim son, and who wandered through Java until he, himself, became a Muslim saint.

Above: This Yogyakarta palace retainer explains a painted relief.

The old man who appeared in this dream held a staff in his hand, a symbol of authority. He extended it to Sultan Agung who took hold of it and was miraculously thrust back to his own court.

As with all events on Java, there is more than one interpretation of this mystic occurrence. Clearly a spiritual relationship with the Islamic personage at Bayat was of importance to Sultan Agung and this relationship is associated with some of the most far-reaching acts of Sultan Agung's reign. We know specifically about some of these events, which can be dated to the year 1633, because there were Dutch observers at the court of Mataram by this time.

In the *Bataviaasch Daghregister* for May 29, 1633, a brief report relates that Sultan Agung had departed the Mataram court to make a special pilgrimage to Tembayat. According to popular tradition, it was on this visit that Sultan Agung had his dream. The significance of this event for Javanese history can be judged by Sultan Agung's reaction. Immediately upon his return to Mataram, he ordered the rebuilding of the burial site at Tembayat. No horses were to be used to haul the stones for the wall or gates. Instead, it is reported that Sultan Agung commanded 300,000 of his subjects to form a human line stretching some 40 kilometers between the Mataram court and Tembayat and, respectfully seated, to pass the materials needed to build the structures to honor the religious lord of Bayat.

At this same time – dated by Western reckoning as Friday, July 8, 1633 – Sultan Agung ordered into existence a restructured Javanese calendar, thus changing the way in which time was calculated on Java. This new calendar was perhaps Sultan Agung's greatest effort at cultural synthesis since it attempts to combine quasi-solar and lunar cycles, an Islamic time sequence with a prior Hindu system of reckoning while still preserving critical elements of a five-, six- and seven-day week.

Immensely complex, this elaborate system of time reckoning consists of a series of interrelated cycles, whose different points of coincidence mark periods of special significance. This means that different activities may follow separate cycles and events become identified by their conjunction amid a number of cycles. Thus the legendary figure of Watugunung presides over a *wuku* cycle of 30 seven-day weeks while the holy days of the Muslim year follow an Arabic cycle of 12 lunar months with either 29 or 30 days.

After honoring the lord of Bayat and reordering the calendar, Sultan Agung celebrated the marriage of his son, who was to succeed him and later become Amangkurat I, to the daughter of Raden Mas Pekik. At about this same time, Sultan Agung also appears to have initiated overtures to officials of the Dutch East India Company in Batavia in an attempt at reconciliation.

All of these events occurred in the same Javanese year. The gates at Bayat, 30 kilometers east of Yogyakarta, still bear witness to this moment in Javanese history. One of these gates still bears an inscription whose numerical interpretation designates the year 1555 as the year of the reordered Javanese calendar. After the death of Sultan Agung, Mataram was continuously encroached upon by the Dutch East India Company and internal dissension among members of the Mataram dynasty led to bitter disputes and the eventual loss and fragmentation of Mataram territory. In the end, what remained of Sultan Agung's kingdom was divided among four courts: a major and a minor court in Yogyakarta and another major and lesser court in Surakarta. However, as Mataram's power declined, its quest for cultural refinement based on ideals of the past increased. This quest gave rise to an elaboration of the standards of linguistic appropriateness, the rules of etiquette and moral conduct, and the subtlety of artistic expression – in short, an entire code of conduct for social and cultural life.

Java Today

In 1997, there were 117.5 million people living on Java. This population, and in particular the Javanese who are the inheritors of Mataram, still value the subtle pleasures of socializing; they show deference to seniors, superiors and strangers; they endeavor to control strong emotions; they tolerate individual idiosyncracies as intrinsic to human nature; and they preserve their sense of a superior civilization. Yet, despite this love of subtilty and ritual, the people of Java are in great rush to modernize, even if it does bring complications and chaos with it.

Java today could perhaps be considered a single, vast settlement – neither urban nor rural. Villages are set close to one another and most rural settlements have population densities greater than the

suburbs of Western cities. By one authoritative account, there are 170 towns on Java ranging in size from 25,000 to over 500,000 inhabitants. There are also the major cities: Bandung and Semarang, with two million and 1.4 million inhabitants respectively; Surabaya with over five million; and finally, the metropolis of Jakarta.

In 1945, Jakarta had a population of barely one million; now it is home to more than 10 million people. However, if one includes the Greater Jakarta area, where in recent years an enormous amount of industrial and housing development has taken place, the population is over 12 million.

What makes Java such a unique settlement is its incredible flow of traffic. The Dutch left the island with a peasant population very much tied to the land in separate subsistence-oriented villages. How-

Above: Hardened lava flows near the Bromo volcano. Right: A Javanese farmer plants the young rice shoots.

ever, within the past twenty years, Mitsubishi and Mercedes-Benz have managed to open up the villages: Mitsubishi with its Colt mini-van that can reach the most isolated villages and Mercedes with huge buses that carry loads of passengers across the island in less than a day.

For people from rural villages throughout Java, work can often be found in towns and cities, and these are the places they go – usually for short periods or between peak seasons of the agricultural cycle. The local differences that make Java so varied are transported to the large cities. Villagers from all the regions of Java come to work in Jakarta's so-called "informal sector." The Madurese come to sell *saté*, while the *bakso* noodle peddlers, with their pushcarts, come from Wonogiri. Workers from Pemalang seem to have a firm grip on the lucrative recycling and disposal industry. One joke even says that soon there will be no one left in Tegal: the men are all working in the construction industry, building Jakarta, while their wives and daughters

have set up food stalls to feed them and anyone else a good, cheap meal.

Cities and towns on Java, despite their urban trappings, are still composed of village-like local neighborhoods. One result of the Japanese occupation of Indonesia has been the adoption of the Japanese system of residential wards. Whether in a city or a village, everyone is officially assigned residence in one of these neighborhood wards.

But it is not only in the cities that one meets the villagers of Java. Over 10 percent of Indonesia's Javanese population now live outside of Java. In Sumatra alone, there are over eight million Javanese. Their new-found mobility has provided the Javans with a safety-valve for controlling development on the island. It is not just poor villagers who leave to seek employment; it is also the ambitious, the frustrated and those in trouble. If a villager has had a quarrel or is suddenly divorced or pregnant, then the bus often offers a means of escaping to a world of new possibilities.

To be understood in this new Javanese world, one must speak Indonesian. Previously, it was possible to live in a large self-contained world of Javanese speakers. Indonesian literacy for Javanese was among the lowest of all of Indonesia's different populations. Although many of the older generation can claim only a "passive" knowledge of Indonesian, the younger generation uses it without hesitation. Government pressure, parental pressure and peer pressure keep children in elementary school and encourage many to remain for further schooling. As villagers have become better educated, they have also become more mobile.

The Indonesian language is also the means by which the outside world reaches the villages of Java. In the 1970s, Indonesia sent its own satellite, called *Palapa*, into orbit, in order to create a modern telecommunications system for the entire country. (At the time, this decision was criticized as an extravagant folly, but now it looks like a brilliant bar-

gain). With this satellite and local transmitter stations, it became possible to broadcast television shows throughout the country.

The government now uses television as a tool to educate the rural masses, particularly for matters concerning the country's development. This includes a farmers' hour, with video clips of farmers from all over Indonesia talking about solutions to specific agricultural problems. Besides this, there are Indonesian dramas and programs broadcasting both popular and traditional singing. American serials like *Kojak*, *Dynasty*, *Lost in Space*, and *Little House on the Prairie* are also broadcast.

Both radios and tape recorders play an important part in village life. Turning up the volume allows one family to share their listening pleasure with their neighbors, creating a desired sense of sociability. Recordings of both popular and

Above: Mother and children out for a day trip.

traditional music are cheap and widely available throughout all of Java.

Traditional entertainment has also been adapted to the new media forms. The master puppeteers from the court centers of Yogya and Solo are still revered. Recordings of their performances are sold on cassettes and on one Sunday night a month, a famous puppeteer is given the opportunity to broadcast an entire *wayang* drama on national TV. However, the shadow-plays are faced with growing competition. Most village families would rather spend their time and money on the education of their children than on elaborate performances of drawn-out family ceremonies.

Village life has its own rhythms. The new "day" begins at dusk, and midday, when it is too hot to work, offers a break in which to nap. Villagers rarely sleep in full eight-hour stints, which means that there is always someone with whom to chat at all hours of the night. In fact, night, especially the hours from midnight to three in the morning, is the time most favorable for obvservation of traditional religious activities. The recent introduction of electricity to many villages and the desire to watch television have begun to fundamentally change these rhythms.

Many houses serve as double households. Different households under the same roof are distinguished as separate "hearths." Married children live with their parents before eventually building another house squeezed in on some vacant plot belonging to a parent or close relative. In most households, it is difficult to keep track of young children who spend their time in the homes of different relatives. Visiting relatives is a way of life and no matter how crowded they may appear, houses always seem to be able to accommodate visitors. This crowded Javanese conviviality makes a place lively and thus worth living in.

Land is at a premium and residential areas have become increasingly densely populated. These residential areas consist of several interconnected hamlets surrounded by fields. Village populations live crowded together on a fraction of their land in order to be able to maintain as much land in active cultivation as possible. Even the land reserved for scttlement is heavily committed to fruit growing – bananas, coconuts and papayas. Nevertheless, a great deal of prime cultivated land has been encroached upon for residential and industrial purposes, and continued loss of valuable irrigated land threatens future rice production.

In the villages of Java it is rice that matters most of all. With an ever growing population, one of Java's main tasks has been to increase its production of rice to keep ahead of the needs of its population. Java has more than doubled its rice production in less than two decades. The effort to do this has affected every rice-producing village on the island.

The government's role has been to provide new high-yielding, quick-growing varieties of rice, provide subsidized fertilizer and guarantee an acceptable purchase price. Irrigation systems have been rehabilitated and extended to permit multiple harvests. Under the Dutch, a large proportion of irrigated land was communal property held by the village and apportioned, in fixed lots, among households. Since land has been scarce in most parts of Java since the 19th century, communal holdings were often informally subdivided into even smaller, Lilliputian-sized plots.

At the beginning of the 1960s, Indonesia passed new agrarian laws that granted individual title to communal landholders. These fortunate landholders, most of them with plots of less than a hectare or two, profited greatly from the government's efforts to stimulate rice production. With some of the richest and most fertile land on earth, even farmers with only one hectare of land are capable of remarkable production. They now harvest an average of over five tons of rice per hectare and often plant two rice crops a year, followed by a third of soybeans or maize. These farmers constitute the elite within their own villages; but increasingly in Javanese villages this elite represents a shrinking minority of the total population. Even in intensive rice growing villages, a majority of villagers are now farm laborers, small businessmen, or have found jobs outside the village.

The enormous productivity of these lowland rice-growing areas of Java depends on preserving the critical watersheds that support the island's irrigation system. In the mountains of Java, where the rush of human activity is less apparent, are the precious forests that protect the integrity of the island's ecology. In Javanese eyes, these mountains have always been the abode of the gods and spirits that safeguard life on Java. Their protective role will be even more important in future as the population and demands for commercial land development continue to grow.

BEYOND THE MYTH
OF BALI

The island of Bali has been much photographed, discussed and described. Guidebooks and photo albums have dubbed it "Island of the Gods," "Island of a Thousand Temples," "Morning of the World" and "Last Paradise." At the same time, scholars have attempted to comprehend its "unique" religion, to describe its social organization, and to understand its history. At least since the 1930s, and with increasing volume and fervor in the recent past, Bali has been romanticized by Westerners seeking an idyllic, unspoiled, pristine paradise to set against their own disillusionment with the emptiness and materialism of modern life. Bali came to represent that paradise, as did Tahiti, Jamaica, and the Seychelles.

The island was perceived as unique and unchanging. It was a last outpost of ancient Indonesian Hinduism in a Muslim country, and a museum of traditional life and thought. While the rest of the world developed, it was thought that Bali remained suspended in the 16th century, endlessly perfecting the beauties of its singular culture with virtually no disturbance from outside. The coming of the Dutch to North Bali in 1849 and to South Bali in 1906-08 was said to have disturbed little. The Dutch respected the "Bali-museum" concept, and sought only to "restore" cultural elements which had become decadent and to "rationalize" a few organizational muddles, while leaving the whole "untouched."

This view of Bali has dominated most of what has been written about it, both scholarly and popular, to the extent that the modern visitor, who will be jostled by

Left: A young boy taking part in a Balinese initiation ceremony in Tenganan, Bali.

thousands of fellow travelers, is still invited to partake of the purity, romance and uniqueness of the Bali experience. The writers, scholars, artists and photographers who have created the prevailing image of Bali are not wrong. The island does strike most visitors as physically beautiful, exotic and special.

Balinese culture is a three-dimensional jigsaw puzzle, whose pieces and layers have been shaped by a variety of intersecting factors. Not all of the pieces fit perfectly; some are duplicated, others are missing, still others fit loosely, or must be jammed into place by the earnest scholar. All of the pieces come from a variety of sources; the Austronesian substratum, India, Indianized Southeast Asia, Lombok and the Lesser Sundas, Java, China and the West. Over time, and with significant local variation, the pieces have interacted; colliding, retreating, rubbing, crumbling and merging along their interfaces. The result is Balinese culture as we experience it today – very much in flux, but nevertheless founded on tenacious beliefs and cultural patterns which are widespread and ancient.

Bali has probably been occupied by man almost as long as nearby Java, where human remains which are over 1.8 million years old have been found. During repeated ice ages, the last taking place over 18,000 years ago, immense bodies of water froze into glaciers. This caused the sea level to drop below today's levels, which exposed Sunda, a large continent that reached from Vietnam to Borneo and across Malaysia, Sumatra, Java and Bali. It would have been easy and relatively comfortable for people to cross and explore this giant land mass, especially since during the last ice age it wasn't uncomfortably cold near the equator. However, details about the prehistory of Bali are all speculation, as no remains of early man have yet been found there. Only with the coming of the Austronesians does evidence become abundant.

The Balinese Language

The Austronesian world, whose boundaries are based on linguistic and cultural affinities, extends discontinuously from Taiwan in the north to New Zealand in the south, and from Madagascar, off the coast of Africa, east to Easter Island, which is closer to South America than it is to Asia. The peoples of this enormous area speak more than 700 different languages, yet a large number of words are identical, and close cognates abound.

The Balinese language is most closely related to those of East and Central Java, Lombok and Sumba, but it shares some of its vocabulary with languages spread across the Austronesian world. The word *lima*, for instance, means "five" not only in Balinese, but also in a host of languages spoken between Taiwan and Samoa. Because it has several "levels" of

Above: A cremation ceremony in Legian, Bali.

speech, Balinese is an extremely difficult language to learn; each caste has its own level, which individuals promptly abandon when speaking to someone of a different caste.

Such subtilties of language signal the importance of hierarchy in all aspects of daily life. Balinese emphasizes this particularly strongly; but the idea is also built into many other Austronesian languages, as well. The word *datu,* or *ratu,* for instance – "lord," "king," or "chief" – is found in various forms over a wide area. Some Austronesian languages even have special ceremonial vocabularies which can be used only on ritual occasions.

The significance of hierarchy is also reflected in their conception of space. Water is sacred to the Balinese, but in their tripartite conception of the cosmos the sea is the lowest level, inhabited by demons and spirits. Opposite this are the volcanic mountains, home to the gods, deified forces of nature and ancestors. Between these is the world of men, where the forces of good and evil are locked in eternal struggle.

Higher, therefore, is better. Temples and great houses are built on pedestals, or in stepped designs. The northerly village of Sembiran, about 30 kilometers east of Singaraja Bali, has been inhabited since Paleolithic times. A number of temples have been found here with giant stone steps, and are still used for special ceremonies. They resemble temples in Java, Cambodia, and even as far away as Polynesia. Their lineal descendants are terraced temples such as Besakih (the Mother Temple of all Bali), Pura Kehen (the old state temple of Bangli), and Pura Penulisan, built on a high point of the rim of the ancient Batur volcano.

Closeness to the mountains denotes power, purity, and status. The Balinese words for the cardinal directions, *kaja, kelod, kangin, kauh*, which are usually mistranslated as "north," "south," "east," and "west," actually mean: "towards the mountains," "away from the mountains or towards the sea," "where the sun rises," and "where the sun sets."

Direction is thus variable according to topography and the season. Other Austronesian cultures share this peculiarity. The Malay/Indonesian word *selatan*, "south," may once have meant "towards the sea," in this case the straits (*selat*) of Malacca, Sunda, and Riau.

Balinese houses are oriented in terms of the mountains and the sea. Domestic altars or family temples for the gods and ancestors are placed in the mountain-eastward part of the compound, followed by the dwelling pavilion of the head of the family, rice storehouses, lesser dwelling pavilions, the kitchen, and so on, down to the pigsties and latrines in the furthest seaward-westward corner of the yard. Stepped pavilions and the position of altars and seats will enable the observant guest to witness Balinese etiquette in action. Polite Balinese always keep their heads lower than those of persons of higher status and never sit too close to the east-mountain side of an empty space.

The entrance to a courtyard is usually a narrow passage reached by a staircase; behind it, a wall, called Aling-Aling, keeps out demons.

Birth and Death Rites

Another Austronesian feature, which is shared with China, is the ancestor cult. Many Austronesians remember long and detailed lineages of their forebears, but the Balinese do not: only some royal and high priestly families keep genealogical records. Instead, the link with ancestors is perceived as a connection between a non-individualized, original clearer-of-the-land and the people who continue to occupy that territory, his/her descendants. Each village has a *pura puseh*, or "temple of origin," where this pioneer/ancestor is venerated. At the same time, each family has its own individual *sanggah*, or domestic shrine, for its own forebears; while clans commemorate their ancestors in a *pura kawitan*, the clan's "temple of origin."

Ancestors are given offerings to ensure their continued progress through the graded ranks of heaven, and therefore their increasing power. Offerings also encourage the ancestors to intercede beneficently in the affairs of their descendants. Ancestors are not quite gods. They are not exactly worshiped, yet they become semi-divine with the passage of time until they merge with the local God of the Soil. In the meantime, ancestors must be remembered, for they constitute a definite link between a given social group and the world of the gods.

Austronesian involvement with the ancestors is expressed in curious funerary rituals found in different forms in Southeast Asia and throughout Indonesia and the Philippines. These practices are known as "double funerals." First, the corpse is buried, cremated or exposed to

the elements. After a time, in the course of a special ceremony, the corpse is interred yet again. This series of rites expresses the continuing and changing tie between the living and the recently deceased. Family ties cannot be dissolved in a single ceremony; there has to be a gradual, formal process of letting go. Ritual offerings ensure that the soul can reach the higher, more pleasant regions of the Hereafter. Some Austronesians placed the remains of their ancestors in jars, hollowed-out tree trunks or stone sarcophagi. Others put them in niches in cliff faces, burned them or painted their bones and left them in caves.

In Bali, burial jars have been found at Gilimanuk and stone sarcophagi abound in the Pejeng-Bedulu area. Today, the preferred method is burning, and the colorful "Hindu"-Balinese cremation ceremony has been made world-famous by

Above: Balinese musicians at a cremation ceremony. Right: Balinese women harvest rice with ani-ani knives, one shoot at a time.

thousands of photographs. Despite Hindu overtones, Balinese funerary practices are clearly Austronesian. Cremation is not immediate, as in India, but follows initial burial, sometimes many years later. Cremation in Bali is accompanied and succeeded by a series of ceremonies in Bali. The families of the rich or important may hold as many as seven. These ceremonies are designed to free the soul from human ties, launch it into heaven and establish it in its proper place in the divine hierarchy. Like many other Austronesians, the Balinese visualize the journey of the soul to the Other World as a voyage in a boat.

Birth, like death, is understood to be a gradual process, and each stage must be ceremonially marked. In Bali, rites begin at the moment of conception, and continue throughout pregnancy, during and after the birth, and at regular intervals until the baby is one Balinese year (210 days) old. Only then can the child be put on the ground for the first time. There are other rites at the onset of puberty, when

the teeth are filed as a sign of adulthood and, finally, at marriage.

Balinese Women

In Austronesia, gender roles are quite remarkable. Despite widespread observation of defilement laws, which require the segregation of men from menstruating women, women enjoy relative equality. Descent is often reckoned bilaterally, so the mother's kin are as important as the father's in determining inheritance. Women can administer property and exercise political and religious power. Women have ruled various Southeast Asian and Polynesian societies, the most notorious in Bali being the 11th-century Queen Mahendradatta, possibly the original of the *Rangda*, the Balinese wicked witch. In Bali and elsewhere in Indonesia, women generally manage the family finances and have many ways of making money in their own right, the most visible and common being the *warung*, or coffee stall.

The influences of Hinduism and Islam have somewhat undermined the traditional equality of the Austronesian woman. Patrilineal inheritance is often preferred in Muslim societies, and even in Bali the divorce laws distinctly favor the man, who, in a dispute, is allowed to take the children as well as the house, leaving the woman to survive alone or return to her parents.

Polygamy was and still is common in Bali. The limit to the four wives allowed to Muslims, and the ruling – in the 1978 Indonesian marriage law – that the husband must have the written permission of his first wife before he can marry again, has progressively reduced the practice. The tendency among young people is to marry once only.

Women visiting Bali can move about easily without any of the many restrictions common in Muslim or conservative Christian societies. Men and women mix freely and happily, but Balinese ways are generally more conservative and modest than Western mores. To avoid offense,

both men and women should make sure to cover their torsos, including their upper arms, and their legs at least to the knee. Shorts and plunging necklines or backs should be avoided, unless one wishes to be labelled *kurang sopan*, "impolite, immodest."

In heavily Westernized enclaves (Kuta, Sanur), anything goes, but Western visitors who hope to make contact with rural Balinese will have better luck if they respect the Balanese cultural mores and don't make social interaction uncomfortable by dressing immodestly or improperly.

When entering any sort of temple, either domestic or public, both men and women should wear the customary attire of a sarong, a clean shirt or blouse with sleeves, and a sash, the Balinese *selendang*, around their waists. It is very important that women visiting Bali respect the defilement laws. It is a serious infrac-

Above: Ulun Danu temple on Lake Bratan, Bali.

tion of religious law for a menstruating woman to enter a temple or the home of a high priest.

Indianization

The second great complex of ideas and influences which contributed to the shaping of Balinese culture is "Indic." It includes elements brought to Bali directly from India, as well as others transmitted via other "Indianized" states, especially Java and Sumatra, but also possibly Champa (Vietnam), and Cambodia (the Khmers).

Scholars have argued much over the "Indianiaztion" of Southeast Asia. Was it brought about by colonists, traders, missionaries or conquerors? Did it represent a wholesale remodeling of the pre-existing cultures, or was it more a case of informal, widespread influences, percolating through already well-established societies in myriad subtle ways? There is no definitive answer, but probably active trade brought many types of Indians to

Southeast Asia, as well as spurring traffic in the opposite direction. Trade goods and ideas, images for conceiving of the divine, patterns for social organization, and a wealth of Sanskrit words and concepts entered Southeast Asia with this commercial traffic over a period lasting several centuries. In Bali, a very recent find on the north coast, near the village of Sembiran, has disclosed pieces of South Indian rouletted ware which date from between 200 B.C. and A.D. 200. This pottery provides a strong indication that there was a nearly direct contact between Bali and India.

When Indian traders and learned men began to arrive in Southeast Asia they certainly did not find a cultural vacuum. Local cultures possessed sophisticated rice agriculture, metal technologies, religious ideas centered on a Lord of the Soil or a local deified ancestor, stepped temple structures and a preference for mountains as particularly holy places. Indians probably never conquered territories in Southeast Asia; the extensive spread of obvious Indic ideas and symbols was most likely facilitated by the nature of indigenous Southeast Asian culture. Indian mythology and imagery could easily be grafted onto locally accepted religious ideas and social structures. The Lord of the Soil became Shiva (Siwa in Bali) or Buddha; the Indian *varna* were added to local hierarchies; the holy mountain became Mahameru, the cosmic mountain, pillar of the world in Indian mythology; Indian ideas about statecraft influenced the idiom of local chieftainship; Indian gods and goddesses were assimilated into the pantheon of deified tree, ground and water spirits. In each instance, the "genius loci" adapted and refashioned the Indian elements so that Hinduism in Bali became vastly different from the parent religion in India.

In Bali, Indic influences are everywhere. The religion of Bali is an eclectic mixture of Hinduism, Buddhism, and indigenous forms of Austronesian animism. Balinese call their religion the *Agama Tirtha*, the "Holy Water Religion," because all its rites involve the liberal sprinkling of water that has been consecrated by a priest. The most important Hindu gods worshiped in Balinese temples are Siwa (Shiva), Wisnu (Vishnu), Iswara (Isvara) and Brahma. They are accompanied by numerous ancestors and Soil-Lord gods and goddesses, as well as the rice goddess, Dewi Sri; the god of the sun, Bhatara Surya; and Bhatari Durga, the goddess of death, who is the malevolent form of Siwa's wife, Parvati. Above and beyond this plethora of divinities, the Balinese conceive of a unitary divine principle, Sang Hyang Widhi Wasa, who is the sum and source of all the lesser deities. Citing this belief in Wasa, some modern, rationally-trained Balinese claim to be monotheists.

Sharing religion and mythology with India, Bali has absorbed a multiplicity of related concepts and symbols from the religious homeland. Gunung Agung, Bali's holiest mountain, is said to have been fashioned by the Hindu gods from a piece of the Indian Mt. Mahameru. The Balinese *meru* (temple towers) mirror the shape of both the cosmic mountain and the layers of heaven. Hindu gods and goddesses are painted or sculpted as they are in India, bearing the same attributes.

Bali preserves much of the literary and linguistic heritage of pre-Islamic Java, to which it was closely related, culturally and politically, for several centuries. Hermits' caves hewn into rock faces at Goa Gajah (the Elephant Cave), near Bedulu, and Tampaksiring are similar to the cave sanctuaries in East Java and India. These caves indicate the presence of monasteries in 10th and 11th century Bali. Imposing rock-cut mortuary *candi* (death shrines) at Gunung Kawi (Tampaksiring) date from the 11th century, and are clearly the formal prototypes of modern Balinese temple towers.

Not all of Bali, however, was Indianized. The famous Bali-Aga villages (Trunyan, Tenganan and the other villages around Lake Batur) did not absorb Indic influences. These villages are still characterized by the ancient worship of stone megaliths, strict endogamy (marriage only within the village) and exposure of the dead, rather than burial and cremation. They are traditionally divided into two parts and ruled by village elders, chosen in equal numbers from both sides. Even in so-called "Hindu" villages, where Indian and Javanese elements are strongest, one shouldn't assume there is a particularly close relationship between the two islands. Balinese culture (especially its music, dance, drama and etiquette) is livelier and less consciously refined than Javanese, and it includes a large number of subtle local components.

Traces of cultural influences from China and Vietnam are much fainter, yet it is evident that they have also been present for a long time. Bronze drums and other implements closely related in form and decoration to those made by the Dong-Son culture of ancient North Vietnam (began ca. 2000 B.C.) have been found in Gilimanuk, Manuaba and Pejeng. The finest of these specimens, the "Moon of Pejeng," can be viewed at the Pura Penataran Sasih, in Pejeng. It is a large (almost two meters) bronze drum of a distinct Dong-Son-style.

Chinese cultural influence, which seems to have been exerted mainly through trade, can be seen in early Balinese literature; Chinese trading vessels are frequently mentioned in Balinese *babad* (traditional histories). Miscellaneous pieces of antique Chinese porcelain are even available for sale today, some of them possibly the remnants of ancient trading ventures. Chinese brass coins, round with a square hole, are plentiful in Bali and are used in many kinds of offerings. The *Barong*, personification of the forces of good, who battles the

Above: Colorful fighting roosters in the village of Tenganan, Bali.

wicked *Rangda* in a popular Balinese dance drama, has much in common with a Chinese dragon, bearer of good fortune.

Evidence of significant Chinese-Balinese contact is provided by the tale of King Sri Adi Jayapangus, who controlled the area around Mt. Batur some time before the rise of the kingdom of Bedulu-Pejeng, which was ruled by his descendants. Unable to wed any local princess as all were inferior to him, he sought out and wooed a Chinese maiden, the owner of a rich vessel which had called at one of his harbors. Enamored of the maiden, the king proposed; but she demurred, reminding him that he was a Hindu, whereas she followed the Buddhist faith. The king swore that both religions would be equal in his kingdom, married the girl, and erected statues of himself and his Chinese spouse in a local temple. Later the couple proved to be childless, so the king dallied with Bhatari Dewi Danu, the goddess of Lake Batur, and founded a dynasty that, under the kings of Bedulu-Pejeng, reached its high point. Jayapangus' act of adultery aroused the divine wrath of Dewi Danu's father, and both the king and his wife were consumed by supernatural fire in the grounds of the Batur temple. The statues honoring the makers of this Balinese mixed marriage can still be seen in Pura Batur. Their love story lives on in the *Barong Landung*, a dance drama performed by men dressed as giant puppets; one a Chinese woman, the other a Balinese man. In some villages, the *Barong Landung* is danced in the streets during Galungan, the Feast of the Gods. At this time, all the Balanese ancestors and divinities descend on Bali for a ten-day period of festivities, to enjoy the offerings provided by their Balinese descendants.

Ties between Bali and its closest neighbors have also existed, intermittently, from the dawn of Balinese history. The connection with Java has been touched on, and is the most important, consistant and long-lasting of Bali's foreign relations. There are indications that Balinese Buddhism may have come from the Sumatran kingdom of Srivijaya, which flourished from the 7th through 12th centuries. At different times, Balinese kingdoms controlled East Java and parts of Lombok and Sumba. There are a few small Muslim communities in Bali, descendants of traders, soldiers and retainers of Balinese rulers, who have stayed where they first settled and clung to their divergent faith. Balinese literature and history show that there were occasional relations between Balinese rulers and Islamic kingdoms, and that the elite, if not the mass of the people, were aware of the need to defend and maintain the Balinese religion as the last bastion of Hinduism in an increasingly Islamic world. Modern Balinese, despite their easy tolerance of other religions, have a sense of the superiority of their own beliefs, especially in comparison to Islam.

Western Influence

Balinese exposure to Europeans occurred sporadically over several centuries and climaxed in bloodshed in 1906-08. The flood of modern European visitors poses some new cultural options, both positive and negative, for the Indonesian government and the modern Balinese. Early visitors to Bali may have included Sir Francis Drake or some of Magellan's men. English and American whalers hunted near Bali during the 18th century. Alfred Russel Wallace, discoverer of the Wallace Line, spent a few days there in 1856. The Wallace Line follows a deep-sea trough which runs between Sulawesi and Borneo, then comes down through the narrow Lombok Strait which divides Bali and Lombok. Wallace opined that it marked the point of division between the tigers, monkeys and jungle trees of Asia, and the marsupials and eucalypts of Australia.

Mads Lange, a Dane, was one of the most interesting of the early Westerners to visit Bali. He arrived in Bali in 1839 and remained until his death in 1856. He had two wives, one Chinese and one Balinese, traded with the Balinese kings and occasionally dabbled in diplomacy on behalf of the slowly encroaching Dutch. He happily adapted himself to Balinese life and was able to function as a mediator, or cultural broker, between the bewildered Balinese *rajas* and the smoothly determined minions of the Dutch colonial government.

The Dutch, installed as colonial overlords in north Bali from 1849, began to encourage organized research into Balinese culture. At the same time, they set about trying to subdue the rest of the island. In 1906, the Dutch used the looting of one of their ships as a pretext to land an armed force on the coast of Bali, near

Above: Tourists waiting for sunset at the sea temple of Tanahlot. Right: A fisherman casting his net near Tanahlot, Bali.

the capital of the kingdom of Badung (modern Denpasar). The Balinese king and royal family, faced with their defeat, committed ritual suicide.

By 1908, the whole island had capitulated and the Dutch began to settle themselves in as the new, "enlightened" rulers of Bali. Misunderstanding much of what they saw and generalizing from conditions in other places, they attempted to "reform," "tidy up," and "rationalize" the apparent confusion of Balinese ranks, rulership, village and territorial boundaries, *adat* (customary law) and so on. They made substantial changes. The Dutch only recognized the Hindu *varna* ranks, and gave preference to members of the upper three *varna* (the *Triwangsa*) when they chose "native" deputy rulers, soldiers and other functionaries. In this way, the Dutch alienated the holders of non-*varna* ranks, barring them from educational advancement or power-holding, and simultaneously drove a wedge between them and the *Triwangsa*. In order to streamline village boundaries, the

Dutch split big villages and combined others to make artificial communities and establish new borders which took no account of village or clan temple membership. This meant that many families found themselves owing money, labor and produce to temples in both their traditional *adat* village and a new government administrative village. Modern Indonesian governments have left most of these colonial arrangements in place.

Positive consequences of the Dutch colonization of Bali center around the bringing of Western scholars and artists to the island. Balinese manuscripts were collected and stored in a library in Singaraja (the *Gedong Kirtya*), where scholars began to translate and discuss them. During the 1930s, a colony of European artists and intellectuals lived and worked in Bali. Walter Spies, Theo Meier and Rudolf Bonnet painted and encouraged Balinese artists — The Puri Lukisan, the art museum in Ubud, provides fine examples of their influence; Margaret Mead, Jane Belo, Gregory Bateson, Katherine Mershon and Miguel Covarrubias all undertook anthropological studies of Bali; Vicki Baum wrote a delightful novel, *A Tale from Bali*, which she set on the island; Ketut Tantri joined the Indonesian freedom fighters; Colin McPhee studied Balinese music.

Bali's romantic image was largely created by these expatriates, and their depiction of Bali as a uniquely beautiful and harmonious place has had tremendous impact over the years. Tourism has reached extraordinary levels and continues to grow without showing signs of stopping. In relative scale and impact, the modern invasion of pleasure-seekers may be comparable to the Islamic invasion of Majapahit, and it may ultimately have the same kind of long-term effects on Balinese culture. Tourism cannot be labeled good or bad: it brings in money and new opportunities, but it also exposes the Balinese to unsettling ideas and influences. So far, however, the Balinese are adapting creatively and with much success to the latest foreign invasion of their island.

A PORTRAIT
OF SUMATRA

Sumatra is a frontier. For the ancient civilizations surrounding the Indian Ocean it was always a mysterious, eastern island of riches – *Suvarna-dvipa*, the golden land, guarding the entrance to all the wealth of Southeast Asia. For Indonesia it is the land of opportunity, vast natural resources and economic dynamism. For the foreign visitor it offers natural beauty, cultural diversity, untamed forests still home to elephants, tapirs, tigers and rhinoceroses, and a rapidly developing tourist trade still full of surprises. Having spent much less of their history under the thumb of colonial powers than other parts of Indonesia, Sumatrans readily admit that they are less cultivated than the well-bred Javanese; but, they quickly add, they are far more egalitarian, enterprising and self-reliant.

The world's sixth-largest island, more than twice the size of Great Britain, Sumatra has been separated from the Asian mainland (and Java and Borneo) for only the last 10,000 years. Its most striking feature is the western mountain range of Bukit Barisan, formed when the northward-moving Indian plate collided with the Asian continent 60 million years ago. The uneasy conjunction of plates continues to cause geological instability along this range, including earthquakes and volcanic eruptions. As the result of a massive eruption 75,000 years ago, which deposited a thick layer of ash all over Sumatra, the Malay Peninsula and distant Sri Lanka, Lake Toba was formed. At the other end of the island, Krakatau was the site, in 1883, of the largest volcanic eruption in recent his-

Left: A Nias islander wearing a remarkable headhunter's ring.

tory. Local accounts say some 36,000 people lost their lives as a result.

The vastness and physical variety of Sumatra give it a wild, open quality in striking contrast to Java and Bali. Both those islands long ago tamed their vast forests, established efficient internal lines of communication and unified their densely settled people into a few large linguistic-political units. Sumatra, by contrast, never approached political unification until Dutch conquest at the beginning of the 20th century. Although its strategic location, great rivers and prized exports provided the foundation for a succession of powerful kingdoms, the eastern marshes and western mountains provided protection for interior peoples who developed their own civilizations barely influenced by the outside world. Despite giving Indonesia its national language, dominant religion (Islam) and modern literature, Sumatra also retained a dozen mutually unintelligible languages, divergent religious and cultural systems of its own.

Srivijaya

Sumatra may have been Ptolemy's legendary "Taprobana," and it was certainly a crucial (though not very distinct) part of the "golden land" of early Indian epics, as well as what Muslim travelers referred to as "Jawah." However, most ancient seafarers, like the inhabitants themselves, had little sense of this island of many kingdoms that lies so close to Java and the Malay Peninsula. They were, however, aware of the kings who controlled the export of gold and dominated the vital straits of Malacca and Sunda. Chinese records tell of successive shadowy kingdoms in the area of southeast Sumatra, but these were all eclipsed by the rise of Srivijaya in the 7th century.

Several Srivijayan inscriptions from between A.D. 683 and 686, discovered near modern-day Palembang, provide the

earliest record of the use of the Malay language. They tell of a Buddhist king who extracted solemn oaths of loyalty from his subjects in exchange for taking responsibility for their spiritual and material welfare. His capital was a major Buddhist center. Although it continued to dominate the Strait of Malacca until the 11th century, Srivijaya left no great monuments to rival Java's Borobudur. The stone temples it did build fell victim to Islamic militants who were more militant than those in Java. Moreover, the empire's rulers didn't bother themselves with scattered interior populations, concentrating instead on dominating the various international ports of eastern Sumatra and the Malay Peninsula. Inscriptions and buried Buddhist statuary have been found in many of these ports. The Srivijayan capital, Palembang, was plundered in an Indian raid in 1025, and dur-

ing the next centuries, independent trade centers grew up in Java, northern Sumatra and the Malay Peninsula. The most important of these centers was located near present-day Jambi.

The chief heir of Srivijaya's glory was Minangkabau, the heavily populated rice and gold producing area in the central mountains. After Java's conquest of the major ports of Sumatra's eastern coast in the 13th century, a prince claiming descent from both Majapahit and Srivijaya established his own kingdom near the headwaters of the Indragiri and Hari rivers, controlling the gold of Minangkabau. Many surviving statues and inscriptions left by this (Tantric) Buddhist king, Adityavarman (1356-75), would seem to indicate that he controlled most of central Sumatra.

Islam

Above: Famous Batak-style houses at Lake Toba. Right: Solemn Toba Bataks during a ceremony in Simanindo, N. Sumatra.

The northwest coast of Sumatra long remained a politicaly independant area. Its rivers were not navigable, its ports

were exposed to the northwest monsoon, and its peoples were reportedly stateless, barbarous cannibals. Its location near the Indian Ocean and the camphor which was collected as resin from trees in the hills above Barus and Sibolga were its only major attractions.

Along the lengthy coast between Barus and present-day Medan were numerous other small, river ports. In 1292, Marco Polo, as part of the expedition carrying a princess from the Mongol Emperor of China to Persia, waited for the monsoon in one of these small ports. He related that his expedition disembarked there and, "for fear of these nasty and brutish folk who kill men for food, we dug a big trench round our encampment . . . and within these fortifications we lived for five months." Despite his fear, Polo and his colleagues lived and traded sufficiently with the locals to give Europe its first account of sago, palm wine, rhinoceroses and cannibalism itself. This was at the port of Samudra (Sanskrit for "sea"), or Sumatra (near modern Lhok-

seumawe), which, during the ensuing two centuries became sufficiently important to give its name to the whole island, at least for Arabs and Europeans coming from the West. In Polo's time, it was still a small kingdom practicing shamanistic animism. He reported, however, that the neighboring kingdom of Perlak (near modern Langsa) had already become Muslim, "owing to contact with Saracen merchants, who continually resort here in their ships."

Judging from the earliest tombstones in the ancient cemetery at Geudong, Samudra itself was Muslim by 1297. When it was visited by the greatest of Arab travel writers, Ibn Battuta, in 1323 it was a sophisticated sultanate with international relations around the Indian Ocean and as far as China. Under its preferred Muslim name of Pasai, it issued gold coins, sent ships to the major ports of Asia and developed a Malay system of writing in Arabic script. For subsequent sultanates, Pasai represented the great Southeast Asian center of Islamic scholarship. Pasai was a producer of silk, and in the 15th century grew large amounts of pepper for the Chinese market.

Despite its commercial and religious eminence, Samudra/Pasai never politically united northern Sumatra. On the arrival of the Portuguese (1509), there were still separate Muslim port-states at (from west to east) Barus, Daya, Lamri, Pidië, Pasai and Aru. After conquering Melaka (Malacca) in 1511, and driving out many of its Muslim merchants, the Portuguese attempted to gain influence in Pasai and Pidië by supporting one side of their numerous succession disputes. The effect was to drive all the anti-Portuguese elements, which included the wealthy Muslim merchant community, to unite under the banner of Aceh, a new sultanate formed around 1500 on the ruins of ancient Lamri at the northwestern tip of Sumatra. Between 1519 and 1524, Sultan Ali Mughayat Syah of Aceh drove the Portuguese out of northern Sumatra and began what was to be a century of bitter conflict with Christian intruders.

When the Portuguese arrived in Sumatra, the most important ports of the region were all already under Islamic authority, and Islam had begun to make inroads into the inland Minangkabau population. Most of these gains can be attributed to the wealth and status of Muslim traders, and the need of an increasingly commercialized people for an easily communicable, universally valid faith. The Portuguese onslaught against Muslim trade, and Aceh's counter-crusade against the Portuguese, introduced the new element of holy war. In the period from 1540 to 1630, Aceh repeatedly attacked the Batak peoples, placing paramount importance upon the latters' acceptance of the Islamic faith.

In northern Sumatra a clear line developed between those who accepted

Right: Praying to Allah in the Grand Mosque of Banda Aceh.

Aceh authority, Islam, and the Arabic script, and those who withdrew into the mountains, took on the designation "Batak," continued to eat pork, use their ancient Indic script and worship their spirits in the traditional manner. The Gayo people around Lake Tawar (in modern Aceh) were in the former group, the Toba and Karo in the latter. In south and central Sumatra, by contrast, Islam spread gradually from the coastal centers to the interior, encountering little or no resistance.

The Aceh Sultanate

Initially, the Portuguese succeeded in disrupting Muslim shipments of Indian pepper to Egypt and the West. Aceh, however, managed to extend pepper cultivation to Sumatra and found ways to transport goods directly to the Muslim ports in the Red Sea, bypassing the Portuguese strongholds along the west coast of India. By the 1550s, Aceh was using this route to supply Europe with about half of its pepper.

Since Turkey was the master of Egypt, this brought the Sultan of Aceh into contact with the Ottomans. In the 1560s, the Sultan sent envoys bearing gifts of pepper to Ala'ad-din al-Kahar ("The Conqueror") Sulaiman, appealing for help against the accursed infidels who had seized Malacca and terrorized Muslim traders and pilgrims in the Indian Ocean.

The Ottomans responded by sending gunsmiths and artillerymen, who contributed much to Aceh's holy wars against the Bataks and the Portuguese. The memory of this assistance from the Caliph of Islam was kept alive by a great Turkish cannon which guarded the palace, a Turkish-style red flag and various popular stories. Economic rivalry with the Portuguese reinforced religious and political hostility. Portuguese Malacca had to endure a dozen attacks from Acehnese fleets between 1537 and 1629.

For the Dutch (in 1598), English (in 1600) and French (in 1602), Aceh was one of the first Asian destinations because of its abundant pepper supply and its aversion to the Portuguese enemy. These Europeans were welcomed, mounted on elephants for their official palace reception and honored with gifts such as *sarung* and *kris*. They found the Acehnese difficult bargaining partners, but continued to visit the busy port. They can also confirm the popular Acehnese memory that the sultanate's peak of power and wealth was reached under Sultan Iskandar Muda ("the young Alexander," 1607-36).

In this period, Aceh was one of the important powers of Asia, with its authority stretching as far as Tiku and Priaman (near modern Padang) in west Sumatra, Asahan in east Sumatra, and Pahang, Johor and Kedah in the Malay Peninsula. Thousands of captives were brought back from its victorious naval expeditions to populate the city, man the war galleys and carry out the heavy construction

work of the sultan's building projects. Unfortuantely, the destruction of war and the natural instability of wooden buildings have combined to erase all but a few traces of Aceh's former splendor.

The last years of Sultan Iskandar Muda were marred by his 1629 defeat by Melaka and signs of paranoia in which he killed many of those closest to him, including his son. His son-in-law succeded him as Iskandar Thani, but died in 1641. Moving away such autocratic extremes, the next four rulers, until 1699, were women.

Foreign traders were now gratified by more predictable conditions and local Acehnese chiefs were able to demand greater autonomy, but Aceh was no longer able to counter persistent Dutch attempts to prise loose the pepper-growing regions and the tin-producing areas of the Malay Peninsula. Aceh managed to remain a great Southeast Asian port and was the only major Indonesian state to retain full trade freedom under the Dutch, but its new major exports, like gold and

elephants, were formerly monopolized by the king and supplies were limited.

Decline of the Harbor Sultanates

While Aceh dominated the coasts of northern Sumatra, similar sultanates arose on the southern rivers. Due to exceptional European demand during the 16th and 17th centuries, pepper growing spread to almost every suitable part of Sumatra. Much of this was grown on the higher ground of central Sumatra by Minangkabau. When they found Aceh's attempted monopoly on the west coast oppressive, they sought other outlets down the Musi and Hari rivers. At Palembang and Jambi, the English and Dutch competed vigorously for this pepper, though the Dutch gained the upper hand by the middle of the century.

The dominance of these port-cities over the vast and varied hinterland of Su-

Above: A Muslim trader goes ashore. Right: A young couple in traditional Aceh dress.

matra was in sharp decline by 1700. The European demand for pepper dropped after 1650, and the Dutch and English companies drove ever harder bargains for guaranteed delivery at fixed low prices. Both companies eventually bought pepper only from suppliers over whom they had monopoly control. Female rule in Aceh was brought to an end in 1699, on the grounds that it was non-Islamic. This initiated a period of dynastic conflict in which the autonomy of the many *uleebalang* (local chiefs) was confirmed.

During the late 17th and 18th centuries, the presence of state authority was hardly noticed by the majority of Sumatrans, who organized themselves in the highlands around kinship-based communities, and in the coastal areas around entrepreneurial chiefs who could open an area to cultivation or trade. Such conditions made it easy for enterprising outsiders to play a role. Bugis from south Sulawesi, Arabs from Hadhramaut and Minangkabau adventurers from Sumatra itself formed many new dynasties.

The biggest players in this league of foreigners were British and Dutch companies, but for them pepper had become a marginal trade item by the 18th century, and Sumatra had become something of a backwater. As a result of the Painan Treaty, in which the Dutch and British agreed to protect local pepper-growing principalities from Aceh in exchange for their harvests, the Dutch established their permanent Sumatran headquarters in Padang in 1663. The British established theirs at Fort Marlborough, Bengkulu, in 1685. Each became a center of rival trade networks along the west coast, but they remained small and vulnerable colonies.

Revival Through Trade and Islam

A new phase of commercial expansion affected Sumatra from the 1780s, as private traders broke the fading monopolies of the Dutch and English companies. Private British and Tamil traders came from India, British and Chinese traders came from the new British free port at Penang (1786), French pepper-buyers and Nias slavers came from Réunion, and Americans came from the maritime centers of New England. American attention focused on the west coast between Sibolga and Meulaboh, where Acehnese river-chiefs created the world's largest center of pepper production in the early decades of the 19th century. In the area around Minangkabau, cassia (a substitute for cinnamon), gambir (for tanning), and, from 1790, coffee, became the new crops that were attractive to Americans and others. In the 18th century, the Chinese began excavating the tin lodes of Bangka.

Since the decline of the powerful Islamic sultans, the chief bearers of Muslim influence have been brotherhoods of Sufis known in Indonesia as *tarikat*, under whose auspices the young men of a village would live and study together in a *surau* (prayer hall). Such *tarikat* schools were especially popular among young Minangkabau men, for whom there was little place in the household or in agriculture, according to the matrilineal inheritance system. These schools provided the basis for a powerful movement of Islamic reform.

The area's new commercialism had increased the social ills this movement attacked, but also the number of Sumatrans able to make the pilgrimage to Mecca. In 1803, three such pilgrims returned after having witnessed the victory in Mecca of the fundamentalist Wahhabis, and they set about trying to reform Minangkabau in a similar direction. Society was quickly polarized, as the reformers (known as Padris) tried to ban such beloved traditional pastimes as cock-fighting and betel-chewing, as well as tobacco and opium use, and at the same time forced the people to pray and adopt Arab dress. In 1815, the movement struck at the remnants of the old Minangkabau

kingdom centered at Pararuyung, killing several princes and burning the palace.

The Dutch Conquest

Despite all of their 17th-century treaties with most of the Sumatran coastal states (notably excluding Aceh), the Dutch had to start almost from scratch after the British returned to their prewar possessions after the Napoleonic Wars in 1816. They were in no position to prevent the dominance over Sumatran trade of the British ports in Penang and Singapore, which continued well into the 20th century. Dutch military advances were slow and were usually provoked by the need to exclude other Europeans. Almost nowhere did Sumatrans accept the extension of Dutch authority without a fight.

The basis of the present Malaysia-Indonesia border is the 1824 Anglo-Dutch Treaty, whereby the British withdrew all their claims to possessions in Sumatra, and the Dutch in the Malay Peninsula. Malacca therefore became British,

Bengkulu became Dutch and the Sultanate of Riau-Johor was divided between British-protected Johor and Dutch-protected Riau. Palembang was considered vital to Dutch interests because of its claim over Bangka tin and its proximity to Singapore, but it took two military expeditions, many casualties and repeated attempts to find a pliable sultan before the Dutch finally abolished the sultanate and ruled Palembang directly from 1825. Rebellions were frequent throughout the 19th century, both here and in neighboring Jambi, where the Dutch established a garrison in 1834.

In Padang, the returning Dutch inherited the Padri headache from the British. Despite their weakness, they were drawn into supporting the opponents of the Padris in a series of protracted operations, from 1820 to 1841, which became known as the Padri War. This made the most densely populated region of Sumatra also the principal Dutch stronghold. The expenses of the garrison were covered by the forced delivery of coffee at fixed prices.

Enterprising Minangkabau took advantage of improved communications and markets to grow their own coffee, as well as tobacco, sugar, cassia and gambir, creating a prosperous, commercially-oriented middle class in many areas. This group enthusiastically welcomed modern-style education, funding their own secular schools from the 1840s on. By 1872 there were almost 1200 Minangkabau children in such schools – seven times more than in Java, where education was a privilege for the aristocracy alone. Sumatra's first generation of Malays who were literate in the Roman alphabet ultimately produced a high proportion of clerks, school teachers, journalists and politicians.

On the east coast of Sumatra, the Dutch advanced slowly. Opposed by

merchants from Singapore, as well as local *rajas*, the most valuable Dutch acquisition proved to be the hitherto insignificant Malay states of Langkat, Deli, Serdang and Asahan in 1865. Jacob Nienhuys began to grow tobacco in Deli, with labor brought from Penang, and within a decade this was acknowledged as the finest leaf tobacco for wrapping cigars. British objections were quickly overcome by the opportunities of supplying the burgeoning new "plantation district" from their Straits settlements. Up to 20,000 Chinese laborers were brought in to cut down the forests and tend the tobacco plants each year, until the 1890s, when cheaper and more tractable Javanese took their place – there were 260,000 contract workers there in the 1920s. Rubber, tea and palm oil estates followed. Prosperous modern towns grew up at Medan, Binjei, Pematang Siantar and Tanjung Balei, and the Malay *rajas* who held the valuable land grew unprecedentedly wealthy from the royalties.

Aceh was by far the biggest challenge to Dutch arms and diplomacy. Proud and free, it had its own wealth and foreign contacts from its pepper and betel nut trade, a self-image as "the verandah of Mecca," and deep suspicion of Dutch advances on both the east and west coasts of Sumatra. In deference to Britain's relations with Aceh, a treaty of mutual defence, which included a 1824 note ensuring continued respect of the sultanate's independence, was agreed to in 1819. However, in 1871, this was annulled by a different Anglo-Dutch Treaty.

The Dutch attack was hastened by energetic Acehnese attempts to form defensive alliances with Turkey, France and the United States. A Dutch force of 3000 men attacked Banda Aceh in April 1873, but withdrew after losing its commander and 80 men. This proved, however, to be only the first chapter of a war which was to last until 1903, exhausting

Right: A night market at Tanjung Pinang.

Dutch reserves of money, morale and men, and leaving a terrible legacy of bitterness in Aceh. By the mid-1880s, resistance leadership had passed to *ulama* (religious scholars) who urged holy war at any cost. The Dutch cemetery in Banda Aceh is a memorial to the more than 10,000 Dutch who lost their lives as a result. For the Acehnese, who lost five times as many, the cemetery is a reminder of their own war heroes, some of whom are now officially recognized as national heroes of Indonesia. As the Japanese approached in 1942, the province rebelled and drove out the rest of the Dutch.

Much of the credit for the eventual Dutch success in imposing their authority over Sumatra was given to Colonel J. B. van Heutsz, Military Governor of Aceh from 1898 to 1904. His policy of relentless pursuit and emphatic assertion of Dutch power was endorsed by a government, which made him Governor-General (1904-09). In that capacity, he sent Dutch troops to every corner of the archipelago where independent *rajas* and villages continued to exist. By 1910 the whole of Sumatra was for the first time under a single authority, albeit a much resented foreign one.

Christian Sumatrans

Though Christian missionaries occasionally visited the ports of Sumatra as early as the 14th century, it was only the isolated peoples who firmly resisted Islam – Bataks and the islanders off the west coast – who offered any real prospect of conversion.

The history of Christian conversion in Sumatra really began with the decision of the German Rhenisch Mission Society to work there in 1861. Ludwig Nommenson, who arrived one year later, was key to the advancement of their cause. Winning confidence as a doctor, mediator and teacher, he extended the mission's work northward from Silindung to Lake Toba, always in advance of Dutch control. Protestant Christianity was melded onto the

Toba Batak identity with great skill, and the reward was the acceptance of Christianity by virtually all of the Batak people between 1880 and 1900. Responding to nationalist movements against Western control in the 1920s, an autonomous Batak church was established in 1930, which helped to maintain the Christian identity of Toba Bataks as they began their successful expansion into commercial and teaching roles all over Indonesia. In contrast to the somewhat marginal place of Christians in Asia, the three million Toba Batak Christians are aggressive and unapologetic about their status.

Sumatra and Indonesia

Economically there were at least three Sumatras in the early part of the 20th century. Each of the three major cities was the center of separate rail and road sys-

Above: The finely crafted sheath of an Acehnese kris. Right: A thoughtful Toba Batak.

tems – Medan in the north, strongly European and Chinese in character, with its closest external links to British Malaysia rather than to other Dutch centers; Padang in the center, the oldest but sleepiest of the major towns; and oil-rich Palembang, whence road and rail systems led southward to the ferry to Java. The trans-Sumatra highway was first planned in 1916, but was not finally completed until 1938. In the same year, the colonial government created the first pan-Sumatran administration, with a governor in Medan supervising ten administrative areas.

In 1917, some Sumatrans formed the Young Sumatran League, centered in the high schools of Batavia, and in 1921-22 they sponsored Sumatra unity conferences in Sibolga, Bukittinggi and Padang. Most of their support came from Muslim Minangkabaus. Christian Batak students became numerous enough in the 1920s to want their own organization, and by 1926 it was apparent that the only acceptable ideals above the ethno-linguistic level would be national Indonesian ones. In fact, Sumatra contributed far more than its share towards the development of Indonesian nationalism, with figures such as Mohammad Hatta (later Vice-president), Soetan Sjahrir (first Prime Minister) and Amir Sjarifuddin (second Prime Minister) playing roles in developing the ideas of national unity.

Even more important was Sumatra's role in developing national literature. For most Sumatrans, Malay had always been the principal written language, and its adoption as the language of nationalism involved major problmes as were experienced elsewhcre. The development of the modern Indonesian novel was almost entirely a Minangkabau affair, with Marah Rusli, Takdir Alisjabana, Nur Iskandar, Abdul Muis and the Muslim leader Hamka dominating the 1920s and 1930s.

Given their large contribution to Indonesian nationalism, and its lack of any inherent unity at an island-wide level, it

is not suprising that Sumatra rejected all attempts to separate it from Java in the turbulent 1940s. The Japanese, in 1945, fostered the idea of an independent Sumatra centered in Bukittinggi, while the Dutch, in 1948-49, tried to foster a Sumatran umbrella for the federal states they had set up in various parts of the island. However, Sumatrans had already decided in the 1920s that they could only bring their diverse ethnic groups together on a national, Indonesian level.

Revolution, Rebellion, Integration

When Indonesian independence was declared in Jakarta on August 17, 1945, Sumatra was governed by ten separate Japanese administrations which had allowed very little Indonesian contact between them. The revolution against first the Japanese, then the British who occupied the three major cities in October 1945 and, finally, the Dutch, had to be fought separately in each residency, with little more than radio broadcasts from Java to provide inspiration. Sumatra underwent some of the most violent aspects of the revolution before it could fit easily within a nationalist framework.

In Aceh the *uleebalang*, who had ruled under the Dutch and Japanese, were violently overthrown in December 1945 by a Muslim-led coalition. Three months later, the Malay sultans and wealthy Simelungun *raja* were similarly overthrown in what was dubbed a "Social Revolution" by the Marxists among its supporters. These movements were not controlled by the republican administration and they led to a breakdown in authority, especially in east Sumatra, where nationalist gangs wrote their own laws.

Even though these excesses caused some groups to seek Dutch protection in 1947-49, Sumatrans were probably more wholehearted in their rejection of Dutch authority than any other major part of the colony. During the period of six months (1948-49) when the Dutch occupied all the cities and towns of Java, Aceh was the only province which the Dutch

71

thought best to leave alone, and Banda Aceh became the capital of what remained of the republic. Despite Dutch attempts to surround republican Java with a ring of minorities that were afraid of Javanese dominance, they were forced to accept the reality of republican sentiments in Sumatra.

Nevertheless, the vast island was far from integrated, politically or economically, when the revolution ended with the transfer of full sovereignty to Indonesia in 1950. Each of the former administrative areas had its own battle-hardened military force which was not eager to return to civilian life, and each felt it had earned the right to play a part in the republic on its own terms. The lucrative smuggling trade to Singapore, which had seemed patriotic during both the Japanese occupation and the revolution, was not easy to turn over to a central government in Jakarta which had little to offer in return.

The first crisis came in Aceh, which objected to incorporation with Christian Bataks into a province of North Sumatra, the failure to declare Indonesia a Muslim state, and the poor rewards for its leaders within the new state. In 1953, the Islamic leadership of Aceh revolted against Jakarta, and declared Aceh part of Darul Islam. Troops sent from Java re-occupied the Acehnese towns, but the rebels controlled the hinterland until 1959, when they surrendered in return for autonomous status for Aceh.

Before, Toba Batak and Minangkabau military leaders had allied with national politicians dissatisfied with the centralism, corruption and the pro-Communist policies of the central government to form the Revolutionary Government of the Republic of Indonesia (PRRI) in February 1958. The central government reacted with great vigor, bombing Padang

Right: Harvesting rubber (latex) from a tree in Sumatra.

and Bukittinggi and sending a large force from Java. The fighting was over within six months; but it left Minangkabau, like Aceh in the same period, feeling like an occupied province in which locals were no longer trusted with high military or civilian office.

Under President Suharto, Sumatran discontent eased. The anti-Communist and free-market policies of the New Order are those which Sumatran leaders in the PRRI had advocated, and the central government had the resources to provide a generous return to the Sumatran provinces for their loyalty. The road system was finally restored, during the 1970s, to prewar levels and better. The Large multi-ethnic provinces were broken up until all except North Sumatra (prewar East Sumatra plus Tapanuli), were back to the old Dutch areas. The military presence became less obvious. However, one still hears grumbles about the *pusat* (center), but these are little different from those heard in Java and elsewhere.

Economic Development

Sumatra has often been called the island of Indonesia's future, with unlimited potential for development of its rich agricultural and mineral resources. It is certainly true that, since the unification of Indonesia at the beginning of the 20th century, Sumatra has grown fastest in population, exports and wealth. Both by immigration (three million of Sumatra's present population were not born there) and natural increase, Sumatra grew by over three percent a year for most of the 20th century, while the rest of the country has been closer to two percent. Medan is the fastest growing of Indonesia's cities, growing from 5800 in 1893 to nearly three million today.

Abundant arable land, as well as a strong entrepreneurial tradition, drew Sumatrans enthusiastically into the rubber

boom of the 1920s and into cloves, pepper, coffee, tobacco, palm oil and other products since. In addition, Sumatra has been Indonesia's biggest provider of oil, with the wells at Langkat and Palembang being followed by newer ones at Pekanbaru and, recently, a vast natural gas field at Lhokseumawe.

Whereas Java provided most of Indonesia's exports in the 19th century, Sumatra did in the 20th. In the 1930s, Sumatran ports handled roughly half the value of Indonesia's exports, but this grew to nearly 70 percent in the 1950s and 1960s, even without counting the large amount of smuggling. The growth of Java-based manufacturing and the greater centralization of the economy has recently reduced this dominance, but Sumatra still provides about 53 percent of Indonesia's ever-expanding exports. Many of those who made their start handling these exports went on to become the biggest *pribumi* (native, i.e., non-Chinese) entrepreneurs of Indonesia in the 1950s and 1960s. However, the centralization of the economy and the importance of political connections have often reduced the role of Sumatrans in the economy in the last 20 years.

This wealth has given Sumatrans a relatively comfortable standard of living, even though the infrastructure of communications, electricity grids and piped water remains less developed than that of Java.

From the 1920s to the 1960s, many Sumatrans earned, on average, more than double the income of the Javanese, but this gap has narrowed, largely because of new, industry-based development in Java, so the poorer southern provinces – Lampung and Bengkulu – are no longer above the national average. However, Sumatrans still attend school longer, own more cars, bicycles and TV sets, and spend more on food and clothing than Indonesians on average. The confident spirit of individual enterprise that has marked Sumatrans through the centuries will continue to serve them and their country well.

73

CITY OF CONTRASTS

JAKARTA

JAKARTA

Sweltering on its humid coastal plain, the vast, sweaty, profuse, multifarious, vibrant city of Jakarta contains all the diveristy of Indonesia. The city center even seems to celebrate this diversity in the almost comic juxtaposition of the white dome of Southeast Asia's largest mosque, **Istiqlal** (1978), the neo-Gothic spires of the **National Cathedral** (1901), and the Grecian columns of the Protestant **Emmanuel Church** (1839) – while the spire of the **Monas National Monument** towers over all three. One Jakarta neighborhood may contain every major Indonesian ethnic group, some Chinese and a European or two. This is the place to acquire a preview or an overview of the vast range of Indonesian regional arts and crafts. **Taman Ismail Marzuki** is the nation's center for the performing arts; **Pasar Seni** at **Ancol** exhibits and sells visual art and handicrafts from all parts of the archipelago. Jakarta, Indonesia's much-maligned capital, also boasts the country's most interesting street life, best selection of eating places, finest museums and numerous historic colonial monuments.

Preceding pages: On the rim of the Bromo volcano. Working the rice terraces.

Jakarta is stereotyped as a city of chaos and contradiction; slums in the shadow of skyscrapers; rickety *becak* jockeying for position next to shining BMWs; barefoot cripples begging outside the closed doors of air-conditioned shopping complexes. Many have seen it as a monument to the yawning gulf between the aspirations of Indonesia's elite and the everyday life of its masses, at once the country's greatest showpiece and its greatest shame. However, for the careful observer, Jakarta embodies Indonesia's unique syntheses as well as its painful antitheses. One block behind the roaring transport arteries lie almost miraculously quiet *kampung* neighborhoods where some of the calm and charm of rural Indonesia lives on, adapted to the new urban setting.

Jakarta was perhaps the first truly *Indonesian* city, a major melting-pot – give or take the odd coagulation of ethnic tensions – of the archipelago's diverse races and cultures. It is the crucible in which the cosmopolitan Indonesian culture of the future is being forged, not only by officialdom and the media, but also by an arcane youth subculture. Jakarta sets the standards of fashion and behavior for all of Indonesia's urban youth, standards which are by no means pure imitations of the West. Few cities have changed more in recent times than modern-day Jakarta.

79

The biggest changes began with the Pacific war, when the invading Japanese inaugurated the city's present name. For more than three centuries the world had known it as Batavia, capital of the Dutch East Indies.

The Dutch city had been a commercial and military center, built around the site of a Muslim port, Jakarta or Jayakarta, on a natural harbor at the mouth of the **Ciliwung River**. Earlier still, the port had been an entrepot for the Sundanese Hindu kingdom of Pajajaran, but in 1527 it was captured by Muslims from Banten and Demak. Little more remains from pre-Dutch days than a single inscribed stone pillar in the National Museum, commemorating a Hindu-Portuguese treaty of 1522. However, today's picturesque **Sunda Kelapa Harbor**, with its magnificent sailing vessels, and the old nautical instruments on sale in the nearby **Pasar Ikan Market**, still recall some of

Above: Sailing vessels at anchor in Sunda Kelapa Harbor, Jakarta.

the atmosphere of the old Asian trading world into which the Dutch intruded all those centuries ago.

Jayakarta was destroyed in 1619 by the VOC (Dutch United East India Company), under the ruthless leadership of Jan Pieterszoon Coen, its fourth governor-general. The small, fortified town built in its place corresponded with the present-day district of **Kota**, and though the walls themselves were mostly demolished in 1810, something of this first Batavia can still be seen. West of the harbor, VOC warehouses from 1652 now house the **Bahari Museum**, with Indonesian maritime exhibits; further south is a large, but dilapidated **VOC wharf**, once used for ship repair. Ruins of other VOC installations can also be seen offshore, on the inner islands of the **Pulau Seribu** (Thousand Islands) Aarchipelago, which is now a weekend beach retreat for wealthy Jakartans. The area of most complete preservation from VOC days, however, is Batavia Town Square, now called **Taman Fatahillah**. The square is dominated by the **City Hall** (*Stadhuis*), which was built in 1719 and restored in 1973/74, and now houses the **Historical Museum of Jakarta**. This solid building, said to have been inspired by its counterpart in Amsterdam, sports horrific dungeons as well as opulent chambers; public tortures and executions were carried out in the square. The museum's collection includes fine furniture and VOC regalia. Also in Taman Fatahillah, are art and *wayang* museums, and a Portuguese cannon from Malacca called **Si Jagur**, said to make barren women fertile if they sit astride it. The canal and houses along Jl. Kali Besar, and the restored **Chicken Market Drawbridge** at its north end, illustrate the doomed attempt to recreate a Dutch environment in this tropical place.

Jan Pieterszoon Coen's fort withstood attacks by huge Javanese armies in 1628 and 1629, but Coen himself, ominously, died of cholera during the second siege. For the next two centuries, Batavia's most feared enemy was not arms but disease. Apart from cholera, the city's stagnant canals bred another deadly threat, malaria. Batavia's pestilences soon earned it the grim epithet of "the Dutchman's grave." By the 1680s, many of the seaward areas of the lower town were practically uninhabitable. In the following century, many Dutch residents abandoned Kota for healthier areas further south which were gradually being cleared of bandits and wild beasts. Thus began a southwards drift of the city's center of gravity which has continued ever since. One beautiful, 18th-century country house is now the **National Archives Building**, halfway along Jl. Gajah Mada on the west side. The **Istana Negara** (State Palace), north of the National Monument, is another. By the early 19th century, much government and social activity had shifted to the city's present-day, symbolic center around **Merdeka Square** (formerly the *Koningsplein*) and **Lapangan Banteng** (*Waterlooplein*),

where a new city rose – literally from the rubble of the old, which was quarried for scarce building material. Impressive public buildings appeared: an empire-style palace, now the **Department of Finance**, begun by Daendels in 1809, but not completed for almost two decades; a theatre, now the **Gedung Kesenian** (1821); the neoclassical **Supreme Court** (1848); and a lavish residence for the commander of the colonial army on Jl. Taman Pejambon, which later became the venue of the *Volksraad* or Indies Parliament and is now famous as **Gedung Pancasila**, the building in which Sukarno first mooted the principles of the Indonesian constitution. The **National Museum**, which is well worth visiting, is on Merdeka Square. It was opened in 1868, by the Batavia Society of Arts and Sciences and is the oldest scientific institution in Southeast Asia (founded 1778). Its collections of sacred Hindu-Javanese art, ethnographic objects, Chinese pottery and its treasure-trove of gold jewlery are world-renowned. The **Istana Merdeka**, or Presidential Palace, on the north side of the square, was completed in 1879; 15 Dutch governors-general ruled here before three Japanese army commanders, then three Indonesian presidents took their place on the well-worn seat of leadership.

A Queen City

With better planning and a number of medical advances, Batavia gradually shed its reputation as a place of death, and was transformed into the *Koningin van het Oosten*, Queen of the East. At the end of Dutch rule, already under increasing pressure from motor traffic and immigration, it was still an orderly, pleasant city of wide streets, shady parks and dignified, if rather stolid, architecture. It was also still of moderate size; southern suburbs like **Kebayoran Baru** were laid out only after the war.

Batavia was Dutch, but most of its inhabitants were not. Its prosperity depended largely upon the enterprise of its Chinese community, who braved persecution to build their homes, businesses and temples here. The district of **Glodok**, immediately south of Kota, was allocated to this pariah community after a notorious massacre of Chinese in 1740, and is still Jakarta's Chinatown. In its narrow, crooked streets, on Jl. Petak Sembilan, is Jakarta's oldest Chinese temple, the **Jin-de Yuan** or **Dharma Jaya**, founded by a Buddhist in 1650. An older name for this temple, Kwan-Im, became the Indonesian word for all Chinese temples, *klenteng*. It boasts fine roof ornamentation and various sacramental antiques. Another interesting *klenteng* is the **Da Bo Gong** on Jl. Pantai Sanur, near the gaudy "dreamland" recreation park of **Ancol**.

A less familiar minority is recalled by the **Portuguese Church**, now known as

Above: A church in Batavia — built in 1736 and destroyed in 1808.

Gereja Sion, on Jl. Pangeran Jayakarta, just south of Kota Railway Station. The "Black Portuguese" were Eurasian flotsam from the breakup of the Portuguese Asian empire. They were brought to Batavia from Malacca and India by the Dutch, who built this attractive, restrained, little (Protestant!) church for them between 1683 and 1695. Much of the interior, including the baroque pulpit, are original. One VOC governor-general, Zwaardecroon, was buried here in accordance with his wish to "sleep among the common folk."

And then there were the Indonesians, the "natives" who came to form the bulk of the population. Distrustful, at first, of the local people, the VOC imported manpower from elsewhere in the archipelago to serve it as craftsmen, slaves and soldiers: Balinese and Macassarese both became familiar languages on the streets of Batavia. The *kampung* between Jl. Bandengan Selatan and Jl. Pekojan, just west of Kota, retains something of the old-world, cosmopolitan atmosphere of VOC

Batavia. Nearby, in Gang Mesjid 1, off Jl. Pangeran Tubagus Angke, the small **Mesjid Alanwar** or Angke Mosque, dating from 1761, incorporates Hindu-Balinese architectural elements. From such milieux emerged the *orang Betawi*; the "Batavian," prototype of the modern Jakartan, whose dialect and customs came to set the tone of everyday life in the city. Even the Dutch adopted *Betawi* ways, donning the *sarong* for home wear and abandoning their stuffy imitations of Dutch town-houses for open bungalows with Javanese roofs and galleries. Much of late colonial residential architecture can be seen in the suburbs of **Menteng** and **Kemayoran**. Today, low dwellings with red clay roof tiles, not high-rise blocks or suburban compounds, still define Jakarta's architectural character.

After independence, the real transformation began. Old monuments were toppled; grander and uglier ones took their place. In-migration and incompetence frustrated the dreams of architects and ideologues; careless destruction and careless construction rendered Batavia almost unrecognizable within two decades.

Many of Jakarta's most famous landmarks date from this period: the **Senayan Sports Complex**, built with Russian money in 1962; the first of its luxury hotels, the **Hotel Indonesia** on Jl. Thamrin; and a remarkable collection of crude, powerful statues in the "Heroes of Socialism" tradition. Many of the latter have attracted deflating nicknames: "Hot Hands Harry", "pizza man" and "mad waiter" for the **Youth Statue** at the south end of Jl. Sudirman, who grimaces as he holds aloft what appears to be a flaming dish; "Hansel and Gretel" for the wholesome couple portrayed by the **Statue of Welcome** on Jl. Thamrin, built for the 1962 Asian Games. Of the striking **Irian Jaya Liberation Memorial** ("the chainbreaker") on Lapangan Banteng, it used to be quipped in Sukarno's time, that the giant's cry was "Empty!" – in

reference to the Department of Finance behind him.

Sukarno's ultimate monumental legacy was the **National Monument** or **Monas**, otherwise known as "Sukarno's last erection." Part Hindu *lingga* (phallic symbol), part marble hymn to progress, it rises 137 metres above the centre of Merdeka Square. Still Jakarta's greatest landmark, Monas offers superb panoramic views and has an interesting museum that depicts the current official version of Indonesian history in 48 dioramas.

Sukarno also bequeathed Jakarta a population that doubled every decade, a phone system which required businesses to employ special staff just to dial numbers over and over again, and a reputation as Southeast Asia's dirtiest, least organized, most dangerous capital. Under Suharto, Jakarta's governor Ali Sadikin set out to change the city's image. He repaired roads and bridges and built schools and hospitals, but also took cruel and much-criticized measures to eliminate the "eyesore" of street peddlers and *becak* from the central areas. A bloody police campaign against urban crime in 1983, repeated the theme of ruthless cleansing. However, Suharto's New Order did not bring an end to extravagant prestige projects. Mrs. Suharto's **Taman Mini Indonesia Indah** ("Beautiful Indonesia in Miniature"), a mammoth theme park in the south of the city, designed to provide a sanitized overview of all of the country's regional cultures, epitomizes the "showcase" mentality.

To the westener unused to the texture of life there, Jakarta still gives the impression of being perpetually on the verge of terminal breakdown. Spreading like some concrete epidemic, Jakarta remains undefeated by its growth. In 1945 there were 900,000 Jakartans; today there are eight million. Yet Jakarta's infrastructure and appearance, though it may be difficult for the newcomer to believe, continue to improve.

JAKARTA (Area Code 021)

Accommodation

LUXURY: **Aryaduta**, Jl. Prapatan 44-46, tel: 3861234. **Borobudur Intercont.**, Jl. Lapangan Banteng Selatan, tel: 3805555. **Jakarta Hilton**, Jl. Jen Gatot Subroto, tel: 5703600. **Horison**, Jl. Pantai Indah, Taman Impian Jaya Ancol, tel: 6406000. **Indonesia**, Jl. MH Thamrin, tel: 2301008. **Jakarta Mandarin**, Jl. MH Thamrin, tel: 3141307. **President**, Jl. MH Thamrin 59, tel: 2301122. **Sahid Jaya**, Jl. Jen Sudirman 86, tel: 5704444. **Sari Pacific**, Jl. MH Thamrin, tel: 3902707.
MODERATE: **Kartika Chandra**, Jl. Gatot Subroto, tel: 510808. **Karya Hotel**, Jl. Jaksa 32-34, tel: 3140484. **Marcopolo**, Jl. Teuku Cik Ditiro 19, tel: 2301777. **Menteng I**, Jl. R. P. Soeroso 28, tel: 3145208. **Menteng II**, Jl. Cikini Raya 105, tel: 3146311. **Sabang Metropolitan**, Jl. Haji Agus Salim 11, tel: 3576221. **Transaera**, Jl. Merdeka Timur 16, tel: 351373.
BUDGET: Concentrated around Jl. Jaksa/Jl. Kebon Sirih, S of Merdeka Square, are **Nick's Hostel**, Jl. Jaksa 16, tel: 3141988. **Bloemsteen**, Jl. Kebon Sirih Timur Dalam 1/173, tel. 323002. **Borneo Hostel**, Jl. Kebon Sirih Barat Dalam 35, tel: 3140095. **Wisma Delima**, Jl. Jaksa 5, tel: 337026. **Djody Hostel**, Jl. Jaksa 27, tel: 3151404. **Jusran Hostel**, Jl. Jaksa, Hall 6, Nr. 9, tel: 3140373. **Tator Hotel**, Jl. Jaksa 37, tel: 323940. **Wisma I.S.E.**, Jl. Wahid Hasyim 168, tel: 333463. **Hostel Norbek**, Jl. Jaksa 14, tel: 330392. **Bintang Kejora Hostel**, Jl. Debon Sirih Barat Dalam 52, tel: 323878.

Restaurants

FOOD STALLS: Warung are everywhere, especially at night along Jl. Kebon Sirik, Jl. Mangga Besar and Jl. H.A. Salim. Singapore-style sanitized versions at **Sarinah** stores on Jl. Thamrin and in Kebayoran Baru.
INDONESIAN: **Ayam Goreng Mbok Berek** (Javanese fried chicken), Jl. Panglima Polim Raya 93, tel: 770652. **Bu Tjitro** (Javanese), Jl. Senen Raya 25A, tel: 371197. **Jun Nuan** (seafood), Jl. Batuceper 69, Glodok. **Pondok Jawa Timur** (Javanese), Jl. Prapanca Raya, Kebayoran Baru. **Sari Bundo** (Padang), Jl. Ir H Juanda 27, tel: 358343. **Satay House Senayan**, Jl. Kebon Sirih 31A, tel: 326238. **Tinoor Asli** (Manado), Jl. Gondangdia Lama 33A, tel: 336430.
CHINESE: **Bakmi Gajah Mada**, Jl. Gajah Mada 92. **Cahaya Kota**, Jl. Wahid Hasyim 9, tel: 3533015. **Istana Naga**, Jl. Jen Gatot Subroto (Kav. 12, Case Bldg), tel: 511809.
WESTERN: **Cafe Batavia**, nostalgic Colonial-style cafe in a historic Dutch buidling from 1805; remarkable parlor of Javan teak; on Taman Fatahillah, Batavia's town square. **Oasis**, excellent restaurant in the Dutch Governor's residence, also offers Rijstafel, reserva-

tions required, Jl. Raden Saleh 47, Kebayoran, tel: 3150646. **Arts & Curios Restaurant**, Jl. Kebon Binatang III 8A, Cikini. **Club Noordwijk**, Jl. Ir H. Juanda 5A, tel: 353909. **George & Dragon**, Jl. Telukbetung 32, tel: 345625. **Sari Pacific Coffee Shop**, Sari Pacific Hotel. **Gaststube**, Jl. Jend. Sudirman, tel: 5712734. **Hard Rock Cafe**, regular live band appearances, Jl. Thamrin 11, Sarinah Bldg, tel: 3903566.

Shopping

TEXTILES & CLOTHES: **Batik Keris**, Sarinah Jaya department store, Blok M. **Danar Hadi**, Jl. Raden Saleh 1A, tel: 342390/343712. **Iwan Tirta**, Jl. Panarukan 25, tel: 349122. Many smaller shops in Tanah Abang, Pasar Baru & Kebayoran Baru.
HANDICRAFTS & CURIOS: **Jakarta flea market**, Jl. Surabaya, Menteng. **Handicraft Center**, Sarinah Jaya dept store, Kebayoran Baru. **Indonesian Bazaar**, Jakarta Hilton. **Pasar Seni**, Ancol. High concentration of smaller shops on: Jl. Palatehan I, Kebayoran Baru; Jl. Kebon Sirih Timur, Menteng; Jl. Majapahit, Kota; Jl. Gajah Mada, Kota.

Museums / Galleries / Zoos

Museum Bahari (maritime), Jl. Pasar Ikan 1, Kota, tel: 6693406/6692476. Tue-Thu 9 am-2 pm, Fri 9-11:30, Sat 9 am-1 pm, Sun 9 am-3 pm, closed Mon. **National Museum**, Jl. Merdeka Barat 12, tel: 360551. Tue-Thu & Sun 8:30 am-2:30 pm, Fri 8:30-11, Sat 8:30 am-1:30 pm, closed Mon. **Ragunan Zoo**, Jl. Raya Ragunan (16 km S of town), tel: 782975. Open daily 9 am-6 pm. **Museum Satria Mandala** (military), Jl. Gatot Subroto 14, tel: 582759. Tue-Sun 9 am-3 pm, closed Mon. **Jakarta History Museum**, Jl. Taman Fatahillah 1, Kota, tel: 679101. Tue-Thu 9 am-2 pm, Fri 9-11, Sat 9 am-1 pm, Sun 9 am-3 pm, closed Mon. **Museum of Fine Art & Ceramics**, Jl. Fatahilah 2, Kota, tel: 671062. Tu-Thu 9 am-2 pm, Fri 9-11 am, Sat 9 am-1 pm, Sun 9 am-3 pm, closed Mon. **Wayan Museum** (excellent collection of Wayang puppets), Jl. Pintu Besar Utara 27, Kota, tel: 679560. Tue-Thu & Sun 9 am-2 pm, Fri 9-11 am, Sat 9 am-1 pm, tours Sun at 10 am, closed Mon. **Textile Museum**, Jl. Karel Satsuit Tubun 4, Tanah Abang, tel: 365367. Tue-Thu & Sun 9 am-2 pm, Fri 9-11, Sat 9 am-1 pm, closed Mon. **Taman Impian Jaya Ancol**, on the border between Kota and Tanjung Priok, amusement park full of attractions, swimming pool, and endless entertainment, open daily, usually after 7 am. **Taman Mini Indonesia Indah** ("Beautiful Indonesia in Miniature"), theme park incl. cultural & zoological museums, Jl. TMII, Pondok Gede, tel: 8400400. Daily 9 am-5 pm.

Cultural Events

Jakarta's and Indonesia's main cultural venue is **Taman Ismail Marzuki (TIM)**, Jl. Cikini Raya 73, tel:

337325. Constantly changing program of shows & performances, daily 8 am-8 pm. **Pasar Seni**, in Taman Impian Jaya Ancol, also has nightly cultural events. **Taman Mini Indonesia Indah** (see Museums) has live dance, music & drama on Sun. **Bharata Theatre**, Jl. Kali Lio 15 (near Pasar Senen) stages *wayang orang* Tue, Wed, Fri & Sat at 8 & 11 pm. University of Indonesia's **School of Folk Art**, Jl. Bunga 5, Jatinegara, rehearses 11 am daily except Sun. *Gamelan* performances every Sun at 10 am at **Wayang Museum** (see Museums).

Tourist Information

Visitors Information Center, Jakarta Theatre Bldg, corner Jl. MH Thamrin/Jl. Wahid Hasyim, tel: 3154094. Mon-Fri 8 am-12 pm & 1-5 pm, Sat 9 am-2 pm. **Directorate General of Tourism**, Jl. Medan Merdeka Barat 16-19, tel: 3838169. Mon-Thu 8 am-3 pm, Fri 8-11 am & 1-3 pm.

Post

Central Post Office, Jl. Lapangan Banteng Utara, Mon-Fri 8am-4 pm, Sat 8 am-1 pm.

Telephone

Kantor Telekomunikasi (24-hour long-distance service), Jakarta Theatre Bldg, corner Jl. MH Thamrin/Jl. Wahid Hasyim. Similar services, long-distance telephone, fax & telegrams, offered by many private *Wartel*, such as **Wartel Duta Dinda Perdana**, Jl. Jaksa 15A, tel: 3143310.

Hospitals

Rumah Sakit Fatmawati, Jl. Fatmawati, tel: 760121-4; or **Pertamina Hospital**, Jl. Kyai Maja 29, tel: 7200290.

Visas / Immigration

Directorate General of Immigration, Jl. Teuku Umar 1, Menteng, tel: 349811/349812. Mon-Thu 8 am-3 pm, Fri 8-11, Sat 8 am-2 pm.

Embassies

Australia: Jl. M. H. Thamrin 15, tel: 323109.
Canada: 5th floor, Wisma Metropolitan I, Jl. Jen. Sudirman Kav 29, tel: 510709.
Ireland: Jl. Gedung Hijau I 11, Pondok Indah, tel: 7690070.
New Zealand: Jl. Diponegoro 41, tel: 330552.
United Kingdom: Jl. M. H. Thamrin 75, tel: 330904.
United States of America: Jl. Merdeka Selatan 5, tel: 360360.

Arrival / Transportation

AIR: Soekarno-Hatta (Cengkareng) International Airport, 23 km W of town, handles all foreign & domestic flights. Taxis & Damri buses (to Kemayoran, Rawamangun, Blok M & Gambir) provide city links.
INTERNATIONAL AIRLINES: **Cathay Pacific**, Jl. Jend Sudirman Kav. 52-53, tel: 5150777. **Thai International**, BDN Bldg, Jl. M. H. Thamrin 5, tel: 3140607. **Quantas**, BDN Bldg, Jl. Thamrin 5, tel: 2300277. **Philippine Airlines**, Plaza Mashil, Jl. Jend Sudriman Kav. 25-29, tel: 5267780. **Swissair**, Plaza Mashil, Jl. Jen. Sudirman Kav. 25-29, tel: 5229912. **British Airways**, Wisma Metropolitan 1, 10th fl., Jl. Jen. Sudirman Kav. 29, tel: 5211490. **Japan Airlines**, MID Plaza, Jl. Jen. Sudirman Kav. 10-11, tel: 5212177. **KLM**, Summitmas Dua, 17th Floor, Jl. Jen Suirman Kav. 61-62, tel: 5212176. **Lufthansa**, Panin Centre Bldg, Jl. Jen. Sudirman Kav. 1, tel: 5702005. **Singapore Airlines**, Chase Plaza, Jl. Jen. Sudirman Kav. 21, tel: 5206933. **UTA**, Summitmas Tower, 9th fl., Jl. Jen. Sudirman Kav. 61-62, tel: 5202262.
DOMESTIC AIRLINES: **Garuda**, Danareksa Bldg, Jl. Merdeka, Selatan 13, 11th floor., tel: 3801901; BDN Bldg, Jl. Thamrin 5, tel: 2311991; Hotel Borobudur, tel: 3100568; Wisma Dharmala Sakti, Jl. Jen. Sudirman 32, tel: 5701292. **Merpati**, Jl. Angkasa 2, Kemayoran, tel: 4225555. **Bouraq**, Jl. Angkasa 1, Kemayoran, tel: 6295150/6595179. **Mandala**, Jl. Veteran 1/34, tel: 368107.
SEA: Passenger vessels berth at **Tanjung Priok Harbor**, 10 km NE of town. Inquire at **Pelni** office, Jl. Pintu Air I, Tanjung Priok, tel: 358398.
RAIL: Kota Station, Jl. Stasiun Kota 1, for *Bima II & Mutiara* night expresses to Surabaya (via Yogya or Semarang), & morning train to Merak & Sumatra. **Gambir Station**, Jl. Merdeka Timur; for other trains to Central & East Java & (with bus connection) Bali, and for Bogor & Bandung. **Tanah Abang Station** for evening train to Sumatra. Some travel agencies, incl. **Carnation**, Jl. Menteng Raya 24, tel: 344027, arrange tickets in advance.
BUS: Pulo Gadung Terminal, corner Jl. Bekasi Timur Raya/Jl. Perintis Kemerdekaan, to Central Java & points E; **Kampung Rambutan Terminal**, ca. 20 km SE of downtown, for Semarang & Bandung; **Kalideres Terminal**, Grogol, for Bogor, W & Sumatra. All three long-distance bus terminals served by local buses from Gambir railway station.
LOCAL: Taxis are metered (*Bluebird* are the most reliable), *bajaj* are not. Buses are frequent and cheap; *patas* are fastest and most comfortable.

PULAU SERIBU

Onrust (Kapal) and **Bidadari** islands have regular ferry services from Tanjung Priok; the **Putri** and **Melinjo** resorts can be reached by charter speedboat from Ancol marina. For tickets contact **Putri Pulau Seribu Paradise**, Jl. K. H. Wahid Hasyim 69, tel: 335535.

WEST JAVA

BANTEN AND THE FAR WEST
SUNDA
BANDUNG
CIREBON

Jakarta happens to be located in Java, but it is hardly of Java. The contrast between the metropolitan capital and the surrounding province is dramatic. For, although West Java contains some big cities of its own, its soul is rural. The least densely populated province of the island, it offers unrivaled scenery, extensive nature reserves and refreshing mountain weather, all within a few hours of Jakarta's confusion. Its prosperity, friendly people and excellent transportation facilities make it one of the most genuinely relaxing parts of rural Indonesia in which to travel. West Java also offers much that is of cultural and historical interest.

West Java was first known to Europe as Sunda – a land, kingdom, language and people all distinct from Java. The 16th-century Portuguese were so impressed by this country that they misapplied its name not only to the island of Java, but to the whole archipelago; to this day, Sumatra, Java, Borneo and Celebes are still known collectively as the "Greater Sunda Islands." The first known kingdom on Java, the Hindu state of Tarumanegara, flourished on the north coastal plain of West Java in the 5th century. A millenium later, the first Por-

Left: Monas, the National Monument built under Sukarno in Jakarta.

tuguese ships to weigh anchor here were welcomed by another great Hindu kingdom, Pajajaran, a contemporary and rival of the great East Javanese Majapahit. Since 1433, the capital had been at an inland location, Pakuan, today's **Bogor**, where Dutch governors-general would later reside. However, in 1522, when Pajajaran concluded an alliance with Portuguese Goa, it was still master of the north coast, including the lucrative ports of Banten and Sunda Kelapa (now Jakarta). The Portuguese were to help protect the Hindu power against Islam's rapid westward expansion along the coast. However, when they returned in 1527, both ports had been captured by Muslims and made vassals of the young sultanate of Demak, 400 kilometers to the east. Landlocked, Pajajaran declined, and 50 years later its capital was conquered by Banten.

While Javanese speakers flocked to the booming coastlands, and Banten became a great trading and military power, the Sundanese retreated to the mountains and high plateau in the south and developed a rural folk culture without cities or courts. In this condition, and so close to Batavia, what now became known as the "Sundalands" were easy prey for the VOC; by 1684, the entire Sundanese-speaking area was under direct Dutch control, while the

87

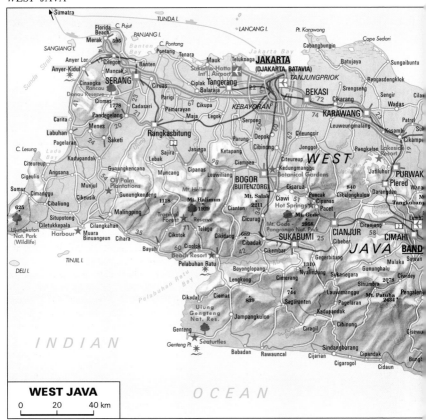

WEST JAVA

0   20   40 km

coastal sultanates of Banten and Cirebon retained nominal independence into the 19th century. In due course, the Sundanese too were Islamized and indeed, became known as purer and stricter Muslims than their Central Javanese neighbours. However, in language, customs and art, and in their own minds, the Sundanese never assimilated with the outgrowth of ethnic Java which had cut them off from the Java Sea.

So, today there are two West Javas; the Javanized, maritime north coast and the Sundanese interior. This human division coincides closely with the most obvious physical one; the north is flat and featureless, a hot, wet, 50 kilometer-wide littoral plain, advancing a little further seawards

each year, laden with the rice which feeds Jakarta's masses, while Sunda proper is a towering, stately mass of welded volcanoes – the **Priangan**, or Parahyangan, "Abode of the Gods," clothed in tea plantations and virgin forest, shrouded in cloud, falling steeply into the sea on the wave-lashed, portless south coast.

The broken island of **Krakatau**, out in the Sunda Strait, is an outlier; many of Priangan's other volcanoes are still active. At Cianjur, Bandung, Garut and Tasikmalaya, the mountains part to cradle high depressions which are meticulously terraced to grow fragrant rice. To the east, the Priangan fades imperceptibly into the more intermittent volcanic terrain of Central Java.

88

The village is dominated by the tiered *meru* roof of the 16th-century **Mesjid Agung**, one of Java's oldest mosques and a good example of transitional Hindu-Islamic architecture. Its peculiar pagoda-like minaret is said to be the work of a Chinese Muslim, and the adjacent shuttered building that of a Dutch Muslim; reflections of early-Javan Islam's ecclectic interpretations. South of the *alun-alun* (central square) are the remains of two large palaces, the **Pakuwonan** and the **Istana Kaibon**. A little further on is the tomb of the third king, Maulana Yusuf, who ruled in the 1570s. Northwest of these remnants of Banten's greatness is a monument to its fall – the ruins of **Fort Speelwijk**, constructed in 1682 to keep the city safely under the Dutch heel. Built overlooking the sea, the fort is now some 200 meters inland; coastal silting has played its part in the decline of Banten. Since 1985, local archaeological finds have been displayed in the **Banten Site Museum** on Jl. Mesjid Banten Lama.

For most visitors, the most important attractions of Java's far west are natural. The national park at **Ujung Kulon** ("West End") is one of Indonesia's prime nature reserves, and a fine example of successful state action to preserve wildlife. This unsullied wilderness shelters hornbill, *banteng* (wild cattle) and crocodile, as well as the only breeding population of Javan rhinoceros to survive Java's long transformation from jungle to market garden. **Krakatau**, 40 kilometers out in the Sunda Strait, is the remains of a great volcano which blew itself to pieces in 1883, in one of the greatest explosions ever recorded. Its scarred, primordial landscapes are reached by sea from **Labuhan**, which is also the usual jumping-off point for Ujung Kulon. Along the coast north of Labuhan are West Java's finest and safest beaches, with accommodations in **Carita**, **Anyer Kidul** and **Florida Beach** (near **Merak**, the terminal for the ferry to Sumatra).

BANTEN AND THE FAR WEST

Ninety kilometers west of Jakarta, via Serang, is the fishing village of **Banten**, known to history as Bantam. Looking at this quiet little place today, it is hard to believe that for a century this was the greatest trading port on Java; the city which Batavia itself was founded to challenge. Wrested from Hindu control in the 1520s, by Gunungjati of Demak, Banten became an independent Muslim sultanate which grew rich on the trade of the Sunda Strait and the pepper of Lampung. Banten attracted English, French and Danish "factories" before a civil war presented the VOC with the opportunity to intervene and end its glory forever in 1682.

SUNDA

Travelling from Jakarta, Sunda proper begins in the rain-drenched town of **Bogor**, 50 kilometers south of the capital, where the first big volcano, **Salak**, begins to rise. The area has a long history of civilization. Fifteen hundred years ago it was part of Tarumanegara, Java's first Hindu kingdom. Fifteen kilometers west of the town, near **Ciampea**, the footprints of a 5th-century king and a miraculously clear inscription adorn the great riverside boulder of **Batutulis Ciampea**. Three kilometers southeast of town, another *batutulis* (inscribed stone) is the only surviving reminder that 15th-century Pajajaran had its capital here; but, Bogor's kings had already vanished into legend before Gustaaf Willem Baron van Imhoff founded a country estate here in 1745. Bogor began its rise to renown as Buitenzorg ("Carefree"), retreat and later offi-

cial residence of the governor-general of Dutch East India. The present **Istana Bogor** (Bogor Palace), elegant and white on its undulating green lawns, dates from 1856, and has seen many a lavish gathering of both Batavia's and Jakarta's elite. Its pre-war furnishings were looted by the Japanese; the present contents are owed to the acquisitive zeal of the late President Sukarno and the generosity of his many benefactors. They include paintings and sculptures, erotic and otherwise, by many of Indonesia's foremost artists. Sukarno was under *de facto* house arrest here from 1967 until his death in 1970.

The real pride of Bogor is the **Kebun Raya**, or Bogor Botanical Garden, which covers a beautiful 87 hectares next to the palace compound. It was founded in 1817, by the Prussian-born, Dutch government naturalist Caspar Reinwardt, with the help of two Englishmen from Kew Gardens. This institution was in the forefront of the Victorian colonial enterprise of documenting, classifying, taming

Above: A manioc vendor at the Bogor market. Right: Fish ponds near Bandung.

and transforming tropical nature. And harnessing it for profit; the *cultuurstelsel* crops were tested and improved here, and the oil palm from Africa (1848) and *Hevea* rubber from Brazil (1883) were introduced. Plantation magnates showered the gardens with funds to keep their money trees pest-free. Bogor is still one of the world's foremost botanical institutions, with 17,000 living specimens from all over Indonesia and the world. The **Museum Herbarium Bogoriensis** and **Bogor Zoological Museum**, as well as extensive library and laboratory facilities, are located on the same site. The gardens, with their ponds and quiet groves, are also favorite venues for picnickers and lovers. The busy, muddy town of Bogor itself has simply sprouted up around the Kebun Raya, and it is the home of one of the few remaining *gamelan* gongsmiths on Java.

Beyond Bogor is the **Tatar Sunda**, the rugged plateau of the Sundanese heartland and the home of the Sundanese arts. The elements are those of Java, but the balance is different. The Sundanese have their own *gamelan*, but they are better known for the more rustic tones of the *kecapi* (a type of lute), *angklung* (a device of bamboo tubes suspended in a frame and shaken, with an almost metallic hollow sound) and *suling* (a soft-toned flute), often accompanying a dreamy female voice. The *wayang golek*, a prosaic but charming three-dimensional wooden version of the *wayang kulit* shadow play, is also known further east, but it is closest to the Sundanese heart. In performance, the romance of the *Ramayana* is preferred here over the philosophy of the *Mahabharata*. The *jaipongan* is a popular Sundanese dance event in which men pay to dance opposite a professional woman performer, very suggestively, but without touching her.

This area was formerly famous for its coffee, which became "Java coffee" to Europe and America. As early as the 1720s, the VOC forced the Sundanese peasantry to pay tax in coffee beans; this archaic imposition was not completely

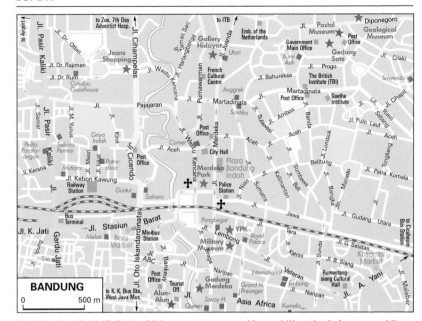

BANDUNG

0   500 m

abolished until 1917. In the 20th century, the place of coffee was largely taken by tea. At **Puncak** ("Peak"), the highest part of the dizzy road from Bogor to the plateau, the hillsides are fragrant with tea. Women pickers still sweat to harvest this valuable crop, sometimes with their children on their backs. Incredibly, another important source of income in this 1900 meter-high mountain pass is fish: *ikan mas* (big carp) are kept in countless fishponds and smaller fish are kept in the shallow water of seasonally empty ricefields. At **Cipanas** there is a famous volcanic spa where the mountains disgorge sulfureous water at a hot 43° C. Many governors-general have sworn by its restorative powers and their country house still stands here. Not far away is the **Cibodas Botanical Garden**, a high-altitude extension of the gardens at Bogor, and beyond that are the forested peaks of two volcanoes that comprise the magnificent **Mt. Gede Pangrango National Park**.

The most isolated and unchanged part of the Sundalands is the westernmost massif, straddling the *kabupaten* of Banten and Priangan Barat. At its center is the vast, rarely visited, **Mt. Halimun Reserve**, with its many trails to various tea plantations. On the western slopes is a cluster of settlements inhabited by the intriguing **Badui** people, a remnant of old Sunda which resisted Islamization by the drastic expedient of isolating itself almost completely from the outside world, both by distance and a series of strict taboos against travel and contact with strangers. The 40 families – never more – of white-robed "Inner Badui" acquired a cultish aura of secrecy and magic which kept outsiders in awe, while the more numerous black-clad "Outer Badui" acted as their ambassadors to the profane world – truly an astonishing piece of social history. The Badui area is usually reached from Rangkasbitung in the north, via the little town of **Lebak** where Multatuli was stationed and sacked, and where his great novel *Max Havelaar* was consequently set. Part of the journey to the Badui must be made on foot. No one may stay in the inner "forbidden area," for although the cult of the Badui is under heavy pressure from education, population growth and tourism, its days are not yet over. A far cry from the Badui is the Halimun massif's eastern window on "civilization;" the seaside resort of **Pelabuhan Ratu**. When Sukarno stayed here, fresh bread rolls were flown in by helicopter from Bandung. At the **Samudra Beach Hotel,** which the late president built, one room is always kept vacant for the Queen of the South Sea, a goddess who lures swimmers to their deaths in the crashing waves of this stormy coast.

BANDUNG

In **Bandung**, the Dutch gave Sunda the capital it had not had since the fall of Pajajaran. The original fiefdom of Bandung was established in 1641, by decree of Sultan Agung of Mataram, but its center was further south; the present city grew up around a Dutch administrative center established on the Great Post Road in 1811. In 1864, it became the capital of the Priangan plateau. Soon conveniently linked to Batavia by railway, it was favored by the colonials for its cool climate and fine location on the mountain-girdled bed of an ancient lake, and became a center for all kinds of Dutch activities not directly tied to the big ports. In 1916, the command of the colonial army was transferred here from Batavia, and Indonesia's officers are still trained here. The **Bandung Institute of Technology (IBT)** was opened in 1920. It is still one of Indonesia's most prestigious universities. With its comfortable bungalows and boulevards lined with flowers, Bandung was Java's most European city – even, some said, the "Paris of the East." In 1942, it was to have been the mountain stronghold which would defy Japan's onslaught; but its defenses crumbled even as the last planes took off for Australia. Today, reclaimed by the Sundanese, but

contested by more than the usual mix of immigrants from other regions, it is a busy, shabby city of almost two million, that thrives on the light industries which came here in the 1970s. Bandung is the site of one of the New Order's most spectacular and controversial industrial projects, the **IPTN Aircraft** plant, and while the old atmosphere has succumbed to the smog, and the newer soubriquet of "City of Flowers" has not been earned, Bandung has managed to retain its historic and architectural interest, its intellectual dynamism and the institutions which make it the seat of Sundanese culture.

The **ITB** campus is in the north of town on Jl. Ganeca; it was an out-of-town location when it was built in 1920. Architect Maclaine Pont used the traditional houses of the Mandailing Batak in North Sumatra as the model for his beautiful and functional design. Sukarno received his engineer's degree here in 1926, but not before helping to found the study club which would grow into the Indonesian Nationalist Party (PNI). To this day, ITB students have a reputation for outspokenness; unapproved political publications have led to trials of student leaders. Not purely a technical university, ITB has an art gallery which is open to the public. Other 1920s buildings include the venerable **Gedung Sate** (1920) on Jl. Diponegoro as well as the **Geological Museum**, opened by the Dutch in 1929, across the street. Nearby is Bandung's tallest and most striking postwar building, the new local government headquarters, that many think looks like some kind of futuristic water tower.

The streamlined curves of the 1930s vision of modernity grace many buildings in the central area and the old elite suburb of Dago, but the most spectacular and well-maintained Art Deco relic is the opulent **Savoy Homann Hotel** on the main thoroughfare, Jl. Asia Africa, once a section of the Great Post Road. However, Bandung's outstandig historic

building, is the **Gedung Merdeka** on the same street – not for its crude, inter-war, civic architecture, but because it was the venue for a grand diplomatic event: the first Asia-Africa Conference, in 1955. Here Sukarno played host to Nehru, Nasser and Ho Chi Minh, and laid the foundations of today's Non-Alligned Movement amid the euphoria of that seemingly distant time of falling empires. "Bandung spirit builds the world anew," blazed a giant slogan from the building's eaves, while the armed Darul Islam rebels watched from the hills and the country lurched towards bankruptcy. Also known as the Asia-Africa Building, Gedung Merdeka houses an interesting museum of photos and other memorabilia from the conference.

Just west of Bandung is the prewar army town of **Cimahi**; nearby, the Tarum river, Sunda's largest, passes over spectacular falls. About 50 kilometers down-

river, the Tarum flows into the huge **Jatiluhur Reservoir**, where a French-built dam and hydroelectric station feed Jakarta's and West Java's ever-growing demand for water and power.

North of Bandung, Dutch-style flower gardens, vegetable plots and even dairy farms grace the slopes of some of Java's highest volcanoes in homely defiance of the wild tropical backdrop. A very Asian use has been found here for fancy European livestock: the locals have discovered that ram-fighting is even more exciting than cockfighting. Here, too, are the famous spa resorts of **Ciater**, with almost Roman-looking hot baths, and **Maribaya**. **Lembang**'s Grand Hotel opened its doors in 1926. The best-known summit of this massif is the readily accessible **Tangkuban Prahu**, with its three craters of blasted boulders and boiling mud.

Even more dramatic landscapes lie on the opposite, southern side of Bandung, though at a greater distance. Thirty kilometers southwest of **Ciwidey**, is a

Above: Fruit and snacks for sale in a typical Cirebon warung.

beautiful cold mountain lake that resembles a Scottish loch. The town itself is a living center of blacksmithing (agricultural tools, as well as decorative knives), something of a rarity even in tribal Sumatra. **Mt. Papandayan**, about 60 kilometers southeast of Bandung via the tea town of **Pengalengan**, is a bigger, angrier Tangkuban Prahu.

There are two routes from Bandung to the east: the old Great Post Road, which returns to the north coast, and a quieter southern route which ultimately winds its way to Yogyakarta. The first town on the southern road is **Garut**, a favorite mountain resort in colonial times, now a quintessentially Sundanese country town which features some of the last pile houses in Java. Sunda retained the old pre-Hindu, Malay-like design long after the houses of Java proper came down to earth, but "Javanization," snobbery and the price of timber are putting an end to it now. North of Garut, at **Lake Cangkuang**, near Leles, is West Java's only significant Hindu temple, imaginatively restored in the 1970s. Perversely (or perhaps appropriately, in syncretic Indonesia), next to the temple is the grave of Arif Muhammad, the pioneer of Islam in the area. The Garut region is even more volcanically active than points west. In 1982, it suffered badly from a series of major eruptions from **Mt. Galunggung**, east of Garut, which covered the countryside in a searing, black blizzard of ash. In **Kawah Talagabodas**, the crater of Galunggung's less deadly twin, a spectacular green sulfereous lake can be seen. After Garut, the next major stop is **Tasikmalaya**, famous for its woven craft products in rattan, pandanus and bamboo. Tasikmalaya also has a *batik* industry; the traditional designs are similar to those of Central Java.

Tasikmalaya's **Tanduy river** roughly marks the linguistic border between Sunda and Java; 40 kilometers further on is the administrative boundary where

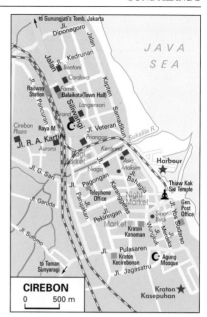

CIREBON

0   500 m

Central Java officially begins. Just before the latter is the turn-off to one of Java's most accessible nature reserves, **Pangandaran**, like Ujong Kulon, a narrownecked peninsula. Pangandaran is also a popular, cheap beach resort.

CIREBON

Some 200 kilometers east of Jakarta, along the coast, beyond the rice town of Karawang, or 100 kilometers from Bandung along the Great Post Road, is the historic city of **Cirebon**. Cirebon was a Muslim city-state, another child of Demak's westward crusade in the early 16th century. Six kilometers north of the city is the holy **Tomb of Gunungjati**, the great Aceh-born warrior who also conquered, Banten and probably Sunda Kelapa (Jakarta) too, before he came to rule Cirebon for Demak. He is revered as one of the *wali songo*, the nine saints who turned Java to the true faith, and his grave is still a place of pilgrimage. Like Banten, Cirebon was a Javanese colony in a Sun-

danese arca. It played an important part in the Islamization of Sunda, but in doing so became partly Sundanese itself. Its deviant Javanese dialect is full of Sundanese words; its music and dance are substantially Sundanese too. Unlike Banten, Cirebon fell prey to the expansion of Mataram under Sultan Agung, and ever since it has remained closely associated with Central Java, whose courts and arts it has emulated. Today it is the *pesisir kliwon*, the western rim of Java proper.

During Cirebon's vassalage to Mataram, one of its rulers, Girilaya, weakened the sultanate in time-honored Javanese fashion by dividing it between his sons. To this day there are two separate palaces or *kraton*: the **Kraton Kasepuhan**, for the sultans of the house of Sepuh, in the southeast of the city, and the **Kraton Kanoman**, for the Anom sultans, more

Above: An old woman paints batik designs in hot wax in a Cirebon factory. Right: Wayang golek puppets during a performance in Cirebon.

centrally located next to the market of the same name. The Kasepuhan houses a small, but worthwhile museum of royal memorabilia. The oldest part of the Kasepuhan dates from 1529; its *sitingghil* (pavilion) features a Hindu-style split gate, while elsewhere the use of Delft tiles is further evidence of the sultanate's eclecticism. In matters of religion, though, the Sepuh sultans were less flexible, as the impressive and equally old **Mesjid Agung** next door demonstrates. This grand mosque is built alongside the *alun-alun* (town square) in Javanese fashion, but it is uncompromisingly skewed towards Mecca; the Central Javanese would have left the building square and simply prayed diagonally once inside. The Kraton Kanoman, of later origin, is run-down, but atmospheric. Many other old buildings line Cirebon's tortuous streets; this is one of Java's better preserved towns.

Battered by the wars of its more powerful neighbors, Cirebon was taken under the muscular wing of the VOC in

1681. It staggered beneath the weight of Dutch exactions, – Cirebon *corvee* laborers even helped build Batavia's roads – but retained its importance as a trade port, thanks largely to its strong Chinese community. There is a fine old Chinese temple, the **Klenteng Thiaw Kak Sie**, near the harbor. The Chinese have made another unique contribution to Cirebon's artistic life; a Chinese architect designed the **Taman Sunyaragi**, a grotesque flight of fantasy in brick and plaster four kilometers outside town, on the southwestern bypass. Built in 1852, this extraordinary, honeycombed folly would come to serve as a pleasure palace-cum-hermitage for Cirebon's royalty, who were intent on following the royalty of Yogya and Solo in their flight from ignominious political reality into what quickly became a culturally tacky dream-world.

A happier artistic synthesis resulted from Chinese participation in the local textile business. Cirebon's renowned *batik* motifs are largely Chinese-inspired; swirling *megamendung* (dark clouds),

rock designs, flying birds, even Chinese lions and dragons are used as decorative themes. The main *batik* centers are in the nearby, semi-rural villages of **Trusmi**, **Kalitengah**, **Kaliwuri** and especially **Weru**. **Indramayu**, a fishing village 50 kilometers to the north, also has its own strong *batik* tradition.

Unfortunately, during the 20th century Cirebon figured in the Indonesian imagination as nothing more grand than *Kota Udang*, the "Prawn City," after its best-known industry; the prewar **Balaikota** (town hall) features the crustacean as an unusual decorative motif. And recently, the town has experienced a kind of artistic renaissance as a center of the *wayang topeng*, masked dance-drama. At **Linggarjati**, 22 kilometers southwest of the city, Java's old masters acknowledged that times had changed by concluding their first diplomatic agreement with the Republic of Indonesia, in November 1946. Their successors have managed to maintain the resort in true Dutch style.

97

BANTEN
(Area Code 0254)

SERANG: Hotel Abadi, Jl. J. Sudirman 36-40, tel: 200641. **Hotel Wisata Baru**, Jl. Maulana Yusuf 16, tel: 200515.

MUSEUM: **Banten Site Museum**, Jl. Mesjid Banten Lama. Tue-Thu 8 am-2 pm, Fri 8-11, Sat 8-12, Sun 8 am-1 pm, closed Mon.

WEST COAST
(Area Code 0254)

CARITA: Mutiara Carita Cottages, Jl. Raya Carita, tel: 81756. **Pelangi Kasih Cottages**, Jl. Raya Carita, tel: 81686. **Carita Beach Resort**, Jl. Raya Carita, tel: 81127. **Desiana Cottages**, Jl. Raya Carita, tel: 81810. **Guna Sangiang**, Jl. Raya Anyer 38, tel: 81078.

ANYER KIDUL: Anyer Beach Motel, Jl. Raya Karang Bolong, tel: Jakarta 367594.

Ujung Kulon National Park: By charter-car from Labuhan to Taman Jaya, the park headquarters at the edge of the park. Regular, twice-weekly boats (& charters) between Labuhan and Taman Jaya. Boats run to the islands Handeuleum and Peucang. There are simple bungalows in Taman Jaya & Handeuleum Island, somewhat nicer ones on Peucang Island. Reservations & permits available from travel agencies.

BOGOR
(Area Code 0251)

MODERATE: **Hotel Pangrango**, Jl. Pangrango 23, tel: 328670. **New Mirah Hotel**, Jl. Megamendung 2, tel: 328044. *BUDGET:* **Elsana Transit Hotel**, Jl. Sawojajar 36, tel: 322552. **Wisma Karunia**, Jl. Sempur 35-37, tel: 323411. **Abu Pensione**, Jl. Mayor Oking 15, tel: 322893.

Restaurants
Asinan Bogor, Jl. Kapt Muslihat. **Fortuna** (Chinese & seafood), Jl. Surya Kencana 130.

Shopping
GONGMAKER: **Pak Sukarna's**, Jl. Pancasan 17. *HANDICRAFTS:* **Batik Keris**, Jl. Merdeka 6. **Nusa Penida**, Jl. Ir H Juanda. **Kenari Indah**, Jl. Bondongan Blok 30. **PP Dobbe & Son**, Jl. Kantor Batu 19. Additional shops in the *pasar.*

Museums / Gardens
Bogor Zoological Museum, Jl. Ir H. Juanda 2, tel: 322177. Sat-Wed 8 am-4 pm, Thu-Fri 8 am-3 pm. **Bogor Botanical Gardens**, Jl. Ir H. Juanda II, tel: 322220. Daily 8 am-5 pm. **Museum Herbarium Bogoriensis**, Jl. Ir H. Juanda 22-24, tel: 322035. Mon-Thu 8 am-2 pm, Fri 8-11, Sat 8 am-1:30 pm, closed Sun.

Tourist Information / Post Office
Jl. Ir H. Juanda 10, tel: 321350. **Post office:** Jl. Ir H. Juanda.

Hospital
Jl. Raya Pajajaran, tel: 324080.

PUNCAK REGION
(Area Code 0255)

LUXURY: **Bukit Raya**, Jl. Raya 219, Cipanas, Cianjur, tel: 512505. **Puncak Pass**, Jl. Raya, Sindanglaya, Cianjur, tel: 512503/4. **Surya Indian Hotel**, Jl. Gadog II/45, Cipanas, tel: 512871.

MODERATE: **Chalet Bali International**, Jl. Raya Puncak, Cisarua, Bogor. **Cibulan**, Cibulan, Cisarua, Bogor. **Sanggabuana**, Jl. Raya 4-6, Cipanas, Cianjur, tel: 512227. **Sindanglaya**, Jl. Raya 43, Pasekon, Cianjur, tel: 512116.

BUDGET: **Kopo Hostel**, Jl. Raya Puncak 502, Cisarua, Bogor, tel: 94296. **Pondok Pemuda Cibodas**, Cibodas botanical gardens.

Restaurants
Countless restaurants, especially Sundanese fish restaurants, along main road (Jl. Raya Puncak).

PELABUHAN RATU
(Area Code 0268)

LUXURY: **Samudra Beach**, Sangkawayana, Pelabuhan Ratu, Sukabumi, tel: 512505. Reserve at Hotel Indonesia in Jakarta, tel: 2301008.

MODERATE: **Pondok Dewata**, Jl. Kidang Kencana 22, tel: 41022. **Cleopatra Hotel**, Jl. Raya Citepus 114, tel: 41185.

BUDGET: **Karang Sari**, Jl. Raya, tel: 41078.

BANDUNG
(Area Code 022)

LUXURY: **Kumala Hotel**, Jl. Asia-Afrika 140, tel: 4205141. **Hotel Panghegar**, Jl. Merdeka 2, tel: 432286, fax: 431583. **Savoy Homann**, Jl. Asia Africa 112, tel: 432244. **Royal Palace Hotel**, Jl. Lembong 21, tel: 4208372. **Grand Hotel Preanger**, Jl. Asia Africa 81, tel: 431631.

MODERATE: **Guntur**, Jl. Oto Iskandarinata 20, tel: 4203763. **Hotel Paniisan**, Jl. Sukajadi 202, tel: 281114. **Setiabudi Guesthouse**, Jl. Dr. Setiabudi 191, tel: 212716. **The Royal Dago Inn**, Jl. Jr. H. Juanda 169, tel: 2502200. **Catellya Guesthouse**, Jl. Dr. Rum 12, tel: 431098. **Edelweiss Guesthouse**, Jl. Sukajadi 206, tel: 282369. **Hotel Endah Parahyangan**, Jl. Raya Cibeureum, tel: 634934.

BUDGET: **Sriwenda**, Jl. Ciliwung 7, tel: 273368. **Losmen Sandara**, Jl. Kebon Jati 51/7B. **Corner Hotel**, Jl. Wastukencana 8, tel: 436871. **Sakadarna International Traveler's Homestay**, Jl. Kebon Jati; Gg. Babakan 55-57B , tel: 4218553.

Restaurants
FOOD STALLS: mainly around *alun-alun* & on Jl. Merdeka and Jl. Haji Juanda. *INDONESIAN:* **Babakan Siliwangi** (Sundanese), Jl. Siliwangi. **Bakmi Raos**, Jl. Kejaksaan 19. **Dago Tea House**, Pajajaran University Campus, off Jl. H Juanda. **Handayani** (Javanese), Jl. Sukajadi. **Koja Sate House**, Jl. Pasir Koja 1. **Naya**

(snakes), Jl. Pasteur. **Pakarjan**, Jl. Pasir Kaliki. **Sate Ponorogo**, Jl. Jen Gatot Subroto. **Ponyo** (Sundanese), Jl. Malabar. **Pak M Uju** (Sundanese), Jl. Dewi Sartika 7A. *CHINESE:* **Queen**, Jl. Dalam Kaum 79. **The Rose Flower**, Jl. Jen Ahmad Yani 32. **Tjoen Kie**, Jl. Jen Sudirman 46. **Tien Tien**, Jl. ABC 82. *WESTERN:* **Tizis**, Haji Juanda 14, near ITB campus. Bakeries & cafes are rare; a few on Jl. Braga.

Shopping

Local specialities include puppets, ceramics, leather goods. Craft shops at Pasar Baru, Jl. Braga, & Jl. Asia-Afrika. **Sarinah** (dept. store), Jl. Braga 10, has a handicrafts section. *PUPPETS:* **Cupu Manik**, Gang Haji Umar 2, near Jl. Kebon Kawung. *FLEA MARKET:* **Pasar Jatayu**, on Jl. Arjuna, 1 km from train station. *DON'T MISS:* the jeans shops on Jl. Cihampelas with their eccentric "Disneyland architecture."

Museums / Galleries / Zoos

Ceramics & Textiles Research Institute, Jl. A Yani 318. **Museum Geologi**, Jl. Diponegoro 57, tel: 2732055. Mon-Thu 9 am-2 pm, Fri 9-11, Sat 9 am-1 pm. **Museum Konperensi Asia Afrika**, Jl. Asia Africa 65, tel: 438031. Mon-Thu 8 am-1 pm, Fri 8-11, Sat 8-12. **Museum Mandala Wangsit Siliwangi** (military), Jl. Lembong 38, tel: 250393. Open weekdays. **West Java State Museum**, Jl. Oto Iskandarinata 638, tel: 250976. Tue-Thu 8 am-2 pm, Fri 8-11, Sat-Sun 8-12. **Taman Sari Zoo**, Jl. Kebun Binatang 7, tel: 282770. Open daily 9 am-5 pm.

Cultural Events

Yayasan Pusat Kebudayaan (YPK), Jl. Naripan 7, city's cultural center: *wayang golek* Sat 9 pm-4 am, other performances weekdays. **State Institute for Performing Arts (SSTI)**, Jl. Buah Batu 212, has some music & *wayang* performances. **Rumentang Siang Theatre**, Jl. Baranang Siang 1, *Wayang golek:* Sat 9:30 pm - 4:30 am; *wayang orang:* Fri after 8 pm. **Pak Ujo's**, Jl. Padasuka 118, tel: 271714. **Pasundan Restaurant** (Hotel Panghegar), Jl. Merdeka 2, dance and music, with dinner, Wed & Sat after 7 pm. **Sanggar Tari Purwa Setra**, Jl. Otto Iskandar Dinata 541A, nightly *jaipongan*.

Tourist Information

Bandung Tourist Office, *Alun-alun*, on Jl. Asia Africa, tel: 256644. Mon-Thu 8 am-8 pm, Fri 8-11 am, Sat 8 am-2 pm. **West Java Provincial Tourist Office**, Diparda, Jl. Cipaganti 151, tel: 281490. Mon-Thu 8 am-2 pm, Fri 8-11 am, closed Sat & Sun.

Telephone

Jl. Asia-Afrika, near Jl. Oto Iskandarinata.

Hospital

7th Day Adventist Hospital, Jl. Cihampelas 161, tel: 282091.

Arrival / Transportation

AIR: Direct links to all Java airports, plus Denpasar & Palembang. **Husein Sastranegara Airport** is 4 km W of town, by taxi or by *bemo* (Angkutan Kota) from bus station on Jl. Kebon Jati. *Airline offices:* **Garuda**, in Grand Hotel Preanger, tel: 431782. **Merpati**, Jl. Asia Africa 73, tel: 439774; **Bouraq**, Jl. Cihampelas 27, tel: 437896.

RAIL: Many services to Yogyakarta, Surabaya (via Yogyakarta), Bogor & Jakarta (but not directly to Cirebon), from main train station.

BUS: Leuwi Panjang Bus Station, in S of city, for Bogor & Jakarta. **Cicaheum Bus Station**, 45 minutes out of town by *bemo* from Kebun Kelapa, for Yogya & East.

PANGANDARAN
(Area Code 0265)

More than 50 *losmen* on the peninsula. More up-market are: **Sunrise Beach Hotel**,tel: 639220, on E side; **Surya Pesona Hotel**, tel: 639428; Adams, tel: 639164, on W side.

CIREBON
(Area Code 0231)

LUXURY: **Cirebon Plaza**, Jl. Kartini 46, tel: 2061. **Patra Jasa Motel**, Jl. Tuparev 11, tel: 209402. **Bentani**, Jl. Siliwangi 69, tel: 203246.
MODERATE: **Grand Hotel**, Jl. Siliwangi 98, tel: 205457. **Aurora**, Jl. R.A. Kartini 27, tel: 204541. **Niaga**, Jl. Kalibaru Selatan 47A, tel: 206718.
BUDGET: on Jl. Siliwangi: **Famili**, no. 66, tel: 207935; **Priangan**, no.108, tel: 202929. Elsewere: **Asia**, Jl. Kalibaru Selatan 15, tel: 202183. **Cordova**, Jl. Siliwangi 87, tel: 204677.

Restaurants

Canton, Jl. Pagongan 8A, tel: 202967. **Kentjana** (Sund.), Jl. Karang Kencana. **Kopyor**, Jl. Karanggetas 9, tel: 204343. **Maksim** (seafood), Jl. Bahagia 45, tel: 202679. **Sinar Budi** (Padang), Jl. Karanggetas 20, tel: 3846. **Jumbo Seafood**, Jl. Siliwangi 191, tel: 203606.

Shopping

BATIK: **Batik Permana**, Jl. Karanggetas 16, tel: 205156. **GKBI** (*batik* cooperative), Jl. Pekarungan 33. Out of town (high quality): **H Mohammed Masina**, Trusmi, near Weru. Cirebon *topeng* masks: **Pak Kandeng**, Suranenggala village, on road to Gunung-jati's grave.

Museums

Museum Kraton Kasepuhan, Jl. Kasepuhan 37, tel: 204001. Open daily 9 am-4pm.

Tourist Information

Tourist information, Jl. Dr. Ciptomangun Kusuma 1.

Post Office

Post office, Jl. Yos Sudarso.

Arrival / Transportation

Train station, Jl. Siliwangi; long-distance bus station, **Kuningan**, 5 km S of city.

CENTRAL JAVA

THE MOUNTAINS
BOROBUDUR
YOGYAKARTA AND
SURROUNDINGS
SOLO AND SURROUNDINGS
THE NORTH COAST

THE MOUNTAINS

The western part of interior Central Java is the land of the **Serayu**, the only large river in Java that empty southwards into the Indian Ocean. Despite its apparently central location, this fertile basin and the coastal plain to its south, formerly known as Bagelen, has historically been isolated both from the north coast *pesisir* and the royal lands to the east. Consequently, this area has retained archaic cultural features that are no longer found in other parts of Java; these include traditional five-village federations and a unique oral imitation of *gamelan* music.

Near the headwaters of the Serayu is the **Dieng Plateau**, a rich source of historical monuments as well as one of Java's strangest and most magical places. Dieng is a treeless moor at 2000 meters, ringed by pine-clad mountains. Here, gentle sunlight can give way to thick blankets of fog or chill rains in the blink of an eye. The earth is equally moody; crystals glitter in pools shining with kaleidoscopic colors; poisonous gas belches from jagged fissures. In the dawn of Indic civilization in Central Java, Hindu kings chose this elemental theater – the name means "Abode of the Gods" – as

Left: A Hindu temple tower at Prambanan.

the setting for their monuments, many of which are still standing today. Apart from the maverick **Candi Bima**, which features rows of staring heads (apparently a unique imitation of an architectural style from Orissa), the seven surviving temples have a restrained, austere aspect. All of the temples are dedicated to Shiva; they date from the end of the 7th century to around A.D. 780. At the east end of the plateau is **Goa Semar**, a cave traditionally used as a place of meditation. In 1974, Goa Semar was the unlikely scene of an infamous private meeting between Suharto and the then Australian prime minister Gough Whitlam, shortly before Indonesia invaded East Timor.

Though **Dieng** is site of the oldest temples, it was at **Gedong Songo** that the "standard model" of the Javanese temple was established, upon which later architecture would elaborate: a cube-shaped central construction containing a shrine chamber, set on a wider plinth, and capped by a tall roof which recedes in steps, to give the impression that it is even taller. The Gedung Songo temples lie 50 kilometers east of Dieng as the crow flies; scattered over the summits of six mountains along the southern flank of **Mt. Ungaran.** They all date from between A.D. 730 and 780, and the main temple in each group is dedicated to

CENTRAL JAVA

0   50 km

Shiva. Because of its exposed location, this is thought to be the most dramatic temple site in Java. Nearby is the hill station of **Bandungan**, mountain resort for wealthy citizens of the north-coast city of Semarang, which is only an hour away.

For all its spectacle, Mt. Ungaran is only a minor outlier of Java's volcanic spine. To its southeast is the swampy basin of **Lake Rawapening** and the town of **Ambarawa**, where train passengers bound for Yogyakarta used to transfer to a remarkable Swiss-type rack-and-pinion railway, to negotiate a long, steep incline. Until the Semarang-Magelang-Yogyakarta line closed in 1977, in the face of competition from road transport, Ambarawa was a lively railway town. In 1978,

its train station became the national **Museum Kereta Api** (Railway Museum), where one can see some 25 Dutch and German locomotives of pre-1930s vintage. Some are still in working condition, including Ambarawa's cogwheel train from 1902, which will, by prior arrangement, haul visitors up the nine kilometer track to **Bedono**.

In the fields two kilometers south of Ambarawa is a big Dutch fortress, today known simply as **Benteng Ambarawa** (Ambarawa Fort). In the mid-19th century, this was intended as the lynchpin of Java's defense against invasion by a European enemy. No invasion came, and the fort was declared obsolete in 1892, but with its squat outlying blockhouses

ously active, and presides over the living heart of the island, where the worldly glory of Java began and where its cultural soul still lies.

BOROBUDUR

Inner Java begins at **Borobudur**; south of the cool, upland town of **Magelang**, in the Progo river valley. It is the world's largest Buddhist monument and arguably the most extraordinary and impressive historic site in Indonesia.

The first two terraces were built at the confluence of two rivers – symbolizing the Ganges and Jumna to the architect – in the middle of the 8th century. Around A.D. 790, the new Buddhist Sailendra dynasty took over the huge project of finishing this temple. A century later, Borobudur fell into disuse when the center of power moved to East Java.

Borobudur is a gold mine of symbols. Some of its messages have been deciphered, others remain obscure. The overall form alone projects multiple associations; in plan, it is a *mandala*, a geometric figure promoting meditation; in profile, it is Meru, the Hindu cosmic mountain, or perhaps a single giant *stupa*, emblem of the Buddha's enlightenment.

The monument is a terraced pyramid of hewn volcanic rock (andesite) with a base 110 meters across. Four of the five lower terraces form square galleries around the periphery of the main structure. Ancient Buddhist ritual demands that pilgrims circle a shrine clockwise before approaching its center; to walk thus around Borobudur's galleries is a stroll of more than five kilometers. The more than 1300 illustrative reliefs on the walls, and some of the 1200 purely decorative panels, once adorned with brightly-painted stucco, were meant to boost the spirits of the perambulating pilgrim.

The reliefs in the first gallery depict historical episodes from the life of Buddha, who died some 1200 years be-

and staring gun ports it is still a formidable sight. Still further south is **Banyubiru**, a notorious concentration camp for Dutch civilians during the Japanese occupation, and still a major jail.

The twin volcanoes of **Mt. Merbabu** (3142 m) and **Mt. Merapi** (2914 m), mid-way between the Java Sea and the Indian Ocean, dominate Central Java at this point. Both offer rewarding panoramas: Merbabu is best viewed from **Kopeng**, and Merapi from **Kaliurang**, Yogyakarta's beautiful hill resort; Merapi can be climbed with a guide, from **Selo**, which lies between the two mountains. Merbabu is an extinct volcano that looks north towards **Semarang**. Merapi, by contrast, is vigorously and danger-

fore Borobudur's cornerstone was laid. Some 120 marvelous reliefs tell the story of the Indian prince Gantama, who became "The Enlightened One;" his mother Maya's miraculous conception; his birth; his first steps; his marriage; his three journeys; his meditative life as a solitary in the forest; his englihtenment under the bodhi tree; the preachings of Benares; and his death after eating rotten food.

Also in the first gallery, is the beginning of a cycle of 720 reliefs, continued in the second and third galleries, depicting Buddha's 500 previous lives. The fourth gallery, on the fifth terrace, shows the son of the well-to-do merchant, Sudhana, on his quest for wisdom and enlightenment, aided by various *bodhisattvas*. In addition, the walls of the four galleries are perforated with niches which contain no fewer than 368 Dhyani Buddhas, arranged in the four cardinal directions. To the west, Buddha Amitabha ("Immeasurable Light") sits in a gesture of meditation. To the south sits Ratnasambhava ("Jewel-Born"), in a gesture of wish-granting. To the east sits Akshobya ("The Unshakeable"), in a gesture of invocation to the earth. Finally, to the north sits Amoghasiddi ("Realizer of Goals"), in a gesture of fearlessness. In the 64 niches of the fifth gallery, one can see Buddha Samantabhadra ("All-Benevolent") in gestures of giving and debating.

The three upper terraces are round and have no walls. Here, within 72 miniature, perforated *stupas*, one can see meditating Adi-Buddhas (the transcendental Over-Buddha), moving the "Wheel of Learning" with his hands. Reaching in to touch one of these figures is supposed to bring good luck.

From here, the plan of the temple becomes increasingly abstract. The simple form of the unadorned central

stupa represents enlightenment. What can't be seen are two small, sealed chambers within the great *stupa*, containing – Nothing; total emptiness; a void.

Apart from being a great religious monument, Borobudur is an important source of historical information. In their pious friezes, its makers gave us priceless stone pictures of their own lost time; here are the houses, the ships, the clothes, the musical instruments and dances not of Buddha's India, but of 9th-century Java. Not until a thousand years later did Europe finally grasp Borobudur's importance. The ubiquitous Raffles discovered it in 1814, under a mountain of volcanic ash. In 1911, the Dutch completed the first restoration. By 1968, the earthen core was rotten and the whole structure in danger of collapse; a major UNESCO program was launched to save it, and the work was completed in 1983.

Two smaller Buddhist temples are also associated with Borobudur. The 8th-century **Candi Mendut**, three kilometers to the east, was once described by a Dutch scholar as, "the jewel among the antiquities of Central Java." Although its exterior has some fine detailed reliefs, Mendut's fame is primarily based on the beautiful statuary in its shrine chamber. Inside, a three meter-tall sitting Buddha preaches the law of suffering. The smaller *bodhisattva* figure seated on his left is Lokesvara, the Bodhisattva who refused to become a Buddha until all men on earth were saved. Offerings are still brought here on *Waicak*, the anniversary of the Buddha's enlightenment. The figure on the right is the *bodhisattva* Vajrapani. **Candi Pawon** is a miniature Mendut located halfway between Mendut and Borobudur.

YOGYAKARTA
AND SURROUNDINGS

South of Borobudur the Progo flows out onto the broad coastlands of the

Right: Detail from the marvellous Borobudur reliefs.

Daerah Istimewa Yogyakarta (Yogyakarta Special Region), the only princely state-within-a-state to survive the national revolution of 1945-49. The region's history begins in **Prambanan**, 17 kilometers east of Yogyakarta. Scattered about this village are some of the finest temples in Indonesia. The oldest are contemporary with Borobudur, and like Borobudur they are Buddhist monuments built during the Sailendra era. **Candi Kalasan**, the first to be encountered on the way out of Yogyakarta, was consecrated in A.D. 778; its Buddha statue is gone, but the external carving is still marvellously intricate, all the more so considering it was originally only a base for even finer detail in plaster. Kalasan represents Indonesian Buddhism in a more sectarian form than Borobudur; it was dedicated to a cult goddess, Tara. **Candi Sewu**, the "Thousand Temples," is another early Buddhist establishment. It features some 240 small shrines which are arranged in a complex *mandala* pattern around a large central building; in its

present state as ruins, it has the air of a lost city.

When the Sanjaya returned to power after A.D. 832, to establish the kingdom sometimes known as "First Mataram," they intermarried with the Buddhist Sailendra and even sponsored the construction of Bhuddist temples themselves. **Candi Plaosan** and **Candi Sari**, stone versions of a two-storey, wooden temple design of the time, are the result. Nevertheless, the new dynasty was a Hindu dynasty, and the greatest of its architectural works, said to have been built to rival Borobudur, is the great Hindu temple complex known as **Candi Prambanan**.

The Splendor of Prambanan

Like Borobudur, Prambanan is often said to surpass even its Indian prototypes. The Opak river was actually diverted to make way for the three extensive precincts which once surrounded this temple. The outer walls and shrines are now

105

a builder's yard of jumbled stone blocks, but the central edifices have been largely restored to their original glory.

Prambanan consists of three major sanctuaries, one for each member of the Hindu trinity: Candi Brahma, Candi Visnu and Candi Siwa. Since Javanese Hinduism tended to make Shiva the highest god and arrange the others around him, the 47 meter-tall spire of Candi Siwa, in the center, is taller and more architecturally perfect than the twin temples to Brahma and Vishnu which stand on either side. An inscription commemorating its consecration in A.D. 856 describes it as, "a beautiful dwelling for the god." Inside the sanctuary stands an enormous statue of Shiva in his four-armed human form; since the normal iconography would have represented him simply as giant penis, this figure may also represent King Rakai Pikatan, who is believed to have commissioned the temple complex.

In other chambers around Shiva are the pot-bellied sage Agastya, Shiva's elephant-headed son Ganesha, and his wife Durga. In local legend, Durga is Loro Jonggrang, a "Slender Maiden" turned to stone by a rejected suitor. "Even Europeans," notes a Dutch textbook from 1919, "come to ask the statue of Durga for some favor or other, or for protection." Today, flowers and other offerings can always to be seen at her feet. Her Javanese name is sometimes given to the whole temple complex. Opposite Candi Siwa is a smaller shrine with a powerful statue of Shiva's mount, the divine bull Nandi. The inner panels of the balustrade around Candi Siwa illustrate the *Ramayana* epic in a series of monumental stone reliefs. In them, Prince Rama's beloved wife Sita is carried off to Sri Lanka by the demon king Ravana; but Rama manages, with the help of the monkey general Hanuman, to free his beloved from the demon's power.

Above: A New Year's offering to the "Teaching Buddha" at Candi Mendut. Right: Keeping an eye on the news at lunchtime.

Prambanan is of timeless beauty. The triple towers which were erected 11 centuries ago, remain weirdly futuristic, providing a stunning backdrop for the **Loro Jonggrang Theater**, an open-air stage where the famous *Ramayana* dance performances are held on four consecutive moonlit nights each month during the dry season.

The Prambanan group is also comprised of several other less important Hindu temples, including the recently excavated **Candi Sambisari**, which is small, was but perfectly preserved by volcanic ash. However, none were built much later than Prambanan. In the first half of the 10th century, King Sindok transferred the center of power to East Java, where it remained for the next 600 years. Then, in the 16th century, after the fall of the last and greatest East Javanese state, Majapahit, the island's historical center of gravity, migrated back to the lands below Mt. Merapi. According to Javanese tradition, this process culminated in the re-foundation of Mataram,

this time as an Islamic kingdom, by Kyai Gedhe Pamanahan. His son, Senopati, initiated the imperial expansion which was to make this second Mataram the last of Java's great indigenous states.

Senopati journeyed to the desolate south coast to meet with Ratu Loro Kidul, the Queen of the South Sea, who promised him the support of her spirit army. The beaches around **Parangtritis** are still the center of the cult of this siren goddess, who lures young men to their deaths by enticing them to swim in her dark ocean. When the ruler of Yogyakarta is crowned, the goddess is offered clippings of the sultan's nails and hair. The coastline here has a windswept, restless beauty.

Senopati's court was at **Kota Gede**, now virtually a suburb of Yogyakarta, five kilometers southeast of the town center. His grave, and that of his son Krapyak, who succeeded him in 1601, can be viewed here, in a dark, flower-strewn chamber – accessible on Mondays and Fridays and subject to the wearing of

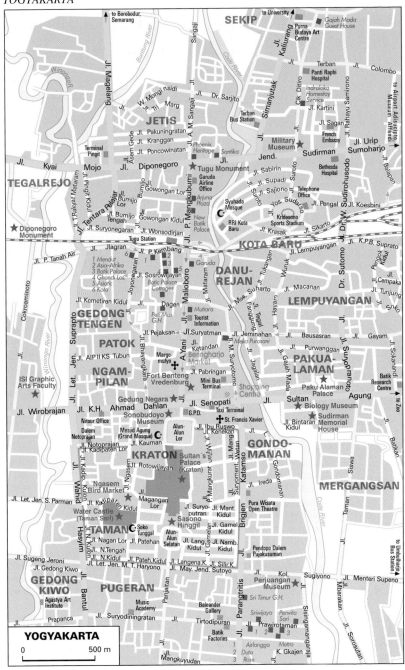

respectful Javanese clothing. The mausoleum was reconstructed after a fire at the beginning of the 20th century, but its musty, incense-permeated interior still reeks more strongly of the past than any sunlit temple. In the quiet grounds is a pool with a sacred albino turtle. Kota Gede is also a known center of silversmithing.

Krapyak's son Agung is buried not with his father and grandfather at Kota Gede, but in a spectacular hilltop mausoleum in **Imogiri**, midway between Yogyakarta and the sea. Agung was the greatest of Mataram's rulers, conquering Surabaya in 1625, besieging Dutch Batavia in 1628 and 1629, and finally taking the title of sultan in 1641. At his death in 1646 he was lord of all of Central and East Java, and the greatest Indonesian conqueror since the time of Majapahit. The burial place which he created for himself reflects his glory. A great, sun-dappled stairway of 345 steps leads to a fortress-like edifice which contains not only Agung's own black tomb, but also the tombs of all his successors. After the sultanate split in 1755, both Yogyakartan and Surakartan rulers continued to be interred here, although in separate wings of the building. The tombs are still objects of veneration and may only be viewed by the public on auspicious Mondays and Fridays.

The City of Yogyakarta

The city of **Yogyakarta** is a unique phenomenon in Indonesia. Apart from being the cultural capital and foremost tourist destination of Java, "Yogya" (pronounced "Jogja") is a city of more than half a million people, a major administrative center, the site of more than 40 universities and academies, and the former capital of the Republic of Indonesia. Yet its sophistication comes deceptively cloaked in the simple garments of a giant village.

Though it stands amid a constellation of earlier royal sites, the modern city dates from only the mid-18th century. The death of Sultan Agung heralded a century of chaos and decline for Mataram. Agung's son Amangkurat I was a tyrant who alienated most of his vassals, with the result that his successor Amangkurat II (reigned 1677-1703) could only claim his throne thanks to the Dutch, to whom the sultanate was now beholden. Three "Javanese Wars of Succession" followed before stability was restored in 1755, by the radical means of permanently dividing Mataram into two kingdoms. Paku Buwono III and his line were to rule Surakarta, while his uncle Pangeran Mangkubumi became the first ruler of Yogyakarta under the title of Hamengko Buwono, which is still borne by his descendants.

One of the first deeds of Hamengko Buwono I was to order the construction of the **Kraton Yogyakarta**, the palace which is Yogya's core. This *kraton* is a city within a city. Thousands of people live and work within its walls – *batik* makers, servants and guards, as well as the musicians, jesters and *polowijo* or "weeds" (albinos and dwarfs) of the sultan's retinue, and the royal family itself. The central buildings, the first of which were completed in 1757, comprise a maze of *pendopo* – open or semi-open pavilions – which are separated by courtyards planted with shady trees. The outer walls, each more than one kilometer long and three meters thick, caused the Dutch much consternation when they were added in 1785; but they did not prevent a thousand or so British Indian sepoys from taking the *kraton* against 11,000 defenders in 1812, with the sole casualty being a Scottish officer who was stabbed by a princess he was carrying away as booty.

Not surprisingly, that debacle was the end of the court's independent military, which then accepted the superior power

of the returning Dutch and devoted itself to self-beautification and the development of the Javanese arts. Although it seems timeless, today's *kraton* is essentially the *kraton* of this "theatrical" period, featuring opulent Indo-Dutch furniture, oil paintings by the 19th-century Javanese artist Raden Saleh, and several huge *gamelan* orchestras. Perhaps it is this very element of artifice which gives the palace its other-wordly atmosphere. The ninth sultan, who reigned 1939-88, brought the court down to earth just in time to secure its future, supporting the republic in 1945-49 and even giving over part of the palace to house the first independent Indonesian university, **Gajah Mada**, now located in the north of the city. Today, the *kraton* houses a museum and stages regular *gamelan* and dance performances.

Taman Sari ("Fragrant Garden"), also known as the Water Castle, is even more

Above: A gamelan orchestra at the kraton.
Right: A Ramayana dance performance.

fanciful. Located to the southwest of the main buildings, this labyrinthine ruin was the opulent pleasure palace of the first sultan. **Ngasem**, the adjacent bird market, is built on the dry bed of an artificial lake, across which Dutch visitors were once rowed, in gilded boats, to a manmade island. Only the smaller, central bathing pools have been restored; the rest is in an evocative state of tropical decay.

Immediately in front of the *kraton* is the **Alun-alun Lor**, the town's main square. It is here that fights between tigers and buffalo were once staged for the entertainment and instruction of European dignitaries; the tiger represented Europe, the buffalo Java, and the steadfast strength of the buffalo seldom failed to overcome the ferocity of the tiger. On the west side of the square is the very Javanese **Mesjid Agung** (Grand Mosque), which was built in the form of a *pendopo*. Three times a year, during the *garebeg* festivals, the sultan takes part in a spectacular procession from the palace to the mosque, accompanied by flower-bedecked heaps (*gunungan*) of rice, evidence of his charity. The greatest of these events is *Garebeg Maulud*, when the square seethes with performers and pedlars, and musicians play on two ancient *gamelan* from the palace, for the entire week leading up to the procession.

Not far north of the *alun-alun* is the original Dutch fort, **Benteng Vredenburg**. In 1765, the first sultan agreed to build a fortress for VOC troops in his city. However, despite his industriousness in the field of pleasure gardens, and the fact that the four-kilometer walls around his own palace were supposedly built in two weeksflat, the sultan did not manage to complete Vredenburg within his lifetime; Governor-General Daendels finally put a firm end to the procrastination in 1808. Opposite the fort is **Gedung Negara**, the handsome 19th-century home of the Dutch Resident. Further east, on Jl. Sultan Agung is the **Paku Alaman**, the palace of Yogya's junior royal house, created by Raffles in 1813, as a counterweight to the court of Hamengko Buwono, which he had just had occasion to storm. The Paku Alaman, which is not open to the public, is a less lavish version of the main *kraton*.

The British attack on Yogyakarta in 1812, ended the military power of the Javanese courts proper, but it was not quite the last stand of the aristocracy as a whole. In 1825, after years of court corruption and intrigue, increasing erosion of aristocratic privileges by the European government, and several ominous natural disasters, a Muslim visionary and scion of the royal family, Prince Diponegoro, raised a rebellion against both the *kraton* and the Dutch which lasted five years and cost more than 200,000 lives.

Retrospectively styled as a freedom fighter, Diponegoro is one of the best-known figures in Indonesian history. He was raised in **Tegalrejo**, five kilometers northwest of the *kraton*, where his residence has been reconstructed as the

Diponegoro Monument; with displays of the hero's relics and realistic paintings of the war. In 1830, Diponegoro was finally captured, 40 kilometers northwest of Yogya at **Magelang**, home to yet another commemorative museum, **Museum Diponegoro**. More than a century of oppressive peace followed, the *rust en orde* (peace and order) of Dutch colonialism, described by one nationalist of the 1930s as "the peace of death." When that peace was broken at last, by Japan and the Indonesian revolution, Yogya was once again at the center of the whirlwind as capital of the infant republic from January 1946 until its seizure by Dutch troops in December 1948. The **Museum Sasmitaloka Jenderal Soedirman** celebrates the most important Indonesian military hero of this time, an Islamic schoolteacher who, wasted by tuberculosis, led the republic's armed forces from a litter, which can be seen here.

Yogya's main street is **Jl. Malioboro**, famous for its stalls that offer souvenirs by day and food by night. *Gudeg*, a mild jackfruit curry, is Yogya's speciality. Central Javanese food is the sweetest and least spicy in Indonesia, and makes much use of the soybean products *tahu* and *tempe*.

Insulated by Dutch policy from the changes sweeping other parts of Java during the late colonial period, Yogya was free to both maintain cultural traditions which had faded elsewhere and to innovate energetically indigenous Javanese themes. The Dutch helped with the preservation, as the **Sonobudoyo Museum**, a cultural museum that was opened in 1935, testifies; the innovation was all Yogya's own. Both tradition and innovation have contributed to the town's present aesthetic wealth. In the field of *batik*, the main trend was towards the conservative. Around **Taman Sari** and in the **Jl. Tirtodipuran** neighborhood, workshops produce a variety of traditional and royal patterns.

Wayang kulit, the ancient shadowplay, is a whole way of life in Yogya. There are numerous craftsmen who produce the intricate leather puppets, and two schools for *dalang* (puppeteers). Several institutions offer regular public performances of this magical spectacle, sometimes even the traditional all-night version. As a repertoire, the Indian epics of *Ramayana* and *Mahabharata* are generally preferred over more recent Javanese and Middle Eastern stories. Yogya's dance, by contrast, tends to be highly untraditional. Although some sacred and court dances are preserved, the masked dance-dramas known from the 11th century and still popular in West and East Java are seldom performed in Yogya. They have been replaced by the unmasked *wayang wong*, an 18th century innovation, and the *sendratari*, a Western-influenced dance spectacle without dialogue. The best-known example of this is the "Ramayana Ballet" performed at Prambanan's **Loro Jonggrang Theater** (see p. 107).

Since the revolutionary, arts-oriented Taman Siswa school system was introduced in 1922, Yogya has developed into a center for the visual arts. Pioneers like Affandi, whose **Affandi Museum** is open to the public, used European oils and perspective, defying the Islamic taboos against human representation and ushering in the first wave of a new, confident and individualistic art.

SOLO AND SURROUNDINGS

The twin courts of Yogyakarta were only two of four princely states to survive the incremental Dutch conquest of Java. The others were in **Surakarta**, more commonly known as **Solo**, at the eastern foot of Mt. Merapi. Not as quick to move with the times as those of Yogya, the Solo courts were unable to reconcile themselves with the republic, and in June 1946 their prerogatives outside the palace walls were abolished forever. Today, their old territories are simply part of the province of Central Java.

Some eight kilometers before Solo, on the road from Yogya, is the village of **Kartasura**, where a single crumbling brick wall is the only reminder that the capital of Mataram was here for 66 years. The Javanese courts were extraordinarily flexible: war, misfortune or the whim of a new king could lead to a capital's being transported (sometimes literally, for important *pendopo* could be dismantled and carried) to a new, safer or more auspicious site, leaving behind a mostly wooden ruin which was quickly reclaimed by tropical nature.

Kartasura was founded in 1680 when the previous capital at Plered (near Kota Gede, Yogyakarta) was occupied by an imposter; in 1746, after three years of disastrous war against the Dutch and their allies, Pakubuwana II decided to abandon the obviously unlucky site, and in 1746 he moved to the **Kraton Hadiningrat** in Solo, the fifth and final capital

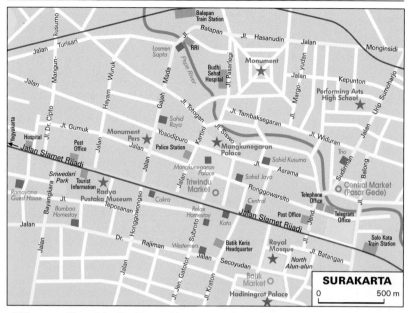

Balapan Train Station
Balapan
Jl. Hasanudin
Jalan
Monginsidi
Jalan Turisari
Jalan Kusumo
Jalan Mangun-
Losmen Sapta
RRI
Monument
Jl. Pepa River
Jl. Pasarlegi
Budhi Sehat Hospital
Jl. Margo-yudan
Kepunton
Jalan Urip Sumoharjo
Performing Arts High School
Jalan Wuruk
Hayam
Jl. Totogan
Gajah Mada
Kartini
Jl. Tambaksegaran
Jl. Widuran
Jl. Dr. Cipto
Jl. Gumuk
Sahid Raya
Yosodipuro
Monument Pers
Jl. Siswa
Trio
Yogyakarta
Hospital
Post Office
Jalan
Police Station
Mangkunegaran Palace
Sahid Kusuma
Asrama
Jl. Sudirman
Balong
Jalan Slamet Riijadi
Mangkunegaran Palace
Sahid Jaya
Sriwedari Park
Tourist Information
Radya Pustaka Museum
Triwindu Market
Ronggowarsito
Telephone Office
Central Market (Pasar Gede)
Ramayana Guest House
Bayangkara
Teposanan
Cakra
Central
Post Office
Telegram Office
Bamboo Homestay
Honggowongso
Relax Homestay
Kota
Jalan Slamet Riijadi
Jend.
Jalan
Subroto
Dr. Rajiman
Westerners
Batik Keris Headquarter
Royal Mosque
Solo Kota Train Station
Jl. Jen. Gatot
Jalan
Secoyudan
North Alun-alun
Jl. Batangan
Jl. Kraton
Batik Market
SURAKARTA
Hadiningrat Palace
0   500 m

of Mataram. Though badly damaged by a fire in 1985, the *kraton* is still worth seeing. It contains a museum of regal pomp, a cannon from Portuguese Malacca (the "wife" of the one in Jakarta's Taman Fatilah), and a peculiar pagoda in which the "emperors" (as the Dutch called them) trysted with the Queen of the South Seas. There is also an important library of Javanese manuscripts. The last of the great Javanese court poets, Raden Ngabei Ronggawarsita, worked here until his death in 1873.

The Solo *kraton* remained the capital of Mataram for less than a decade. The king's brothers were still in revolt, and his son not only saw Mataram divided between Yogya and himself, but also had to suffer the foundation of a new junior court, the **Mangkunegaran**, under his very nose. Since the fire in Kraton Hadiningrat, this palace has upstaged the main *kraton* as a tourist attraction; sporting an imposing central *pendopo* of Javanese teak with an Italian marble floor, a famous *gamelan*, and a museum of *topeng*

masks and *wayang* puppets. It was twice restored by a Dutch architect, Thomas Karsten, before the war, and remains the best maintained of Java's *kraton*. The Mangkunegaran Palace is north of the Kraton Surakarta, across the railway tracks. Further north is an independent cultural museum, **Museum Radyapustaka**, which was founded in 1890.

Indonesia's first railway line, begun in 1867, linked Solo with Semarang. In earlier days the Solo river, Java's longest, carried boat traffic from Solo to the Strait of Madura, about 300 kilometers away.

In those times, Solo's wealth derived from the fertility of its lands and the labor of its subjects. Today, light industry is increasingly important. Solo's *batik* industry is organized on a larger scale than in Yogya. Some of the largest *batik* companies in Indonesia, including **Batik Keris**, have their headquarters here. Traditional Solo *batik*, famous for its natural, soft brown dyes against a mellow yellowish background, is still available at **Pasar Klewer**, the the main *batik* market.

113

Solo has no great temple complex in its vicinity to match Yogya's Prambanan. However, 36 kilometers to the east, on the slopes of Mt. Lawu, is one of the island's most intriguing and unusual antiquities, **Candi Sukuh**. Though within present-day Central Java, this temple historically belongs to East Java and Majapahit. Built around 1430, during the declining years of the empire, Sukuh is the end of the process of architectural and religious assimilation which began at Dieng; still a Hindu temple of sorts, but with the Indian elements all but overwhelmed by Javanese innovations. The central monument is a stepped pyramid, almost like a Mexican ruin. Some see this as a resurgence of a form of terrace used for ancestor worship long before Indian influences ever arrived in Java. Sukuh seems to be associated with a cult of the *wayang* hero Bima; in addition, a wealth of sexual imagery suggests a fertility cult. A realistic set of male and female genitalia carved in stone, fragrant with recent flower offerings, adorns the floor of one of the entrances. Despite the airy views from 910 meters and the erotic humor of the reliefs, Sukuh is an unsettling, almost demonic place in its setting of dark pines. With its images of animals – giant turtles, elephant men, staring pigs – it is reminiscent of a painting by Bosch.

Candi Ceto, built 50 years later, is also on Mt. Lawu, seven kilometers further north and 600 meters higher. Little remains of the original structure, but the *pendopo* and Balinese split gates have recently been reconstructed on the old terraces. Near **Karangpandan**, on the road to Sukuh and Ceto, is the spot which former-President Suharto has chosen as his final resting place. He was born and raised in the Yogya area, but **Makam Suharto** looks out over the broader *sawah* of the Solo valley. Suharto's elaborate mausoleum *pendopo* was completed in 1977, but will not be open to the public until he lies there in state.

Beyond Karangpandan, a road winds through misty forests to the mountain resorts of **Tawangmangu**, which has marvelous gardens, and to **Sarangan**, the usual starting-point for an ascent of Mt. Lawu. Sarangan is beyond the boundaries of the Yogyaharta Special Region, and commands views over the old railway town of **Madiun**.

Sangiran, 15 kilometers north of Solo, is an important anthropological site that was first excavated in the 1930s. The 1.8 million-year-old skulls found here have given rise to heated debate as to wether they represent a link between *Pithecanthropus erectus* and *Homo sapiens*. The **Sangiran Site Museum** displays replicas of these skulls, as well as plant fossils.

THE NORTH COAST

Tegal and **Pekalongan** are the first towns on the Central Javanese coast east of Cirebon. Tegal is a growing, light industrial center known mainly for its ubiquitous emigrants, who sell food from their *war-teg* (*warung* in Tegal) from Jakarta to Surabaya. Pekalongan, however, is *Kota Batik* (Batik City), where the wives of generals and diplomats order their *batik*. Before the war, Eliza van Zuylen, a Eurasian working in Pekalongan, set technical standards for *batik* manufacture which have never been equalled, with her Dutch-inspired floral patterns. During the war, Japanese models inspired the town's famous *Hokukai Batik*. Today, Javanese, Arab, Chinese and European entrepreneurs design and produce *batik* here and, while there is reputedly such a thing as "traditional Pekalongan *batik*," the real "tradition" is one of innovation. The very best workshops, which take as much as eight months to complete a single piece, are in surrounding villages like **Kedungwangi**.

The port of **Semarang**, not the old royal town of Solo, is the provincial capital and biggest city in Central Java. From

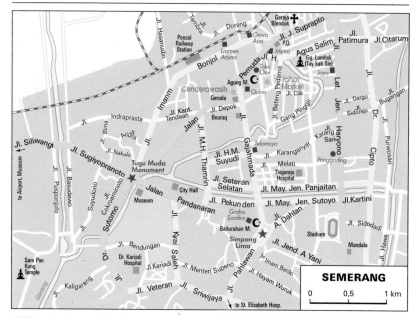

1678, when it was the first part of Mataram to be ceded to the VOC, until 1948, when it was the base for an airborne assault on Yogya, Semarang was a Dutch beach-head on the Javanese heartland and a conduit through which its wealth was extracted. Dutch warehouses and offices are still much in evidence downtown. An 18th-century church, **Gereja Blenduk**, with a green copper dome and an imposing classical portico, is still in use, although the baroque organ is no longer in working order. Much of its congregation is Chinese; Chinese traders were here long before the Dutch made Semarang their own, and have outlasted them as masters of Semarang's commerce. The **Sam Poo Kong Temple** in the southwest of the city, is dedicated to a sanctified Chinese Muslim said to have visited this coast in the 15th century – Chinese and Indonesians worship together here. **Klenteng Gang Lombok** is a more conventional Chinese temple, dating from 1772. Although the old Chinatown is still distinguishable around the

klenteng, the richer Chinese businessmen have abandoned the blackout-ridden, old town center to join their Indonesian patrons in the elite suburb of **Candi Baru**, on the hills overlooking the city.

Because of the massive social changes it has witnessed, Semarang's 20th century history has been turbulent. Henk Sneevliet, the Dutchman who introduced Marxism to the Indies in 1913, was active in the Railway Workers' Union here; he and his Javanese comrade Semaun made Semarang the capital of early Indonesian radicalism. Thirty years later, 2000 nationalist rebels died here in one of the most bizarre and tragic battles of the Indonesian revolution. After initially allowing Indonesians to take over, Japanese troops, on British orders, recaptured the city in October 1945. However, six days later the Japanese were relieved by "British" troops who were in fact Indians, themselves not-so-willing colonial subjects. The **Tugu Muda Monument** in the city center commemorates the Indonesian dead.

115

Every year, Java's north coast advances imperceptibly seaward. Semarang owes its growth partly to the fact that it has not suffered as badly from the creeping mud as old rivals further east. When the Europeans first arrived, the greatest trading ports of Java were not Banten, Jakarta, Cirebon and Semarang, but obscure places, now almost forgotten by the world, on the curve of coast between Semarang and Surabaya.

Demak, whose fleets once conquered most of the coastal kingdoms of Java – and founded the rest – is now stranded 12 kilometers from the sea. Apparently founded by a Chinese Muslim, Demak was Java's first Islamic state and first exponent of *jihad*. In the late 1520s, it snuffed out the last fading embers of Majapahit's glory and became the first Islamic link in the chain of Moslem dynasties through which Solo and Yogya trace their legitimacy back to the ancient Hindu empire. Tradition has it that four

Above: All in a day's work.

116

of the engraved pillars of Demak's **Mesjid Agung Mosque** were brought from the Majapahit court. Certainly they are very old, although the remainder of the building was completely rebuilt in 1845 and again in 1987, when then-President Suharto presided over its reopening. This is Java's most holy mosque; traditionally, seven pilgrimages here during the annual feast of *Garebeg Besar* are supposed to be worth one complete *hajj* to Mecca.

Even more interesting is the mosque at **Kudus**, which is of pure pre-Muslim design. Not only are the split gates reminiscent of a Balinese temple, but the redbrick minaret in front is so similar to a Hindu *kulkul* (gong tower) that it may actually have been one. "Kudus" is a corruption of the word *al-Quds*, meaning Jerusalem; the only place in Java to have an Arabic name. The mosque, which bears the date 1549, is known as *al-Manar* or *al-Aqsa*, after the one in Jerusalem. It was founded by Sunan Kudus, who is said to have been the head of the mosque at Demak before he moved here.

Sunan Kudus is one of the *wali songo*, the "nine saints" who are given popular credit for the Islamization of Java. His carved, curtained grave behind the mosque has been a revered shrine for 400 years. The old port area of northeastern Java is also the homeland of anther *wali*; Sunan Kalijaga, is buried at **Kadilangu**, about two kilometers south of Demak.

The domestic architecture of Kudus is more Middle Eastern than its mosque, with high, whitewashed, windowless streetside walls. Many of the female population work in the town's clove cigarette factories. The rich, sweet scent of *kretek* smoke was first introduced in the 1890s, and only started to make converts on a large scale in the 1920s; yet now it seems a timeless and essential part of Indonesia. Kudus was the first center of the *kretek* industry. Its cottage producers lost out to new factories elsewhere after the war, but the big Chinese-owned Djarum plant has regained much of the ever-growing market from Kediri-based Gudang Garam.

Jepara comes closer to remaining a port than Demak or Kudus, but still misses the sea by a couple of kilometers. In the 16th century, ships from China, Burma, India, Persia and Arabia moored in its now vanished harbor and its own navy besieged Portuguese Malacca three times. Today it is a quiet, rather isolated place, best known for its woodcarvings in teak and mahogany.

The most famous child of this part of northern Central Java is Raden Ajeng Kartini, Indonesia's foremost national heroine, whose birthday is celebrated as "Kartini Day" on April 21st.

Born in 1879, in **Mayong** near Kudus, where there is a commemorative monument, Kartini was a daughter of the Regent of Jepara, who allowed her to attend European school at a time when most Javanese aristocrats found female education unacceptable. Her wholehearted enthusiasm for the ideals of Ethical Policy dumbfounded even the Dutch themselves. In moving letters later published as *Door Duisternis tot Licht* (Through Darkness to Light), she expressed in lucid Dutch her desire to bring education and emancipation to Javanese women. Kartini died tragically at 25, a few days after the birth of her first child. Her life and works are celebrated in Jepara at the **Museum Kartini di Jepara**, and in **Rembang**, where she spent her single year of married life, at the **Museum Kartini di Rembang**. She is buried near the old mosque in **Mantingan**, 19 kilometers south of Rembang, on the road to Blora.

A few kilometers east of Rembang is the little-known *batik* center of **Lasem**, where 50 small factories produce hand-drawn designs, often floral in theme, for sale in Surabaya. The industry is controlled by the Chinese, who have been here for seven generations, and it resembles a 19th-century southern Chinese town.

Though separated from the historic coastland by only a low range of chalk hills, the **Lusi river valley** has always been one of Java's backwaters. This is almost the last place where one can see the rare *wayang* form called *krucil* or *klitik*, which uses flat, toy-like wooden puppets. At the beginning of this century, the villages around **Blora** were the scene of an extraordinary type of anticolonial resistance movement. An illiterate peasant named Surantika Samin founded a nativist religion stressing family and village loyalty, rejection of the money economy, and passive resistance to any form of external authority. Fueled by resentment against forestry regulations in this teak-growing area, the movement spread; taxes remained unpaid, schools unattended. The Messiah himself was exiled in 1907, but seven years later his followers were still keeping Dutch troops busy and Saminism survived into the 1960s. **Museum Grobogan**, near Purwodadi, contains historical, ethnographic and handicraft exhibits from this area.

DIENG AND GEDONG SONGO
DIENG PLATEAU
Accommodation

Several small *losmen* and a restaurant on the plateau, but many prefer to stay in Wonosobo, 1 hour down the mountain.

WONOSOBO
(Area Code 0286)
Accommodation

MODERATE: **Surya Asia**, Jl. J. A. Yani 137, tel: 22292. **Sri Kencono**, Jl. J. A. Yani 81, tel: 21522. **Nirwana**, Jl. Resimen 18/36, tel: 21066. *BUDGET:* **Citra**, Jl. Angkatan 45, tel: 21880. **Wisma Duta**, Jl. R. S. U. 3, tel: 21674. **Widuri**, Jl. Resimen 18/44.

Restaurants

Dieng Restaurant, Jl. Angkatan 45/37. **Asia Restaurant**, Jl. Angkatan 45/33, tel: 21165.

GEDONG SONGO

Usually visited from Semarang, but nearby **Bandungan** has several hotels. You can see other historic sites on day excursions from Yogyakarta.

AMBARAWA AND MAGELANG
(Area Codes 0298 & 0293)
Museums

Railroad Museum, Jl. Stasiun, Ambarawa. Daily 8 am-5 pm. **Museum Palagan Ambarawa** (military), Jl. Major Sugiopranoto, Ambarawa. Daily 7 am-6 pm. **Museum Diponegoro** (Prince Diponegoro Memorial Museum), Jl. Diponegoro 1, Magelang, tel: 2308. Sun-Wed 8 am-2 pm, Fri 8-11, Sat 8 am-1 pm, closed Thu. **Museum Soedirman** (General Sudirman Memorial Museum), Jl. Ade Irma Suryani C7, Magelang. Mon-Sat 8-12, closed Sun.

YOGYAKARTA
(Area Code 0274)
Accommodation

LUXURY: **Ambarrukmo Palace**, Jl. Adisucipto, tel: 588488/588984. **Garuda**, Jl. Malioboro 60, tel: 566353. **Mutiara Hotel**, Jl. Malioboro 18, tel: 563814. **Puri Artha**, Jl. Cendrawasih 9, tel: 563288. **Sahid Garden**, Jl. Babarsari, tel: 587370. **Sri Manganti**, Jl. Urip Sumoharjo, tel: 2881. **Sriwedari**, Jl. Adisucipto, km 5, tel: 588288.
MODERATE: On Jl. Prawirotaman – **Airlangga Hotel**, no. 6-8, tel: 372829. **Sriwijaya Guesthouse**, no. 7, tel: 371870. **Wisma Indah Guesthouse**, no.16, tel: 376021. **Duta Guesthouse**, no. 20, tel: 372064. **Metro Guesthouse**, no. 7/71, tel: 372364. **Rose Guesthouse**, no. 22, tel: 377991. **Arjuna Plaza**, Jl. Mangkubumi 48, tel: 513063. **Gajah Mada Guesthouse**, Jl. Bulaksumur, Gajah Mada university

campus, tel: 563461. **Hotel Mendut**, Jl. Pasar Kembang. **Pura Jenggala Guest House**, Jl. Cendrawasih 2, tel: 512238. **Indraloka Homestay Service**, Jl. Cik Ditiro 14, tel: 513614, arranges boarding with Indonesian families. **Yogya International**, Jl. Adisucipto 38, tel: 564727.
BUDGET: Mostly in travellers' ghetto S of train station. Gang I: **Beta Losmen, Lucy Losmen, Hotel Jogya, Dewi Homestay**. Gang II: **Bagus Hotel, Ghandi Losmen. Ratna Hotel**, Jl. Pasar Kembang 17A, tel: 561851. **Hotel Kota** is at end of Jl. Pasar Kembang on Jl. Gandekan Lor. South of Jl. Pasar Kembang: **Hotel Asiatic**, Jl. Sosrowijayan 6. **Indonesia Hotel**, Jl. Sosrowijayan 7. **Intan Hotel**, Jl. Sosrokusuman 1/16. **Prambanan Guesthouse**, Jl. Sosrokusuman 18/20, tel: 513303.

Restaurants

FOOD STALLS: Along Jl. Malioboro, late-night *gudeg*, *sate & sop kaki kambing* (goat-foot soup) stalls.
INDONESIAN: **Ayam Goreng Nyonya Suharti**, (fried chicken) Jl. Adi Sucipto 208, tel: 515522, Jl. Solo (beyond Ambarrukmo Palace Hotel). **Juminten** (Javanese) Jl. Asem Gede 22, Kranggan 69. **Bu Citro** (Javanese), Jl. Adisucipto, near airport entrance. **Warung Makan Sederhana**, Jl. Mangkubumi 61B. **Sinar Budi** (Padang), Jl. Mangkubumi 41.
CHINESE: **Moro Senang**, Jl. Solo 55 (beyond airport). **Sintawang**, Jl. Magelang 9. **Tiong San**, Jl. Gandekan 29, a block W of Malioboro.
TOURIST SPOTS: Indo-western eateries in *losmen* area S of station. Favored are **Superman** on Gang I & **Anna's** on Gang II. Better and pricier approximations to western food at **Legian Garden Restaurant**, Jl. Perwakilan 9 (corner Jl. Malioboro/Jl. Suryatman).

Shopping

Pasar Beringharjo (city market) off Jl. Yani/Malioboro. **Art & Craft Centre** in Pura Wisata, Jl.. Brigjen, Katomso.
LEATHER GOODS: Many shops are on Jl. Malioboro, eg **Toko Setia**, nos. 79 & 165.
WAYANG KULIT PUPPETS: **Ledjar**, Jl. Mataram D. N. I 370 (E of Malioboro). **Mulyo Suhardjo**, Jl. Taman Sari 37B (W of Winongo river). **Swasthigita**, Jl. Nga-dinegaran MD 7/50 (off Jl. Panjaitan, S of *kraton*).
SILVER (Kota Gede): **Tom's Silver**, Jl. Kota Gede 3-1A. **MD Silver**, Jl. Keboan, Kota Gede.
ANTIQUES & CURIOS: Many shops on Jl. Malioboro, incl. **Toko Asia**, and in Taman Sari area. For higher prices, but more reliable antiquity: **Jul Shop**, Jl. Mangkubumi 29. **Ardianto**, Jl. Pejaksan 21.
BATIK: Hundreds of outlets. Fixed prices at **Terang Bulan**, Jl. Ahmad Yani 76. Two dozen factories around Jl. Tirtodipuran, S of *kraton*, sell *cap* (printed) *batik*. Taman Sari/Bird Market area is center for cheap

batik painting; for more expensive originals, see "Art Galleries."

Museums / Zoos

Biology Museum of Gajah Mada University, Jl. Sultan Agung 22, tel:514011. Mon-Thu 8 am-1 pm, Fri 8-11, Sat & Sun 8-12. **Museum Dirgantara Mandala** (air force), Adisutjipto Air Force Base, tel: 513647-9. Mon-Thur 8 am-1 pm, Sat & Sun 8-12, closed Fri. **Yogyakarta Kraton Museum**, tel: 512036. Sat-Thu 8:30 am-1 pm, Fri 8:30-11. **Gembira Loka Zoo**, Jl. Gembira Loka. Daily 7 am-6 pm. **Museum Perjuangan** (national history), Jl. Sugiyopranoto 24. Tue-Thu 9 am-1 pm, Friday 9-11, Sat & Sun 9-12, closed Mon. **Museum Pusat TNI Angkatan Darat** (military), Jl. Jen Soedirman 47, tel: 586417-8. Mon-Thu 8 am-1 pm, Sat & Sun 8-12, closed Fri. **Museum Sasana Wiratama**, Tegalrejo, tel: 513068. Daily 7:30 am-6 pm. **Museum Sasmitaloka Panglima Besar Jen Sudirman**, Jl. Bintaran Wetan 3, tel: 512663. Mon-Thu 8 am-1 pm, Fri 8-11, Sat 8-12, closed Sun. **Museum Sonobudoyo**, Jl. Trikora 3, tel: 512775. Tue-Thu 8 am-1 pm, Fri 8-11:30, Sat 8-12:30, Sun 8-12, closed Mon.

Art Galleries

Museum Affandi, Jl. Solo 167, tel: 588526. Daily 8 am-4 pm. **Amri Yahya Gallery**, Jl. Gampingan 67 (close to ASRI). **ASRI (Indonesian Academy of Fine Arts)**, Jl. Gampingan (W of city center, beyond Winongo River). **Bagong Kussudiardjo**, Jl. Singasaren 9, off Jl. Wates.

Cultural Events

GAMELAN: **Kraton Yogyakarta**, rehearsals Mon & Wed am. **Pakualaman Palace**, every 5th Sunday at 10 am. **Ambarrukmo Palace Hotel**, 10:30-12:30 & 3:30-5:30 pm daily, in lobby.

WAYANG KULIT: **Agastya Art Institute**, Jl. Gedong Kiwo MJ 1/996 (off Jl. Bantul in SW of town), every day except Saturday, 3-5 pm. **Sasono Hinggil** (pavilion S of *kraton*), 2nd Sat of each month, 9 pm-dawn. **Ambar Budaya**, Yogyakarta Craft Center, near Ambarrukmo Hotel, daily 8-9:30 pm.

DANCE: **Pendopo Dalem Pujokusuman**, Jl. Brig Jen Katamso 45, Mon/Wed/Fri 8-10 pm. The kraton dancers rehearse every Sunday morning 10:30-12. Several dance schools open rehearsals to visitors: **Krido Bekso Wirama**, Jl. Wahid Hasyim; **SSTI (State Dance Academy)**, Jl. Colombo (N of city); **Bagong Kussudiardjo**, Jl. Singosaren 9, off Jl. Wates. **Ramayana Ballet** staged on full-moon nights at Prambanan May-Oct. Reservations and information: tel: 96408, or at the tourist information center.

DRAMA: **Pura Wisata Open Theatre**, Jl. Brig. Jen Katamso, tel: 563605. Every night, 8-9:30 pm.

Tourist Information

Jl. Malioboro 16, tel: 566000. Mon-Sat 8 am-7:30 pm, closed holidays.

Currency Exchange

Bank Niaga & Bank Bumi Daya on Jl. Sudirman, & **Bank Negara Indonesia 1946**, next to post office. **Hotel Garuda** changes money on Sunday & after hours. Additionally, several exchanges on Jl. Pasar Kembang and Jl. Sosrowijayan.

Post / Telecommunications

Post Office, Jl. Senopati 2. Mon-Thu & Sat 6 am-10 pm, Fri 6-11 am and 2-10 pm. **Perumtel** (tel, fax, telegrams, telex) behind the post office, open 24-hours.

Hospital

Rumah Sakit Bethesda, Jl. Jen Sudirman 81, tel: 881774. Open 24-hours.

Arrival / Transportation

AIR: Adisucipto Airport, Jl. Solo, E of town. *Airline offices:* **Garuda**, Jl. Mangkubumi 52, tel: 61440; **Merpati**, Jl. Sudirman 9-11, tel: 514272; **Bouraq**, Jl. Mataram 60, tel: 882664.

RAIL: Train station has 12 trains to Jakarta daily, 6 to Bandung, 8 to Surabaya.

ROAD: For buses to surrounding towns, **Terminal Umbulharjo**, 5 km SE of center near Kota Gede, though some buses for Borobudur leave from **Terminal Pingit**, Jl. Magelang. Long-distance buses leave from bus company offices on Jl. Mangkubumi & Jl. Diponegoro, or on Jl. Sosrowijayan, by the ticket agencies.

LOCAL: You can find taxis on Jl. Senopati by post office, or at bigger hotels. **Horsecarts** *(andong)* available at station, post office or public market. **Becak** are everywhere, esp Jl. Malioboro. **Minibus** terminal off Jl. Senopati, behind shopping center. **Bicycles** can be rented from **Hotel Aziatic** or some *losmen* on Gang I & II (see Accommodation).

SOLO (Area Code 0271)
Accommodation

LUXURY: **Cakra Hotel**, Jl. Slamet Riyadi 201, tel: 45847. **Sahid Kusuma Hotel**, Jl. Sugiopranoto 20, tel: 46356. **Sahid Raya Hotel**, Jl. Gajah Mada 82, tel: 44144. **Solo Intan Hotel**, Jl. Slamet Riyadi 366, tel: 746075. **Riyadi Palace Hotel**, Jl. Slamet Riyadi 335, tel: 717181.

MODERATE: **Putri Ayu**, Jl. Slamet Riyadi 331, tel: 711812. **Ramayana Guest House**, Jl. Dr Wahidin 22, tel: 712814 (near Putri Ayu). **Hotel Wisata Indah**, Jl. Slamet Riyadi 173, tel: 43753. **Malkana Hotel**, Jl. Gajah Mada 29, tel: 712233. **Hotel Dana**, Jl. Slamet Riyadi 286, tel: 711976.

BUDGET: **Hotel Central**, Jl. A. Dahlan 32, tel: 42814. **Mawar Melati**, Jl. Imam Bonjol 54, tel: 636434. **The Westerners**, Jl. Kemlayan Kidul 11, tel: 633106. **Solo Homestay**, Jl. A. Dahlan, Gg. Bandar 2. **Losmen Sapta**, Jl. Gajah Mada 182. **Relax Homestay**, Jl. Gatot Subroto. **Mama Homestay**, Jl. Yos Sudarso, Kauman Gg. 3/49, tel: 52248. **Bamboo Homestay**, Jl. Setyaki 1, tel: 635856. **Matahari Hotel**, Gandakan Kiwo RT02/RW1, Nr. 8. **Hotel Trisari**, Jl. A. M. Sangaji 4, tel: 635959.

Restaurants
FOOD STALLS: Best on **Jl. Teuku Umar**, off Jl. Slamet Riyadi.
INDONESIAN: **Andalas**, Jl. Ronggowarsito (near Mangkunegaran Palace Hotel). **Bakso Taman Sari**, Jl. Gatot Subroto 42C (between Secoyuden & Slamet Riyadi). **Sari** (Javanese), Jl. Slamet Riyadi 351 (3 km from town center). **Segar Ayem** (Javanese), Jl. Secoyudan (opp Pasar Klewer). **Timlo Solo** (Javanese), Jl. Urip Sumoharjo 106. Lots of small eating places around train station and on Jl. Achmad Dahlan.
CHINESE: **Centrum**, Jl. Kratonan 151. **Orient**, Jl. Slamet Riyadi 337A (near Sari). **Populair**, Jl. Achmad Dahlan 70. **Ramayana Restaurant**, cornor Jl. Imam Bonjol/Jl. Ronggowarsito (off Jl. Slamet Riyadi).

Shopping
Pasar Gede (general market), end Jl. Urip Sumoharjo. **Jl. Secoyudan** is main shopping street. Fleamarket **Pasar Triwindu** (9 am-4 pm), Jl. Diponegoro, in front of Kraton Mangkunegaran.
ANTIQUES & CURIOS: **Eka Hartono**, Jl. Dawung Tengah 11/38. **Parto Art**, Jl. Slamet Riyadi 103. Several more on and just off Jl. Slamet Riyadi & Jl. Urip Sumarharjo. Reproduction furniture: **Mirah Delima**, Jl. Kemasan RT 11. WAYANG PUPPETS: **Usaha Pelajar**, Jl. Nayu Kidul (N of bus station). DANCERS' REQUISITES: **Toko Bedoyo Serimpi**, Temenggungan 116 (corner Hayam Wuruk/Ronggowarsito). BATIK: **Batik Danar Hadi**, Jl. Slamet Riyadi. **Batik Keris**, Jl. Yos Sudarso 37. **Batik Semar**, Jl. R.M. Said 132. Textiles market is **Pasar Klewer**, by main kraton.

Museums / Zoos
Museum Kraton Surakarta, tel: 632889. Sat-Thu 9-12:30, closed Fri. **Museum Istana Mangkunegaran**, Mon-Sat 9-12, closed Sun. **Museum Radyapustaka**, Jl. Brig. Jen. Slamet Rijadi 235, tel: 632306. Tue-Thu & Sun 8 am-1 pm, Fri & Sat 8-11, closed Mon. **Sriwedari Zoo**, Jl. Ir Sutami 109, tel: 636379. Daily 7 am-5 pm.

Cultural Events
GAMELAN MUSIC: **ASKI**, Pagelaran Alun Utara rehearsals most days 9 am-2 pm. COURT DANCING: **Mangkunegaran Kraton**, Wed 10-12.

WAYANG ORANG & KETOPRAK: **Taman Sriwedari**, Jl. Slamet Riyadi, Mon-Sat 8-11 pm. **Taman Hiburan Bale Kambang**, nightly 8 pm, matinee Sun 10 am.
WAYANG KULIT: **Radio Republik Indonesia** (near train station), 3rd Sat each month.

Tourist Information
Jl. Slamet Riyadi 275, tel: 711435.

Currency Exchange
Bank Bumi Daya & **Bank Niaga**, Jl. Slamet Riyadi (nos. 8 & 18), & **Bank Negara Indonesia 1946**, Jl. Jen Sudirman 19.

Post / Telecommunciations
Jl. Sudirman, open daily 7 am-9 pm. Jl. May Kusmanto, tel: 40108.

Arrival / Transportation
AIR: **Garuda** and **Merpati** in Cakra Hotel, Jl. Slamet Riyadi 201, tel: 630082. Mon-Fri 7:30 am-4:45 pm, Sat, Sun & hol. 9 am-1 pm. Sempati, c/o Solo Inn, Jl. Slamet Riyadi 266, tel: 46240. **Adi Sumarmo Airport** is 9 km W of town. **Silk Air**, BCA-Bldg, Jl. Slamet Riyadi, tel: 41374, Mon/Wed/Sat direct to Singapore.
RAIL: 15 trains each day to Yogya, 1 to Semarang, 8 to Surabaya, all from **Solo Balapan** station.
BUS: For inter-city buses, **Terminal Tirtonadi**, 3 km N of center on Jl. Setiabudi. Some night bus companies operate from Jl. Urip Sumoharjo, and some minibuses to Yogya from Jl. Yos Sudarso.
LOCAL: **Minibus station** opp. Pasar Klewer near Kasusuhunan palace. **Taxis** nearby at Jl. Kratonan. Bike rental at **The Westerners** (see Accommodation).

PEKALONGAN
(Area Code 0285)
Accommodation
LUXURY: **Nirwana Hotel**, Jl. Dr Wahidin 11, tel: 22446. MODERATE: **Hayam Wuruk**, Jl. Hayam Wuruk 152-158, tel: 24322. **Hotel Istana**, Jl. Gajah Mada 23-25, tel: 23581. BUDGET: **Hotel Asia**, Jl. Wahid Hasyim 49, tel: 22125. **Gajah Mada**, Jl. Gajah Mada 11A, tel: 41185. **Sari Dewi**, Jl. Hayam Wuruk 1, tel: 21248.

Restaurants
Pekalongan Remaja, (Chinese) Jl. Dr Cipto 20, tel: 21019. **Serba Ada**, Jl. Hayam Wuruk 125. **Hayam Wuruk**, (seafood, Chinese) Jl. Hayam Wuruk 69, tel: 25233.

Batik
Ahmad Yahya, Jl. Pesindon 221, tel: 22413. **GKBI** (National Batik Cooperative), Jl. HA Salim 39, tel: 25811. **Tobal Batik**, Jl. Teratai 7A. Many other shops on Jl. KH Mansyur & Jl. Hayam Wuruk. Out of town: **Oey Soe Tjoen**, Jl. Raya 104, Kedungwuni.

Arrival / Transportation
Minibus station: Behind Pertamina gas station, Jl. Hayam Wuruk. **Intercity bus station**, 2 km out of town.

SEMARANG
(Area Code 024)
Accommodation
LUXURY: **Metro**, Jl. H Agus Salim 2-4, tel: 547371. **Patra Jasa Hotel**, Jl. Si Singamanaraja, tel: 314441-7. **Graha Santika**, Jl. Panadanaran 116-20, tel: 413115. *MODERATE:* **Bukit Asri**, Jl. Setia Budi 5, tel: 475743. **Candi Baru**, Jl. Rinjani 21, tel: 315272. **Muria**, Jl. Dr. Cipto 73, tel: 516355. **Quirin Hotel**, Jl. Gajah Mada 44-52, tel: 547063. **Telomoyo**, Jl. Gajah Mada 138, tel: 545436. *BUDGET:* **Jaya**, Jl. MT Haryono 87, tel: 543604. **Oewa Asia**, Jl. Kol. Sugiono 12, tel: 542547. **Losmen Arjuna**, Jl. Imam Bonjol 51, tel: 544186.

Restaurants
There are many restaurants in the shopping centers on Simpang Lima. *INDONESIAN/SEAFOOD:* **Sate Ponorogo**, Jl. Gajah Mada 107, tel: 540637. **Soen**, Jl. A Yani 164, tel: 316174; **Kompleks Warna Sari** (food centre), Jl. Gajah Mada. *CHINESE:* **Gajah Mada**, Jl. Gajah Mada 43, tel: 543753. **Pringgading**, Jl. Pringgading 54, tel: 288973. More on Gang Lombok, in Chinatown, next to *klenteng*. *WESTERN:* **Toko Oen**, Jl. Pemuda 52, tel: 541683.

Shopping
Shopping Centers around the central square Simpang Lima: Gajah Mada Plaza, Plasa Simpang Lima, Matahari Department Store.
Bird market: Jl. Kartini, near stadium.
BATIK: **Cenderawasih**, Jl. Pemuda 66, tel: 545986. **Batik Danar Hadi**, Jl. Gajah Mada 186, tel: 545999. **Batik Keris**, Pertokoan Complex, Gajah Mada Plaza. *ANTIQUES & CURIOS:* **Pandjang**, Jl. Widoharjo 31A, E of bus station; also several shops on Jl. Pemuda.

Museums
Central Java State Museum, Jl. Abdul Rahman (1 km from airport). **Museum Jamu Nyonya Meneer** (Museum of Herbal Remedies), Jl. Raya Kaligawe km 4, tel: 285732. Mon-Fri 10 am-3:30 pm.

Cultural Events
WAYANG ORANG & KETOPRAK: Nightly at **Ngesti Pandowo**, Jl. Pemuda 116, **Sri Wanito**, Jl. Dr Dipto, & **Wahyu Budoyo**, Kopleks Tegal Wareng, Jl. Sriwijaya. *DANCE:* Performances at **Taman Raden Saleh**, Jl. Sriwijaya.

Tourist Information
Municipality Tourist Office, Dinas Pariwisata, in Taman Raden Saleh, Jl. Sriwijaya 29, tel: 311220.

Mon-Thu 8 am-2 pm, Fri 8-11, Sat 8-12. **Central Java Prov. Tourist Office**, Jl. Dadukoro, Blok BB, PRPP Complex, tel: 607182, Mon-Thu 8 am-2 pm, Fri 8-11, Sat 8-12.

Post / Telecommunications
Post office, Pasar Johar, above Jl. Pemuda. **Telecom office** next door, open 24-hours.

Hospital
St. Elizabeth, Jl. Kawi 1, Candi, tel: 310076.

Arrival / Transportation
AIR: Ahmad Yani Airport, 8 km W of Semarang. Airline offices: **Bouraq**, Jl. G. Mada 61D, tel: 543065. **Garuda**, Graha Santika Hotel, Jl. Pandanaran 116-20, tel: 310045, 413217. **Merpati**, Jl. Gajah Mada 17, tel: 517137. Mandala, Bangkong Plaza, Jl. Letjen M.T. Haryono 864, tel: 444737.
RAIL: Tawang station is on the main Jakarta-Cirebon-Surabaya line.
BUS: Inter-city bus terminal is **Terminal Bis Terboyo**, 6 km from center, reached by *mikrolet* from Terminal Sendowo (see below).
SEA: Pelni, Jl. Emu Tantular 25, tel: 555156.
LOCAL: Main internal bus station is **Terminal Sendowo** on Jl. Suari, S of Gereja Blenduk. Taxis with air conditioning and meters at **Atlas Taxi**, Jl. Telaga Bodas 1, tel: 412412.

KUDUS
(Area Code 0291)
Accommodation
MODERATE: **Hotel Notosari Permai**, Jl. Kepodang 12, tel: 21245. **Hotel Air Mancur**, Jl. Pemuda 70, tel: 22514. **Kudus Asri Jaya Hotel**, at the bus station, 4 km S of town center.
BUDGET: **Losmen Duta Wisata**, Jl. Sunan Muria, Gg. Barongan 2/194, tel: 22694.

Restaurants
Garuda Restaurant, Jl. Jen Sudirman 1; good food stalls on *Simpang Tujuh* in front of *kabupaten* office.

JEPARA, REMBANG, PURWODADI
Museums
Museum Kartini di Jepara (Raden Ajeng Kartini Memorial Museum), Jl. Kartini 1, Jepara. Mon-Sat 8 am - 2 pm, Sun 9 am- 1 pm.
Museum Kartini di Rembang (Raden Ajeng Kartini Memorial Museum), Jl. Gatot Soebroto 8, Rembang. Mon-Thu 9 am-2 pm, Fri 9-12, Sat 9 am-1 pm, holidays 9 am-5 pm.
Museum Pemerintah Daerah Grobogan (Grobogan Regional Museum), Grobogan, Purwodadi. Mon-Thu 8 am-1 pm, Fri 9-11, Sat 8-12, closed Sun.

EAST JAVA

THE NORTH COAST
SURABAYA
MADURA
SURABAYA TO MALANG
MAJAPAHIT AND
THE BRANTAS
PENATARAN
BROMO AND BEYOND

East Java is vernacular Java, country Java, deep Java. It was here that Javanese art finally mastered its Indian models; ancestor-worship and mysticism triumphed over theology, and a peasant bandit was able to found a great dynasty. East Java saw the most powerful of all Javan kings, but there have been no kingdoms here now for almost three centuries; no courtly arts, but also no empty pomp, no grovelling deference and no eclipse of folk traditions. Devoid of living *kraton*, far from the capital and relatively poor in tourist facilities, East Java attracts fewer visitors than the other two Javanese provinces. Yet in many ways, it offers a fairer and more diverse view of the island's life and people.

THE NORTH COAST

To the north of the volcanic spine is a wide plain where the twin rivers Solo and Brantas wind through teak forests, sugar fields and rice paddies to their sprawling deltas on the Strait of Madura. A final modest ridge of dry limestone, the "North Chalk Hills" (of which Madura Island is an extension) separates the Solo river valley from the Java Sea. In terms of culture and history, as well as physical geog-

Left: Panoramic view of the Merapi volcano.

raphy, the seaward part of this area is a continuation of the Central Javanese *pesisir*. **Tuban**, 100 kilometers along the palm-shaded beach from Rembang, is another ancient port, once Majapahit's main harbor. It boasts the grave of a minor *wali*, Sunan Bonang. Inland is **Bojonegoro**, where the **Sendangduwur Mosque** features a beautiful *gapura*, an ornamental doorway, from the 16th century. Its intricately carved reliefs above the lintel are mostly flowers and coral.

On the broken northeast corner of Java, the ancient port of **Gresik** rivals Demak in the brilliance of its past. According to Chinese records, Gresik was founded in the 14th century by traders from Canton. Blessed with a fine, sheltered anchorage, it became a major international trading center and was the first port of Java to be visited by Europeans – Portuguese traders en route to the Moluccas. The Portuguese writer Tome Pires, who lived in Malacca between 1512 and 1517, described Gresik as "the jewel of all Javan trading ports." Also like Demak, Gresik was a major, early center for the dissemination of Islam, not only in Java, but throughout eastern Indonesia. **Makam Maulana Malik Ibrahim,** in Desa Candipuro, is the revered tomb of the very first of the *wali*, Malik Ibrahim, and his family. The tomb-

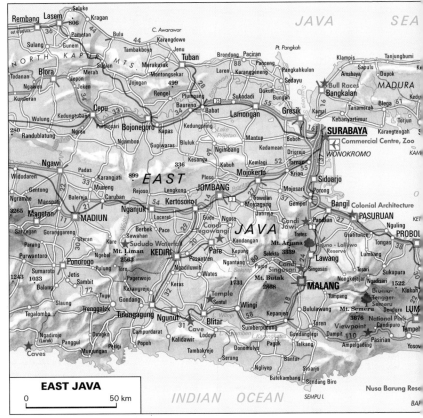

EAST JAVA

0   50 km

stone was probably imported from Gujarat, India; according to its inscription, the saint died in 1419. Two kilometers south of the town center, on a hill called **Giri**, is the even more famous grave of **Sunan Giri**. Unlike the other *wali*, Sunan Giri founded a line of spiritual lords to continue his authority after his death. These were feared both by the Dutch, who called them "the popes of Java," and by the rulers of Mataram, who respected their learning and spiritual power. In 1680 the line was finally exterminated by its combined enemies, but Giri has remained a place of pilgrimage. In life, the *wali* could work miracles; in death, they are still *kramat*, thought capable of bestowing divine favors on the devotees.

Still, Gresik is losing its sacred aura. The kind of Islam which moves today's youth has more to do with morals and loudspeakers than with saints and graves. Sawmills are the new face of Gresik, where Kalimantan's razed forests are reduced to plywood and pulp. The old Gresik lingers only in the narrow streets of the "Arab quarter," and around the holy tombs themselves.

SURABAYA

It was not silt which led to Gresik's eclipse; plenty of exotic sailing craft still bob on the polluted waters of its harbor. The culprit was the mighty colonial port of **Surabaya**, just 25 km along the coast

to the southeast. Ceded to the Dutch by Mataram in 1743, Surabaya was still smaller than Gresik in 1800. However, it had been selected as the chief Dutch entrepot and administrative center for East Java; and the massive growth of the colonial economy in the 19th century made Surabaya the busiest port and the biggest city in the Dutch Indies, outstripping even Batavia and ranking almost alongside Singapore in international importance. Today, Surabaya has again been overtaken by Jakarta in size, but at 5.1 million people it is the second largest in the country and growing fast. Surabaya's sweet name belies a reality of heat, dirt and noise, but it is an interesting and gripping place. This is a living cultural center, both in the formal sense of plays and performances and in the sense of the fusion and regeneration of folk cultures.

Surabaya is cosmopolitan, but without the jarring pseudo-Western glitter of Jakarta. Give or take an air-conditioned shopping complex or two, Surabaya's atmosphere is more purely Indonesian, with a special east Indonesian flavor. For as Surabaya grew as an export point for Javanese products, it also became the hub of the maritime trading network for the eastern archipelago as a whole. Much of its population is from nearby Madura, but there are also large numbers of Banjar from Kalimantan, Bugis and Minahasans from Sulawesi and Ambonese from the Moluccas.

Surabaya's colonial boom was in a sense, a renaissance, for the port has a long history. In 1620, it was a fortified trading city over 30 kilometers in circumference, a state in its own right with lordship over Gresik and Sidayu. However, five years later Mataram took it by siege, thus ending Surabaya's luster for more than two centuries. According to tradition, the conquered king's son took on the life of an ascetic at the holy grave of Surabaya's founder – yet another *wali*, Sunan Ngampel, who was a pupil of Malik Ibrahim of Gresik. His grave can be seen in **Kampong Ngampel**, the birth place of the city, now lost in the old commercial district between the forks of the Kali Mas.

A little to the south, where Jl. Rajawali crosses the west branch of the river, is the famous **Red Bridge**, once the heart of Dutch Surabaya. In 1920, rush hour was, "an indescribable press of four- and two-wheeled carriages, carts loaded with merchandise, travelling sailors, native and Chinese merchants, coolies..." Today's roaring motorized battle leaves one at an even greater loss for words, but the neighborhood is now evocatively dowdy, with run-down Dutch warehouses and prewar offices.

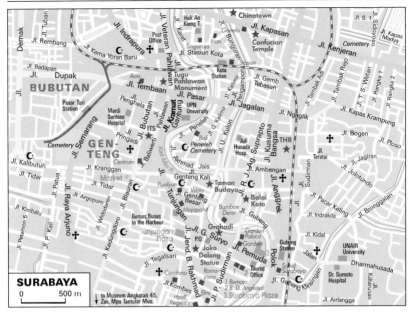

When the Red Bridge neighborhood was in its prime, it was the geographic center of the city, halfway between the docks in the north and the gracious suburban administrative precinct served by **Gubeng Station** in the south. The dock complex at **Tanjung Perak** remains much as it was, except for its new air-conditioned passenger terminal. Coolies still unload sacks of copra, pepper and cloves from boats from such places as Tarakan, Tolitoli and Ternate. Scrubbing, hammering sailors struggle to keep ageing warships seaworthy; as in Dutch times, this is Indonesia's main naval base. But in the south, urban growth has swamped the old civic boulevard, **Jl. Pemuda / Jl. Gub Suryo**, now a commercial thoroughfare lined with banks and hotels. Nevertheless, **Grahadi**, the residence of the Dutch governor, still stands here on immaculate lawns, an island of tranquillity preserved by the

Right: A classic pose from a Ramayana dance in Surabaya.

presence of today's Governor of East Java. On a plinth opposite the residence stands the corpulent figure of **Joko Dolog**, a 13th-century statue from the Malang area which has long been Surabaya's trademark.

Around the corner on Jl. Tunjungan is a building which recalls both the heyday and the end of colonialism in Indonesia. **Hotel Majapahit Mandarin Oriental**, which opened in 1910 as Hotel Oranje, was Surabaya's finest. Countless settlers, ship owners and cruise ship passengers were served *rijsttafel* in its palatial dining room and sipped Bols on its polished terraces. The unsightly air-conditioning units bolted to the more expensive rooms are a concession to modernity, but otherwise, this pavilion-style hotel retains its old-world grace. In 1942 the invading Japanese renamed it Hotel Yamato and after their defeat an attempt to make it Oranje again precipitated an incident which helped spark off the biggest and bloodiest battle – indeed, some say the only real battle – of the national revolu-

126

tion. The blurred, monochrome photographs of this event have not lost their power to move; they show Indonesian youths scaling the building's squat tower to tear off the blue strip from the Dutch tricolor on the flagpole, leaving the *merah putih*, the red and white flag of the republic.

At this time, there were only a few Dutchmen in the city; order was officially in the hands of 6000 British troops, who were mostly Indian. When these seemed about to be massacred by more than 100,000 Indonesian fighters bent on various combinations of revolution and *jihad*, the British flew in Sukarno and Hatta to arrange a ceasefire. However, there was more fighting, and on November 10, 1945, a day now commemorated as *Hari Pahlawan* (Heros' Day), the British began a bloody, punitive sweep through Surabaya, supported by naval and air bombardments. Many of the defenders fought in the ancient state of selfless frenzy which has entered the English language as "amok;" the fighting lasted three weeks. Though the Republicans lost thousands of men, the Battle of Surabaya was a turning point in the revolution, convincing the outside world that the republican leaders were not simply a group of isolated collaborators who would soon be denounced by their own people. Those who fought and died on the Indonesian side are commemorated by the **Tugu Pahlawan** (Heroes' Monument), and the whole city is often honored with the epithet *Kota Pahlawan* (City of Heroes). An army museum containing relics of the revolution, the **Museum Angkatan 45**, is located in the far south of town.

East Java is the original home of much of the island's classical cultural heritage. The first great works of old Javanese literature were composed here, including the *Arjunawiwaha*, the *Bharatayuddha* and the *Ramayana*, all classic Old Javanese versions of ancient Sanskrit

myths. Episodes from East Java's history supply the raw material for the *Panji* and *Damar Wulan* romances, which provide lighter alternatives to the Indian epics of *wayang* repertoire. Panji is a perfect knight whose pursuit of his true love, the equally flawless Dewi Anggreni, gives him ample scope to demonstrate his courage and honor. Damar Wulan, a more demotic hero, is a stable boy who manages to marry a princess of Majapahit.

The East Javanese have their own genres as well as their own scripts. The Panji cycle is often played by the *wayang gedog* – essentially a form of *wayang kulit*, but with a slightly different style of puppet and accompaniment from a seven-tone *pelog gamelan* rather than the customary five-tone *slendro* type. Sunan Giri himself is said to have introduced this *wayang* form. *Ludruk* is a special Surabayan form of drama in which the settings are contemporary urban households and the human actors speak the local *arek* dialect. Coarse, realistic and satirical, *ludruk* epitomizes the strong

127

populist vein in East Javanese art and society. The whole range of the region's performing arts can be sampled in Surabaya, although for dance, the most prestigious venue is the **Candra Wilwatikta Open Air Theatre** near Pandaan, 45 kilometers south of the city. Traditional arts form a living part of folk culture in Surabaya in a way that is being lost in Jakarta. The decrepit red light districts of **Jarak** and **Bangunrejo**, for instance, are still the haunt of *ronggeng*, dancing-girls-cum-prostitutes who dance by the roadside just as they centuries years ago.

Surabaya is also a good place to watch *reog*, one of Java's oldest and strangest entertainments. *Reog* is the local name for the ancient trance dance which occurs in different forms and under different names from Banten to Bali. In West and Central Java, the main performer rides a flat hobby horse of woven bamboo and is literally whipped into his trance state while weird clowns look on, a surreal scene which sets the imagination roving. In East Java and Bali, grotesque monster masks are worn. The *Reog Ponorogo* (after Ponorogo, a small town south of Madiun) performed in Surabaya combines both types in a spectacle of orchestrated madness.

MADURA

The barren island of **Madura** lies off Surabaya like a stray piece of maritime eastern Indonesia somehow towed to the Javanese coast. Madura has a pronounced dry season, and when the rain does fall it is quickly swallowed up by the limestone hills. One result is that the inhabitants eat more maize and cassava than rice, and breed cattle instead of water buffalo. Another is that the Madurese have always been more dependent upon the sea and more orientated towards the lands beyond it, than the Sundanese,

Right: A Maduran racing bull and his owner.

Javanese or Balinese. Madura is an island of picturesque fishing villages, blinding white salt pans and multicolored *prahu* drawn up on golden beaches. The north coast is the best place in Indonesia to spot traditional *prahu*, and the last place on earth where some designs are still built.

Oppressed by Javanese dynasties and dissatisfied with the dry poverty of their own island, the Madurese seem to have spent much of their history vainly trying to master Java. Sultan Agung of Mataram conquered Madura in 1624, forcing its petty states to unite under the line later known as Cakraningrat. However, as Mataram grew weak, the tables were turned. Again and again, Madurese armies were the crucial factor in the wars for the Javanese throne. However, they were never numerous enough to be more than just a factor. Twice – in 1677 and 1742 – they actually took the court of Mataram, only to lose it again. Today, emigration seems to be succeeding where arms failed. Of the 12 million Madurese, Madura itself supports barely three million; the rest live on the mainland, and in parts of the north coast east of Surabaya they make up virtually the whole of the population.

The Madurese are the epitome of Indonesian martial valor, but, unfortunately for their place in modern schoolbooks, their only consistent antipathy has been towards Java, against which they have more often fought alongside Dutchmen than opposite them. The regents of Madura were granted extravagant titles and privileges by the Dutch in return for services rendered. The Cakraningrats became official custodians of the remote *Oosthoek* of the East Java mainland, and even bore the title of sultan for a time. Several Cakraningrats are buried in the **Air Mata** cemetery near **Arasbaya**. This contains richly decorated Muslim graves in pre-Islamic style, including one backed by a huge carved stone screen in the form of the *gunungan* which signals

the end of a *wayang kulit* performance. In the east of the island, a separate dynasty ruled for the Dutch in **Sumenep**, where their 18th-century palace, **Kraton Sumenep**, still stands. Part of it has been converted into a small museum housing royal regalia. The royal tombs of Sumenep are at the **Asta Tinggi Cemetery**, one kilometer outside the town. One of the princes of Sumenep was a personal friend of Stamford Raffles, and supplied much of the information which Raffles used to put together his classic *History of Java*, still selling after almost 200 years. The **Mesjid Jamik Mosque** is roughly contemporary with the palace and features the graceful Hindu roof which was superseded on later Javanese mosques by the squat Arab *qubbah*. Also remarkable are the classical colonnades gracing many colonial buildings in this quiet, country town.

For many, Madura seems to bear out the supposition that harsh lands produce harsh people. Others say that the Madurese of today are simply like the Javanese of old, before their courts became effete and their people deferential to the Dutch: proud, brave, vengeful, quick to anger and fascinated by long knives. These characteristics are perhaps reflected in the Madurese approach to religion. Madura was not one of the first areas to be Islamized, but it took on the new faith with the zeal of many a late convert. In the 20th century it was one of the bastions of Islamic politics. Madura is undoubtedly *kasar* (coarse), the cultural antipode of the Javanese *kraton*. However, the angular, ascetic faces and loud, aspirated speech of Madurese men inspire wary respect on the mainland. Their unpredictable temperament is also said to render approaches to Madurese women a matter for extreme caution. This is widely regretted because Madura's beautiful womens are the sole guardians of the secret of *goyang Madura*, a supposedly indescribable lovemaking technique.

A more accessible attraction is the unique sport of bull-racing, Madura's prime tourist attraction. Pairs of massive

pedigree bulls cover 130 meters in ten seconds flat while their "jockeys" hang grimly on to light wooden sleds lashed between each pair. Honor, life and limb, and a great deal of money are at stake. The cash prizes were introduced 80 years ago by the local Dutch government in order to encourage the breeding of better stock; since then, both the bulls and the prizes have continued to get bigger. Qualifying races are held throughout the island before the October final in **Pamekasan**, the administrative capital. This tournament is a major social and cultural event, complete with *gamelan*, dancing and armed brawls.

The Madurese also have a distinct version of *batik* which features highly stylized bird, fish and leaf motifs in an almost autumnal, reddish-brown color derived from tree bark. It smells different from *batik* produced elsewhere. In Ma-

Above: Untamed nature on Java. Right: "...by the sweat of your brow" – vegetable cultivation.

dura, *batik* is exclusively a cottage industry, and all the wax is applied by hand. The main center of production is **Tanjungbumi** on the north coast. Despite its proximity to the teeming city of Surabaya, the northern interior of Madura is one of the most traditional parts of western Indonesia. Obvious examples include the *destar* headdress still habitually worn by older men, the *sarong kebaya* worn by the women and the preponderance of ox- and horsecarts on the roads.

SURABAYA TO MALANG

South of Surabaya, 40 kilometers of flat, teeming, glistening, rice-laden delta country separate the city from the mountains. In **Sidoarjo**, half-way across this delta, estuarine fish are farmed in brackish pools and *krupuk* (expanded rice crackers) are manufactured. A dozen workshops also make finely traced red- and white-*batik*. Surabaya's most popular resort is **Tretes**, 22 kilometers beyond Sidoarjo on Mt. Arjuna, the volcano which, on a clear day, seems to loom over the streets of the city itself. The summit is part of the little-known **Arjuno-Lalijiwo Reserve**, with many difficult, but spectacular hikes. Tretes is comfortable and scenic, but not one of the retreats of the elite. It also features a large number of Madurese prostitutes.

In topographic make-up, East Java is more straightforward than the rest of the island. The mountains of Central Java still have something of the tangled, interlocked confusion of the Sunda highlands. However, in the east, this storm of rock gives way to an even, powerful swell. Over the 400 kilometers between Solo and the eastern tip of Java, majestic peaks alternate with fertile basins in a single stately row of volcanoes, none less than 2000 meters high. All have multiple peaks, but each is clearly a single massif. Each basin cradles one major town – from west to east: Solo, Madiun, Kediri,

Malang, Lumajang, Jember and, finally, Banyuwangi on the Bali Strait.

The great oscillations of altitude, combined with a climate much more seasonal than that of the rest of the island, make this backbone of East Java a land of predictable but nonetheless jarring extremes; heat and cold, rain and aridity, barrenness and lushness.

The historic core of East Java is not as tightly concentrated as Central Java's Magelang-Yogya-Solo arc. The old kingdoms spread and shifted over a wide area, and their remnants are scattered in a broken circle around the **Arjuna-Butak-Kelud** mountain group, which straddles the island between Surabaya and the south coast. Although there are signs of Hindu civilization in East Java from the 8th century, the area only entered the mainstream of history with the mysterious shift of power from Central Java in the early 10th century. The first kings of the East Javanese era are hazy figures and the site of their capital has never been found, but their earliest substantial

monuments are in the foothills of **Mt. Arjuna**, not far from Tretes.

One of these foothills, **Gunung Penanggungan**, is of special interest, for it was regarded as a miniature of Mt. Meru, the Hindu world-mountain.

Not content with creating artificial Mt. Merus in their architecture, the Hindu Javanese also sought holy mountains in their natural environment. The shape of Penanggungan, with four foothills around a central peak, rendered it especially suitable, and it is still a dramatic and appropriate backdrop for performances at the **Candra Wilwatikta**, an open-air theater near **Pandaan**. On the slopes of Penanggungan are more than 80 shrines, most of them very small and weathered. The earliest, but also the most attractive and complete, are, of all things, royal bathing places.

Candi Jalatunda and **Candi Belahan** were the tenth-century prototypes for many such elaborate *mandi* elsewhere in East Java and in Bali. Both consist of mossy tanks of eroded stone set back into

sculpted hillsides – dark, magical places. At Belahan, the blessed water spouts from the nipples of the goddesses Sri and Lakshmi, the wives of Vishnu. It is not known exactly what ceremonies were performed here, but a 14th-century text hints at erotic rites. Whatever their connotations, these bathing places were important enough to receive the ashes of kings. An urn containing ashes and gold was found during the excavation of Jalatunda. In 1049, Belahan was converted into a funerary monument for one of Java's most famous rulers, Airlangga, whose statue as Vishnu once stood between the goddesses, but is now in the Mojokerto Archaeological Museum.

Airlangga was a half-Balinese hermit-king who reunited East Java in 1019 after a divisive war, and ruled it until his death in 1049. Before he died, however, he divided the country again by splitting his lands between his two sons. The new bor-der was known as the *pinggir rekso* (guarded frontier). Running north and south from the summit of **Mt. Kelud**, it coincides with the real linguistic division between Central and East Java. The western kingdom was Kediri, centered in the town of the same name. Also known as Daha, this was at first the dominant of the two. Kediri did much for Javanese literature, but left precious few monuments.

The eastern kingdom created by Airlangga was called Janggala. By the beginning of the 13th century it was a mere vassal of Kediri, but in 1222 a usurper called Ken Arok, who had murdered the regent of Janggala, seized power in the east and founded **Singosari**, a dynasty that overthrew Kediri; its name is still borne by a village north of Malang. It lasted only 70 years, but left behind a rich monumental legacy.

Singosari Temples

One of the most complete Singosari temples, **Candi Jawi**, is not far from

Above: Candi Jawi, one of the Singosari temples.

Jalatunda. This is neither a Buddhist nor a Hindu shrine, but a combination of both. The foundation is Hindu, but a Buddhist stupa crowns the monument.

In the Singosari period, syncretism superseded coexistence in the relationship between the two faiths. Religious thought became less rigorous, more mystical, more emotional, more Javanese. Hinduism was now fully identified with worship of the god Shiva. Shiva was Buddha and the human kings were incarnations of both. The builder of Candi Jawi, King Kertanegara (1268-92), had it house a statue of himself as a "Siwabuddha" – Shiva on one side and Buddha on the other. Almost without exception, East Javanese temples are monuments to kings as well as deities.

As religion drifted from its Indian moorings, so did architecture, with stunning results. A far cry from the squat Indian reproductions at Dieng, Jawi is a further development of the free, soaring style beginning to emerge at Prambanan. Its waisted silhouette has the tropical weirdness characteristic of the East Javanese temples and projections of the unfettered Javanese imagination.

Other Singosari temples can be found south of Candi Jawi in the high country around Singosari itself. **Candi Kidal**, near Tumpang, was even more audacious than Jawi, and has paid in, earthquake damage, for the presumptuous skill of its architect. It is currently being restored to its full 12.5 meter height.

Candi Jago, in Tumpang, has a different form, with a high three-level base and a smaller, off-set shrine building. It is most remarkable for its reliefs, executed in a two-dimensional style quite unlike the rounded realism of the Borobudur carvings and probably influenced by the *wayang kulit* shadow puppets — more evidence of the progressive "Javanization" of Java's art. Some of the figures shown, like the grotesque *panakawan* clowns, are still popular *wayang* charac-

ters. Heads and feet are turned sideways, as in an Egyptian mural. Other panels depict the wooden architecture of the 13th century, so like that of modern Bali. **Candi Singosari** is almost the only visible remnant of the old capital. The last and most elaborate of the dynasty's temples, it was never quite finished. The sculptors worked from the top down, for the final detailed ornamentation is complete only on the upper parts. Disaster overcame Singosari in 1292 or 1293, when it was overthrown by a king called Jayakatwang from Kediri. A hundred meters from the temple are a pair of huge, menacing *raksasa* (giant) statues which may once have stood ineffectual guard at Singosari's gate.

Malang, which has been described as the most attractive town in Java, is the natural base for exploring the Singosari temples and the mountains around them. Like the Sundalands, Malang's high valley is perfect for growing coffee and the town grew up in the 19th century on the wealth which the government coffee system squeezed from the soil and its children. When compulsory cultivation ended, both locals and Europeans preferred to plant the tobacco and fruit for which the place is now known; while its cool climate attracted the Dutch which kept its fortunes from flagging. Malang is hilly and varied, without the dreary, straight, shuttered main street of many towns of its size. Along with the Dutch architecture, it also seems to retain a ghost of Dutch civic discipline and concern for neatness.

Still, Malang is a Javanese town – much more so than kaleidoscopic Surabaya – and something of a cultural center in its own right. *Topeng Malang*, for instance, is a special local form of the masked dance genre, enacting stories from the Panji cycle. Once one of Java's most widespread dramatic genres, *wayang topeng* has retained its popularity in only two disparate geographic settings, Cirebon and Malang. In Malang it is a

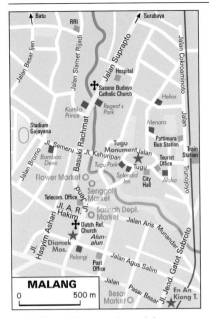

MALANG

0   500 m

real folk tradition, used to celebrate marriages and circumcisions. At the **Sasono Budoyo Catholic Church** in Malang, *gamelan* music and even Javanese dance are used in services. Protestant churches in Indonesia, from the Dutch Reformed to the American Baptists, have tended to be agents of cultural assimilation; with Catholics, the assimilation is the other way around. This tactic has certainly paid off in Java, where Catholicism has profited from the drift to Christianity caused by the combination of government insistence upon adherence to an official religion and widespread Javanese antipathy to rigorous Islam. Not that religious antipathies are much in evidence in Malang, where the central mosque and the Protestant church stand side by side on the main square.

Other faded colonial idylls lie in the vicinity of Malang. **Lawang**, 18 kilometers to the north, along the main road, was

Right: Javanese women selling their colorful wares in Trowulan.

even more popular than Malang as a retirement place for Dutch civil servants and rich Chinese businessmen. Lawang's town square is probably the most attractive and tranquil in Indonesia, with grass, fountains, a restrained stone monument and a dignified white town hall on one side. **Kebun Raya Rurwodadi**, a little beyond Lawang, is an outstation of the national botanical gardens at Bogor. The beautifully located swimming pool and restaurant at **Selecta**, 23 kilometers northwest of Malang via Batu, was once the very symbol of the good life to which ordinary Dutchmen could aspire in the colonies while stiff respectability and economic recession ruled at home.

Near Selecta is the source of the great **Brantas river**, Java's second river after the Solo. The Brantas sources lie barely 40 kilometers from the sea, but reaches it by following an extraordinary route which gives it a length of 252 kilometers. First it flows southeast to Malang, then down through a sharp defile to a west-east section parallel with the south coast, then back north and east via Kediri and Mojokerto to form the great delta south of Surabaya. This delta was the stage for the greatest act in Hindu Javanese history after the fall of Singosari.

MAJAPAHIT AND THE BRANTAS

A few months before his end the last Singosari king, Kertanegara, had the temerity to offend Kublai Khan, conqueror of China. Kublai sent an ambassador to demand Java's acknowledgement of the suzerainty of the Middle Kingdom; Kertanegara sent him back with a mutilated face. By the time the inevitable punitive expedition arrived in Java, Singosari had already been sacked and the king killed by his own rebels from Kediri. Ironically, the Chinese army was to ensure that a new and greater Javanese dynasty arose from the ashes. Wijaya, one of Kertanegara's sons-in-law, was devious enough

to persuade the Chinese to help him defeat the rebel Jayakatwang. He then turned upon them and drove them back to their boats to become undisputed lord of East Java. In 1294, Wijaya founded a new capital on the delta of the Brantas, and called it **Majapahit**. The lower Brantas valley was exceptionally fertile, rich in rice and sugar, and one of the most densely populated places on earth. At the same time, access to the sea meant access to the trading wealth now represented by Surabaya. Majapahit became a great walled city of palaces, temples and canals. What remains of it is scattered over 15 square kilometers around the village of **Trowulan**.

Like other Javanese capitals, Majapahit was mostly wooden. Unfortunately, because even its more permanent monuments were built of red brick instead of stone, not much has survived. A lot of imagination is needed to picture it as it was when the court poet Prapanca described it in 1365, as being as, "beautiful and unearthly as a Balinese temple, but immeasurably grander and finer." The dry sump of **Segaran** was a six-hectare pool of limpid water. In the surrounding fields were gilded pavilions where King Hayam Wuruk and his *patih* (prime minister) Gajah Mada received guests and watched tournaments and sacrifices. The gateway of **Bajang Ratu** led to the courtyard of a vanished temple, where flowering trees produced the petals which were strewn in the king's path wherever he went. **Candi Brahu** was the greatest of the city's temples, overlooking the field of Bubat where envoys from West Java once camped, bringing a Sundanese princess to be Hayam Wuruk's bride. **Candi Tikus** was a royal bathing-place.

The **Museum Purbakala Trowulan** contains hundreds of archeological finds, including terracotta heads which look so Greek that some have speculated on European influence. One stormy, masculine face has been identified, justifiably or not, as that of Gajah Mada himself, and its image graces Indonesian textbooks and even government buildings. Because

Majapahit seems to have had dependencies throughout the archipelago, it is important to modern Indonesians as a historical precedent for their state. Some of the city's monuments have been more reconstructed than restored, and the army has built a huge new **Pendopo Agung** on an original foundation.

The Muslim graves at **Tralaya**, two kilometers south of the museum, have revolutionized traditional views of the history of Java. They date from 1376 onwards, and, bar one found in Trowulan itself, they are the oldest Muslim burials in Java. It used to be accepted that Islam spread from the bottom up, spreading first among traders and commoners oppressed by Hindu caste and kingship. Yet, the Tralaya graves seem to belong to Majapahit nobility, perhaps even members of the royal family, suggesting "top-down" Islamization. One of them still has the form of a Hindu *lingga*.

A regent of nearby **Mojokerto**, Kromodjojo Adinegoro, was responsible for the upsurge of interest in the Majapahit ruins at the beginning of the 20th century. He founded an archaeological museum which was transferred to the government in 1912 and is open today as the **Museum Purbakala Mojokerto**.

In what sense Majapahit "ruled" the outer islands in the 14th century is open to question, but it certainly ruled East Java and its kings and priests made processions around the religious sites in all parts of the land. Apart from continuing to honor Singosari shrines, they also built outlying temples of their own. **Candi Tegowangi** and **Candi Surowono**, near **Pare**, are both Majapahit sites. Pare is a typical East Javanese small town – so typical that Clifford Geertz immortalized it under the pseudonym "Mojokuto" in his classic *The Religion of Java*. **Museum Purbakala Tirtoyoso**, in **Kediri**, also has Majapahit exhibits. Kediri was

Right: A silversmith with his traditional tools.

the last refuge of Hindu-Javanese power during the period of Islamization. Racked by disorder after the death of Hayam Wuruk in 1389, Majapahit staggered on until hemmed in by Islamic sultanates. When the Portuguese arrived in 1512, the "pagan" state had retreated to Kediri – whether it still called itself Majapahit is not known. Fifteen years later it was conquered by Demak, ending the Hindu-Javanese era. Today Kediri is home of the clove cigarette empire, Gudang Garam.

PENATARAN

Further up the Brantas, beyond Kediri, in the region around **Tulungagung** and **Blitar** is rich in antiquities. The less important ones date from the Singosari period and before. **Candi Sawentar**, in the village of the same name near Blitar, is a temple like Jawi and Kidal. **Goa Selamangleng** near Sanggrahan, southeast of Tulungagung, is a hermit's cave carved with scenes from the temptation of Arjuna. However, the real attraction is the Majapahit sacred site, **Penataran**. Located above Blitar, on the slopes of Mt. Kelud, Penataran is East Java's largest and finest surviving temple complex.

Whereas the great monuments of Central Java seem to aim at power through mass, the emphasis at Panataran is on space. There are three wide courtyards, which are linked by ornamental gates and rise progressively in the direction of the mountain. Appended to the rear of the complex, in the tradition of Jalatunda and Belahan, is a bathing place, and another has been fully restored in the nearby village of **Penataran**. The main sanctuary was at the top and back, but only the foundation remains. In better condition are Candi Naga on the second level, with guardian serpents draped along its eaves, and the restored **Dated Temple** on the first level, a perfect miniature version of Candi Jawi or Candi Kidal. So called be-

cause an inscription records its construction in 1369, the Dated Temple is now the symbol of the Brawijaya army division.

The stone reliefs decorating almost every surface at Penataran, including the sides of humble foundation structures, represent the highest development of that medium in East Java. As at Candi Jago, the illustrations are highly stylized. Their themes are bewilderingly various, and include such curiosities as the Bubuksha-Gagang Aking story, as well as the more classical Indian epics. Gagang Aking ("Dry Stalk") is a Hindu ascetic who starves his way to wisdom; his younger brother Bubukshah ("Glutton") is a Buddhist who reaches enlightenment in comfort. Less narrative iconography features animals, especially mythical ones; weird, unearthly, power-laden creatures. East Javanese art is infused with an awareness of the supernatural world beyond observable phenomena.

At **Sentul**, not far from Blitar, on the way to Penataran, is the tomb of Sukarno; Indonesia's greatest 20th century shrine, **Makam Proklamator**. Sukarno was the man chosen to ride the tide of revolution and lead a new, apparently impossible to rule, nation through its first, most difficult years. Hardly known as self-effacing in life, Sukarno nevertheless had the humility to ask to lie as a commoner in death; alongside his mother in the small town where he spent much of his youth. Or perhaps he was already beyond both humility and pride? For eight years no inscription marked the simple grave; it was distinguished by only a sun-faded parasol, an ancient symbol of power. Sukarno's resting place makes a provocative contrast with the lavish mausoleum which his successor, Suharto, completed for himself in 1977, at the age of 56. In 1978, the events of 1965 were judged far enough gone to allow Sukarno's rehabilitation as a national hero. An elaborate monument was built over the grave, and today it is a large and lucrative tourist destination, complete with restaurants and souvenir stands.

BROMO AND BEYOND

East Java, as far as Malang, has always been somewhere near the mainstream of Javanese history. Even after the coming of Islam and the return of power to Central Java, the old eastern core remained part of Mataram's *mancanegeri*, or outer domains; an important source of tribute as well as rebellion. However, east of Malang was a land so remote from the world of most Javanese that they classed it with the outer islands, calling it the *tanah sebarang wetan*, the "land on the far side in the east." The Dutch later called it the *Oosthoek*, the "eastern salient." Java's eastern peninsula consists mostly of rugged mountains; there are no big cities, no ancient monuments, just wild, tropical landscapes – Java in the raw.

No landscape is rawer than that of the famous **Mt. Bromo**. At 2392 meters, Mt.

Above: Semeru volcano. Right: Orchards in blossom.

Bromo itself is actually the smallest of three peaks rising from the center of a vast extinct crater, the **Tengger** caldera. Over the last two centuries, Mt. Bromo's mouth has alternated between crater lake and gaping vent; today, unlike its two neighbors, it is active. The volcano-within-a-volcano configuration is like Mt. Batur in Bali, but while Mt. Batur has a blue lake at its foot, Mt. Bromo has a sea of sand. Not for nothing is Bromo East Java's most popular tourist destination. The view into the volcano's crater is as humbling as anything found in nature, and the landscapes of the Sand Sea are like the end of the world, or the beginning. The scale of the outer caldera is such that visitors feel like ants in the ruins of a cathedral. Bromo is usually ascended before dawn, on horseback or on foot, from the village of **Ngadisari**. An alternative route begins at the old Dutch health resort of **Tosari**.

Mt. Bromo is the holy mountain of the remarkable Tengger, a 60,000-strong ethnic group native to the surrounding

Tengger Highlands. Once a year they gather for a ceremony of appeasement on the razor-sharp rim of the mountain, hurling fruit, vegetables and flowers into the steam below. At one time it was a human sacrifice which was cast into the fire. The Tengger are not Muslims, but the last surviving fragment of the culture of Majapahit. Hayam Wuruk himself exempted the Tengger villages from tax and ordered them to worship Bromo (Brahma); six centuries later, they are still fulfilling their obligation. The Tengger retain a pre-Muslim calendar, and their priests or *dukun* possess beakers engraved with zodiac signs and 14th-century dates. Rice will not grow well in the cool, mountain air and the main crops of the Tengger are maize, onions, carrots and cauliflower. Until recently, they built wooden longhouses unlike any other dwellings in Java; now they live in tin-roofed shacks.

Vast as it is, Tengger is only part of the massif separating Malang from the next valley to the east. The southern part is formed by the perfect cone of **Mt. Semeru**, at 3676 meters the highest mountain in Java. Also called Mahameru, this is the island's definitive Meru, or world-mountain. The rest of Java's mountains are supposed to have been pieces which crumbled from Mt. Semeru when the gods fumbled its transplantation from the Himalayas. The anomaly of a having second Meru, at Mt. Penanggungan near Pandaan, is explained by the theory that the top of Mt. Semeru was also lost in flight and fell to form the smaller mountain. Mt. Semeru is more or less continuously active and has caused considerable devastation at times; ash from the eruption of 1911 fell even on Bali.

The north coast of the *Oosthoek* is an unexciting stretch of ricefields and mangrove forests, interrupted only by the sands of **Pasir Putih**, a beach resort near **Situbondo**. The coastal population is made up almost entirely of Madurese,

who have come here through history as soldiers, traders, plantation laborers and farming settlers. The Madurese in **Bondowoso** have developed a new sport for their favorite animal: bull fighting. This is bloodier for the bulls than the racing practiced on the home island, but not so dangerous to human life: bull fights bull, not matador.

The Madurese were able to make much of this part of Java their own because of the repeated wars which swept and depopulated the area during the 17th and 18th centuries. **Blambangan**, a name which now refers only to a small peninsula in the far southeast, was once a powerful Hindu kingdom extending westwards as far as Mt. Bromo. Caught between expansive empires to the west and their stubborn Balinese enemies to the east, Blambangan could not maintain a stable independence. It became a no-man's-land where bandits and refugees built precarious kingdoms between the power blocks. Sultan Agung conquered Blambangan in 1639, but, unable to hold

139

it against the Balinese, he decided to transport as much of its population as possible to Central Java as slaves. In 1697 the reformed kingdom was conquered again by the ex-slave Surapati, arch-enemy of the VOC. Amid the chaos, Blambangan retained the Hindu religion, the last major region of Java to do so. In an interesting cultural twist, it was the Dutch who ensured its ultimate Islamization, sponsoring two Muslim princes as rulers of Blambangan in order to reduce Balinese influence there; nevertheless, they had to fight a war in 1771-72 to have their way.

Today, almost the only remnant of Blambangan is the Balinized dialect spoken by the 400,000 *Osing* people who live around **Banyuwangi** on the Bali Strait. Until 1881, Banyuwangi was the base from which the Dutch handled all relations with Bali and Lombok, then still

Above: Harvesting bananas in East Java.
Right: Proud owner and his fighting rooster.
Right: Traditional Maduran dance.

independent. In 1920, it was still a substantial port, exporting bananas and copra to Australia. Coconut trees still line the coast, and the incongruous place name of **Glenmore**, which is located on the road from Banyuwangi to Jember, is a reminder of the international plantation investors who were once drawn to these lowlands. The ferry to Bali now leaves from **Ketapang**, eight kilometers north of Banyuwangi, but the older port remains a common stoping place for travelers.

Behind Banyuwangi, the land suddenly sweeps upwards towards the **Ijen Plateau**, the dead crater of Java's eastern-most volcanic massif. Like Tengger, Ijen now contains a number of sub-craters, of which **Kawah Ijen**, by virtue of its periodic activity and spectacular appearance, is the best known. The sheer walls of this crater enclose an eerie lake of opaque, blue-green water from which a bitter river flows. Several thousand people live on the Ijen Plateau. Some hunt the peaks for volcanic sulfur, which

they collect with hand tools like the medieval miners of Europe; oil refineries and fertilizer plants buy the acid. Others plant and pick coffee, exactly as it was done a century ago in the mountains of West Java.

In some ways, the eastern tip of Java is remarkably like the western tip. Sparsely populated and wild, both have served as refuges for threatened wildlife as the advancing ploughs and chainsaws have driven the wilderness back to the extremities of the island. The environments are, however, very different. **Baluran National Park**, on the northeast tip of the *Oosthoek*, gets no more rain each year than parts of England, and it is much less evenly distributed. In the dry season, which lasts from April to October, much of it is like an African savannah, with crackling dry grass and herds of *banteng* and deer gathering warily around the waterholes. The Baluran reserve also encompasses other environments including, vast mangrove swamps and upland forests.

Banyuwangi Selatan Reserve is a newer park on Blambangan peninsula and it is the cartographic mirror-image of West Java's Ujung Kulon National Park. Its protected fauna includes the *ajak*, a wild dog that was once universal in Java, but has been ruthlessly hunted by farmers.

Plengkung, located at the point of Grajangan Bay on the west side of the peninsula, is said to offer the best surfing waves in Indonesia.

Meru Betiri National Park, on a remote section of the south coast which can be unreachable in the wet season, was set up in 1972 to protect the last few tigers on Java. This is one of the most unspoiled places on the island. Only the coffee and rubber plantation at **Sukomade**, itself a remnant of pre-war Java, intrudes upon a wilderness where turtles breed on the beaches and hornbills in the trees. Yet, despite help from World Wildlife Fund, the reserve has failed in its primary goal: the Javanese tiger is gone forever.

141

SURABAYA
(Area Code 031)
Accommodation
LUXURY: **Elmi**, Jl. Panglima Sudirman 42-44, tel: 5322571. **Garden**, Jl. Pemuda 21, tel: 5320951. **Garden Palace**, Jl. Jos Sudarso 11, tel: 5320951. **Hyatt Regency Surabaya**, Jl. Basuki Rachmat 124-128, tel: 5311234. **Majapahit Mandarin Oriental**, Jl. Tunjangan 65, tel: 54543351.

MODERATE: Near Gubeng Station: **Bina Dirga Angkasa**, Jl. Embong Kenongo 52, tel: 5342687. **Remaja**, Jl. Embong Kenongo 12, tel: 5341359. **Royal**, Jl. Panglima Sudirman 68, tel: 5343547-8. **Tanjung Indah**, Jl. Embong Cerme 1, tel: 5353030. **Lasmana**, Jl. Bintoro 16 (not far from zoo), tel: 5377152.

BUDGET: Near Gubeng Station: **Bamboe Denn**, Jl. Ketapang Kali 6A, tel: 5340333. **Gubeng**, Jl. Sumatra 18, tel: 5341603. **Santosa**, Jl. Embong Kenongo 40, tel: 5343306. Elsewhere: **Olympic**, Jl. Urip Sumarharjo 65, tel: 5343216. **Stasiun**, Jl. Stasiun Kota 1; **Paviljoen**, Jl. Genteng Besar 98, tel: 5343449.

Shopping
Jl. Tunjungan/Jl. Basuki Rachmat is the main shopping street.

ANTIQUES & HANDICRAFTS: concentrated on Jl. Tunjungan (incl. 3rd floor of **Pasar Tunjungan Surya**), around Hyatt Hotel. Also on Jl. Raya Darmo: **Bangun**, no. 5; **Rokhim**, no. 27; **Whisnu**, no. 68-74.

Museums / Zoos
Museum Angkatan 45 (military), Jl. May Jen Sungkono. **Loka Jala Srana Naval Museum**, AAL Morokrembangan Complex. Mon-Wed 8 am-1 pm, Fri 8-10, Sat 8-12, closed Sun. **Museum Mpu Tantular** (East Java Provincial Museum), Jl. Taman Mayangkara 6. Tue-Thu 8 am-2:30 pm, Fri 8-11, Sat 8-12:30, Sun 8 am-1:30 pm, closed Mon. **East Java Art Museum**, Jl. Pemuda 3, tel: 45608. Mon-Thu 9-12, Fri 9-10, Sat 9-1, closed Sun. **Surabaya Zoo**, Jl. Setail 1, Surabaya. Daily 7 am-6 pm.

Cultural Events
Taman Hiburan Rakyat (THR) (People's Amusement Park), Jl. Kusuma Bangsa. Various dramas, nightly 8 pm. **Taman Budaya**, Jl. Genteng Kali 85. For more highbrow culture & music, nightly 8 pm; morning rehearsals often open to public. **Candra Wilwatikta Open Air Theatre**, Pandaan. Stages *sendratari* dance on 1st & 3rd Sat of each month, Jun-Nov.

Tourist Information / Post
East Java Province Tourist Office, Jl. Pemuda 118, tel: 5472503. Mon-Sat 8 am-7 pm. **Post office**, Jl. Kebon Rojo (near Tugu Pahlawan), Mon-Fri 8 am-4 pm, Sat 8-12:30, closed Sun. Branch office Jl. Gub. Suryo.

Arrival / Transportation
AIR: Important domestic air transport hub, flights to most Indonesian cities. **Juanda Airport** is 15 km S of town; taxis are sole link. Airline offices: **Garuda**, Hyatt Regency Hotel, Skyline Bldg, tel: 5457347; Branch office: Jl. tunjungan 29, tel: 5457347. **Merpati**, Jl. Raya Darmo 111, tel: 5688111; **Mandala**, Jl. Raya Diponegoro 73, tel: 5687157; **Bouraq**, Jl. P Sudirman 70-72, tel: 5452918.

SEA: Many departures daily from **Tanjung Perak** & adjacent **Kalimas** harbor. **Pelni** office: Jl. Pahlawan 20, tel: 3551092, open Mon-Fri 8 am-12 pm and 1-4 pm, Sat 8 am-1 pm. Ferry for Madura leaves from Ujung Baru in Tanjung Perak, or catch bus direct from Purabaya (Bungurasih) bus terminal..

RAIL: 3 stations. **Pasar Turi** handles services to Jakarta via Semarang. **Kota** (aka **Semut**) & **Gubeng** are terminals for inland route W (via Solo, Yogya & Bandung) and for Malang & Banyuwangi. All trains from Kota go via Gubeng. Surabaya is unavoidable transfer point for rail passengers for Bali; Fares to Bali include ferry & road transfer Banyuwangi-Denpasar.

BUS: 2 main stations. **Jembatan Merah** for N coast towns from Gresik to Semarang. **Purabaya** (aka **Bungurasih**), S edge of city, for rest of E Java (incl. Madura) & Solo as well as long-distance (Jakarta, Bali, etc.) bus trips. Some bus lines have offices on lanes off Jl. Basuki Rachmat and at Purabaya station.

LOCAL: Taxi Super, Jl. Ngemplak 20, tel: 5342096; **Taxi Zebra,** Jl. basuki Rahmat 129, tel: 5618888, with meters. Very dense and regular *bemo* network. Main terminals: **Jembatan Merah** (beside intercity buses) & **Wonokromo**, near zoo. Larger *bis kota* also do some routes in town.

MADURA
SUMENEP: (Area Code 0328) *BUDGET:* **Damai**, Jl. Jen Sudirman 35, tel: 62687. **Wijaya I**, Jl. Trunojoyo 45-47, tel: 62433, is pricier. **Wijaya II**, Jl. K. H. Wahid Hasyim 2, tel: 62531.

FOOD STALLS: on *alun-alun* in the evening.

RESTAURANTS: **17 Augustus**, Jl. DJl. Jen. Sudirman 34, tel: 62255. **Mawar** (Chinese), Jl. Diponegoro 105, tel: 62215. **Kartini**, Jl. Diponegoro 83, tel: 62431. **Mawar**, Jl. Diponegoro 47A.

SHOPPING: **Mustika Kempang**, Jl. Trunojoyo 78, for *batik*. **A Ba'bud**, Jl. A Yani, for crafts & antiques.

MUSEUMS: **Museum Daerah Bangkalan**, Jl. Letnan Abdullah 1, Bangkalan. Mon-Thu 8-12, Fri 8-10, Sat 8-11, closed Sun. **Museum Pemerintah Daerah Tingkat II Sumenep**, Jl. Dr. Sutomo, Sumenep. Daily 7 am-4 pm.

MALANG (Area Code 0341)
Accommodation
LUXURY: **Tugu Park Hotel**, Jl. Tugu 3, tel: 363891. **Kartika Prince Hotel**, Jl. Jaksa Agung Suprapto 17, tel: 361900. **Regent's Park Hotel**, Jl. Jaksa Agung Suprapto 12-16, tel: 363388.

MODERATE: **Pelangi**, Jl. Merdeka Selatan 3, tel: 365156. **Splendid Inn**, Jl. Majapahit 4, tel: 366860.
BUDGET: **Bamboo Denn**, Jl. Arjuno 2, tel: 366256. **Helios**, Jl. Pattimura 37, tel: 362741. **Losmen Simpang Tiga**, Jl. Arif Margono 56.

Shopping

BATIK: **Wisma Batik** (Danar Hadi), Jl. Basuki Rachmat. *ANTIQUES & CURIOS:* Several stores on Jl. Basuki Rachmat; also try **Pasar Besar** market, Jl. Pasar Besar. *OTHER:* **Pasar Burung** (Bird Market), Jl. Tjembaran.

Tourist Information

Tourist office, Jl. Tugu (next to town hall). Mon-Thu 9 am-2 pm, Fri 9-11, closed Sat & Sun.

Post / Telecommunications

Post office, Jl. Agus Salim, S side of town square. **Telecommunications office**: Jl. Basuki Rachmat.

Medical

Doctors: Large practice at Jl. Kawi 13; **Hospital** on Jl. Suprapto.

Arrival / Transportation

AIR: Only **Merpati** flies to Malang. Merpati office, Jl. Jaksa Agung Suprapto 50, tel: 327962; taxi service to airport. Flights only to Jakarta & Denpasar/Bali.
RAIL: Trains to Surabaya are once a day direct to Solo, Yogya & Jakarta via Blitar & Kediri.
BUS: Arjosari, large terminal on N edge of city for long-distance busses and minibusses to the N of East Java. **Dinoyo**, in the NW of city, for minibusses to Kediri via Batu. **Gadang**, S of city, for busses/minibusses to S destinations in East Java.
LOCAL: Pattimura Station, Jl. Pattimura.

MAJAPAHIT

TROWULAN: No *losmen* in Trowulan; visitors wanting to be closer than Surabaya stay in **Jombang: Losmen Melati**, Jl. Pang Sudirman 63. **MOJOKERTO:** (Area Code 0321) Cheap accommodation at **Losmen Merdeka**, Jl. Pramuji 73. **Penginapan Mutiara**, Jl. Setia Mulio, & **Losmen Nagamas**, Jl. Pahlawan 23. **Sriwijaya**, Jl. Desa Pacot, is more expensive.
MUSEUMS: **Museum Purbakala Mojokerto**, Jl. Ahmad Yani 14. Tue-Sat 7 am-1 pm, closed Mon. **Museum Purbakala Trowulan**, Jl. Mojokerto 349, Mojokerto, tel: 544. Tue-Sun 7 am-4 pm, closed Mon. **Museum Purbakala Tirtoyoso**, Jl. Jen A Yani, Kediri. Mon-Wed 8 am-1 pm, Fri 8-11, closed Thu/Sat/Sun. **Museum Balai Penyelamatan Arkeologi**, Jl. Syodanco Soeprijadi 40, Blitar, tel: 81365. Sun-Thu 7 am-1 pm, Fri 7- 11, Sat 7-12.

MT. BROMO

Via **Ngadisari**: Leave North coast road at **Probolinggo**, catching minibus to **Sukapura** or if possible **Ngadisari**; both have simple accommodation. From Ngadisari, 3 km walk to **Cemoro Lawang** on caldera lip, 2 more hrs on foot or 1 hr by hired pony to Bromo summit. Only accommodation above Ngadisari is moderately-priced **Bromo Permai Hotel** at Cemoro Lawang – book in Probolinggo, Jl. Raya Panglima Sudirman 237-42, tel: 0335/427451. Via **Tosari**: Bus inland from **Pasuruan**, then overnight in **Tosari**. From Tosari, 2 hrs to rim and another 2 to Bromo. Guide advisable.

MT. SEMERU

Usual approach is from Malang by minibus via **Tumpang** & **Gubugklakah** to **Ngadas**, then on foot via **Rano Pani** (where guides are available) & **Rano Kumbolo**. Very strenuous, requires full camping equipment, food & water.

BANYUWANGI (Area Code 0333)

MODERATE: **Kumala Hotel**, Jl. A. Yani 21B, tel: 23287.
BUDGET: **Baru**, Jl. M.T. Haryono, tel: 21369. **Bhakti**, Jl. Jen Sudirman 115, tel: 21129. **Wisma Blambangan**, Jl. Dr Wahidin 4, tel: 21598.
KETAPANG: Manyar, Jl. Situbondo 110, tel: 24741.

Museums

Museum Daerah Blambangan Banyuwangi, Jl. Sri Tanjung 1, Banyuwangi. Tue-Sun 8 am-2 pm, closed Mon.

Tourist Information

Jl. Diponegoro 2, tel: 24761.

Arrival / Transportation

SEA: Ferries leave for Bali from 2 terminals at Ketapang, 8 km N of town, every half-hour.
RAIL: Train station is the easternmost terminus of Java's rail system: trains run to and from Yogya & Surabaya.
BUS: 3 bus stations. For Blambangan & the S, **Terminal Brawijaya** in the S. For Ijen Plateau, **Terminal Banjarsari** in the W. For Surabaya & the N, **Terminal Blambangan** on Ketapang Rd.

NATURE RESERVES / PARKS

Conservation Office (PHPA) at Jl. A Yani 108 in Banyuwangi, tel: 41119, issues entry permits; permits for Baluran also available in **Wonorejo**, at park entrance (HQ). **BALURAN:** park entrance and headquarters are at Wonorejo; but there's a simple guesthouse at **Bekol**, 12 km inside park, and one at Bama, 2.5 km farther, on the beach. **BLAMBANGAN** *(Banyuwangi Selatan)*: No roads South of Grajangan, 52 km from Banyuwangi by road. Surfing camp & park interior must be reached on foot or by boat from Grajangan or direct from Bali. **MERU BETIRI:** Access along dirt roads from **Genteng** (via Pasanggaran) or from **Glenmore**. Accommodation at Wisma Sukomade in the Sukomade estate, or at the PHPA Resthouse at Rajegwesi.

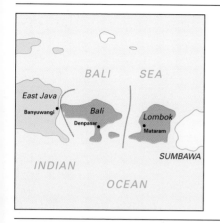

BALI / LOMBOK

DENPASAR
SANUR AND KUTA
THE BALINESE HEARTLAND
UBUD
MOUNTAINS
NORTH COAST
KARANGASEM
LOMBOK

DENPASAR

Denpasar is Bali's "big city," the valve through which the power and culture of Jakarta enters this most self-contained and self-assured of dominions. It is in Denpasar that one also finds Jakarta's lurid cinemas; its deafening, sugary made-in-Indonesia-style pop music; its ubiquitous government billboards; teeming *bemo* stations. Despite all this, glimpses of an older, Balinese Denpasar still gleam through. And, even in Bali, the fine arts and high culture need the patronage of the state, so like other provincial capitals, Denpasar is not without its contemporary highbrow offerings.

Badung is the local name for Denpasar. Before its colonial conquest, Badung was one of the richest and most powerful of the Balinese kingdoms. Its fertile territories stretched northwards as far as Lake Bratan in the central mountains. The very old, but restored temple of **Pura Maospahit** is one of the few surviving remnants of the town's pre-Dutch history. The name refers to the Javanese dynasty of Majapahit, from which all Balinese royalty claim descent. Although the first Dutchmen set foot on Bali as early as

Left: For the pleasure of the gods: Balinese women carrying temple offerings.

1597, the island offered few international trade products and hence never fell within the deadly sights of the VOC. In the 19th century, diplomatic relations were established and north and east Bali were forced to become Dutch vassals while most of the southern kingdoms remained independent. By the beginning of the 20th century, however, the colonial government stepped up its imperialist claims and Badung was the first to learn how radically the military balance had changed. A plundered wreck provided a pretext for war and, in 1906, the **Puputan** (main) **Square** in Denpasar became the site of one of the most tragic and poignant events in Indonesian history. Realizing that they had no chance of victory, the Balinese elected to make an honorable end to the earthly dynasty and to rebuild it together in heaven. Armed only with spears and *kris*, they marched towards the Dutch lines. The king, his family and hundreds of his subjects were mown down by repeater rifles.

After this sad beginning, the Dutch governed Bali with restraint. Roads were built and slavery and widow-burning banned; but settlers and businessmen, and for a long time missionaries, were deliberately excluded from the island as threats to its cultural identity – and its political stability. Denpasar was rehabilitated as an administrative center. The **Puri Pemecutan Palace**, destroyed in 1906, was rebuilt in authentic style in 1907; it is now used as a hotel. The **Bali Museum**, on the square, was set up by a museum society in 1931 to showcase the archaeological and artistic wealth of an island then only just emerging from centuries of isolation and oblivion. Today it exhibits contemporary tools and handicrafts as well as dance costumes and ancient artefacts and sculptures. The architecture of the museum buildings includes imitations of temple and palace styles from all regions of the island.

In 1945, Denpasar succeeded Singaraja as the capital of the whole island. Though most of the Balinese rajas accepted the authority of the revolutionary republic, Bali was quickly back in Dutch hands. In 1946 Denpasar hosted the conference at which a federal "State of East Indonesia" was called into being.

After Bali was reunited with the Republic, President Sukarno had a **bronze monument**, in memory of the martyrs who died fighting the dutch, erected in the center of the square. In the northwest corner of the square, at the large intersection of Jl. Gajah Mada and Jl. Udayana, sits the four-faced, five-meter tall **Batara Guru**. From his elevated podium, he looks in all four directions at once and is worshiped as Shiva, the great teacher.

The state has also sponsored the development of indigenous Balinese arts, a lucrative national resource as well as a unique cultural phenomenon. **Kokar**, the state academy for instrumental and performing arts, established in 1960, trains musicians and dancers. Rehearsals are open to the public. At the newer **Werdi Budaya Arts Centre** (formerly Abiankapasis) new choreography for ancient temple dances is developed, as well as completely new dance programs. These are fascinating year-round, but especially so during the Bali Arts Festival, in June and July.

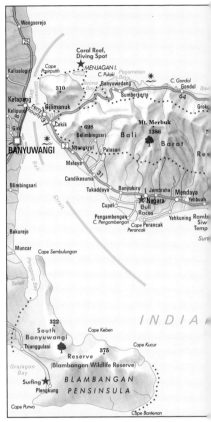

The **Pura Jagatnata** state temple next door to the museum is an interesting modern building. Unusually, this temple is dedicated to Sanghyang Widi, worshipped here as the Balinese supreme being, the highest god. Sang Hyang Widi is undoubtedly a genuine original feature of Bali's complex, multi-faceted religion, appearing on old manuscripts as a strange, small white figure with a three-pronged penis and flames shooting from his joints. However, in prewar Bali he only played a small role in popular ceremony and temple ritual. The holiest shrines, if dedicated to a specific deity at all, were for Shiva of the Hindu trinity, or Surya, the sun god. Popular religion was robustly polytheistic. The change in em-

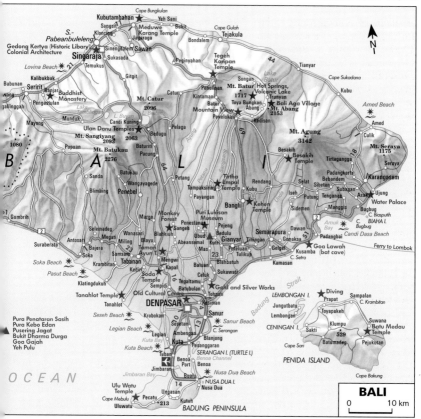

phasis, however, has to do with external pressures placed upon Bali since Indonesian independence. In modern Indonesia, polytheism is neither intellectually nor politically respectable. Hinduism, as a state-sponsored religion, Balinese must toe the *Pancasila* line and worship one, specific highest god.

Tourism in modern Bali began in Denpasar. Before the war, the Bali Hotel, known today as the **Natour Bali Hotel**, used to cater to Dutch vacationers and well-heeled world-travelers. At that time, however, the town still lay outside the reach of the transport arteries of the Indies. Southern Bali had no port suitable for large vessels, so visitors disembarked from their steamers at Singaraja, on the

north coast, and traveled to overland to Denpasar. All this changed with the jet age and the opening of the **Ngurah Rai International Airport**, just 12 kilometers south of the city center. The world came to Denpasar – but soon learned to pass it over. At first, everyone stayed in the town and traveled to the sea or the mountains during the day. Then, as Denpasar grew busier, noisier and less like the paradise people expected of Bali, an exodus to new resorts directly on the beaches began.

SANUR AND KUTA

Modern-day lotus-eaters have settled on almost all of the sandy beaches south of Denpasar, on both sides of the southern tip of Bali. This is where the overwhelming majority of Bali's visitors are "de-planed," accommodated, sunned, massaged, intoxicated, lightly edified by suitably abridged cultural performances, and put back on board when their time or money run out.

Even in paradise money is real, and the neighborhoods are divided by class. Broadly speaking, the east coast is for the well-to-do, the west is for those traveling on tighter budgets. **Sanur Beach**, the closest to Denpasar, is first class; the **Bali Hyatt** and similar hotels are here. In the 1930s, quiet Sanur was the home of some of the European intellectuals who anticipated and inspired the West's love affair with Bali. The beachside house of one of them, the Belgian painter Le Mayeur, has been converted into the **Museum Le Mayeur**, and displays his works. Today it is squeezed in between two big hotels, one of which, the **Grand Bali Beach Hotel**, is the island's only skyscraper. After it was completed in the 1960s, the gruesome prospect of a Balinese Miami Beach growing out of the sand prompted the authorities to enact a far-sighted law prohibiting the construction of any new buildings "taller than a palm tree."

Sanur is a very old port. At **Blanjong**, a short distance inland, an inscribed pillar records the victories of a 10th-century king over unidentified enemies. Discovered in 1932, the inscription is written in Sanskrit and Old Balinese and dated A.D. 914. Contrary to common belief, Indian civilization established itself on Bali long before the 14th-century reign of Majapahit. On nearby **Serangan Island**, on the other hand, **Pura Sakenan** has Bali's closest approximation to a Javanese *candi*.

The **Nusa Dua** luxury beach resort on the **Bukit Peninsula**, hangs like a bulbous pendulum from the southern tip of Bali. Created with the help of the World Bank, in 1970, Nusa Dua is a beautiful sea resort for well-heeled package tourists. The rest of the peninsula is a barren limestone plateau edged by spectacular sheer cliffs falling into the sea. Perched on the westernmost headland is the beautiful **Pura Luhur Ulu Watu**, the "temple high above the rocks," one of the most important in Bali. Nirartha, a Brahmin saint who sought refuge in Bali after the fall of Majapahit in Java, is said to have achieved *moksa* – miraculous union with the godhead – in this temple.

Kuta, the bargain basement beach, has given its name to a whole rag-tag culture of surfboards and *batik* shorts, ramshackle *losmen* and rickety motorbikes, *nasi goreng* and yoghurt, rice wine and marijuana.

Kuta faces west and has some stunning ocean sunsets, as does its slightly more up-market northern extension, **Legian**. Since its discovery by surfers in the early 1970s, Kuta has become the liveliest and most popular tourist destination in Indonesia. Blissfully devoid of historical interest, it lives in an eternal "now" of sea, sweat and music. Everything is for sale in its streets, from the classiest fashion in southeast Asia to the tackiest souvenirs. Even the bodies of Balinese boys are for sale, and find plenty of takers among Australia's young female upper class – a new twist on three centuries of the exploitation of Asian women by European men.

Bali's southern playground is changing quickly and it is not easy to know what will become of it. Though there will always be cheap *losmen* in Kuta, the young, raw, wide-eyed, world-smitten, ragged, outcast travellers' scene of old is rapidly passing away. In its place are hard-headed, young, one-season gypsies getting their tropical rites of passage before going on to work as secretaries or stockbrokers in London or New York.

Right: The magic of Balinese Hinduism still holds its spell.

THE BALINESE HEARTLAND

The heartland of Balinese culture is only a few kilometers from Kuta beach, in the compact foothills at the base of Bali's volcanos. The outside world loves Bali's warm seas, but for the Balinese themselves salt water carries connotations of departure and death; they have never been a seafaring people. Theirs is a terrestrial, agrarian civilization, nurtured and tended along with the emerald rice paddies on the terraced slopes which rise, first gently, then with increasing urgency, dramatically towards the north. A chain of volcanos forms a beautiful, little amphitheater, that acted like a greehouse for the cultivation of a singular, exotic culture. The volcanic soil is fertile and countless streams provide constant water for irrigation. Some 80 percent of Bali's population live in this semicircular bowl where six of the nine states of ancient Bali had their capitals.

A highly developed system of agricultural management, based on the *subak*, a sort of traditional irrigation cooperative, allows the Balinese to devote much of their time to the sacramental art and ceremony which seem to dominate their lives and society. They have ceremonies for everything: to mark events in life- and agricultural-cycles; to propitiate gods and spirits good, bad and indifferent; to expel evil from a person, a village or the whole island; to commemorate the foundation of a house, a palace or a temple. There are celebrations for which the celebrants themselves disagree on the reason. In the past, there was yet another stratum of ceremonies, now largely vanished, for maintaining the theatrical pomp of the royal courts. The development of Bali's massive artistic wealth was tied up with its need for ritual music, dance, decoration and architecture, all of them reaching their highest development in the southern piedmont area.

The most striking and tangible manifestations of Balinese culture are the temples. They are the means by which the Balinese leave their cultural imprint

upon the landscape as does no other group in Indonesia. Even in the most historic parts of Java, graceful buildings are few and far between, but the hills of south central Bali are encrusted with 15,000 temples. Each village needs at least three for different ritual purposes, and there are many more corresponding to other social communities both smaller and larger than the village, including some which are of significance to everyone on the island. Nothing contributes more to Bali's unearthly beauty than this forest of tiered *meru* towers, carved gateways, roofed shrines and guardian statues. Like Penataran in East Java, the temples of Bali are not stone masses but spacious walled compounds enclosing various wooden and brick structures. The *candi bentar* (split gate), which usually serves as an entrance, has become a symbol of the island and of Indonesia as a whole: a giant reproduction greets people

Above: High above the sea – the temple of Pura Luhur Ulu Watu.

entering Jakarta on the road from Cengkareng airport.

Lovely though they are, not many of the temples are very old. Some deliberately sham antiquity: a new one at **Tegaltamu**, just beyond **Batubulan** on the main road out of Denpasar, features 11th-century reliefs copied by their sculptor from an archaeology textbook. However, a concentration of genuine antiquities can be found in the district of **Pejeng**, between the **Petanu** and **Pakerisan** rivers. This seems to have been the center of Hindu civilisation in Bali before the coming of Majapahit. Until recently, the Balinese regarded this period as a dark and barbarous age; traditionally, the true history of Bali begins with the East Javanese administration and clergy installed by Gajah Mada after the invasion of 1343. The last independent king is remembered as a pig-headed monster.

Nevertheless, **Pura Penataran Sasih**, the central temple of the old Pejeng kingdom, is still venerated. Penataran Sasih is famous for the "Pejeng Moon," which is kept in an elevated pavilion at the rear of the temple. It is an outsized bronze gong measuring more than a meter in diameter and almost two meters in length, of a type first developed by the Dong-son culture of Indochina after 1000 B.C. Possibly 1000 years older than the temple itself, the gong is moulded in one piece and expertly decorated with staring faces and geometric designs. Its name relates to a Balinese account of its origin, which portrays it as a fallen celestial body, unrelated to human history. When the first Dutchman climbed up to examine and measure it in 1906, the locals professed amazement that he came back down alive.

Near Penataran Sasih, the small compound of **Pura Kebo Edan** contains a 3.60 meter-tall statue known as the **Pejeng Giant**. The remarkable protuberances on the dancing giant's penis have often been interpreted as indications of his miraculous powers. However, there is a more realistic explanation: the use of one or more "penis pins," inserted through the organ at right angles and secured with knobs on both sides, was widespread in pre-Hindu Indonesia and until very recently in Borneo. Such pins increased female sexual pleasure and their insertion provided a formidable initiation rite for the male.

The name of **Pusering Jagat** ("Navel of the World"), another temple nearby, recalls the former importance of the Pejeng area to the whole of Bali. This temple houses the so-called **Pejeng Vessel**, an intricately engraved stone container for holy water, which bears a chronogram indicating the date 1329. Water is central to Balinese religious practice; indeed, the whole religion is sometimes called *agama tirtha*, "holy water religion." The water formerly held in the Pejeng Vessel represented *amrita*, the elixir of immortality which the Hindu gods produced by churning the primeval ocean. **Bukit Dharma Durga**, southeast

of Pejeng, near **Kutri**, is the site of another fine historical relic, a statue of the six-armed Hindu goddess Durga standing on a slain demon bull. Unusually fluid and lifelike, this is probably a posthumous image of the 10th-century Balinese queen who was the mother of Airlangga, the first great ruler of East Java.

The best-known of all the Pejeng antiquities is **Goa Gajah** or "Elephant Cave," near Bedulu. An entire rock face has been chiselled into a baroque frieze of fantastic plants and animals; the cave itself forms the gaping mouth of a mad-eyed demon, which was mistaken for the eponymous elephant when the site was rediscovered in 1923. This strange monument was probably a hermitage for 11th-century priests. Few would describe Goa Gajah as beautiful, but it is certainly extraordinary and contains some splendid workmanship. A Balinese, it is said, likes threatening temple decorations; the ugly faces repel any dangerous powers and make him feel safe. The elaborate bathing place below the cave was excavated in 1954. The resemblance to Belahan, in East Java, suggested by the nymph-shaped spouts is not accidental, but a result of early dynastic links. **Yeh Pulu**, one kilometer from Goa Gajah, between the Petanu and Jurang rivers, is an enigmatic, giant rock relief, two meters high and 25 meters long. It has no parallels in Indonesia, but is thought to date from after the Majapahit conquest. The **Museum Purbakala Gedung Arca**, north of Bedulu, offers a good overview of the archaeology of the Pejeng area.

The most striking of Bali's pre-Majapahit monuments, however, stands a few kilometers down, where Pakerisan valley becomes a steep ravine cutting into the rising flank of the Mt. Batur massif. At **Gunung Kawi** in **Tampaksiring**, nine full-scale *candi* façades, each set in a deep niche for protection, have been hewn out of two solid rock walls facing each other across the river. Nearby is an

elaborate cloister, also of solid rock, for the monks who once tended them. Painstaking Dutch scholarship has revealed that the five main monuments probably commemorate King Anak Wungsu (1049-1077) and the wives who burned themselves on the royal pyre to be with him in the next life (the last such suttee took place on Bali in 1903). The carving is more conventional than at Goa Gajah, but the scale of the undertaking far more impressive. River water, diverted through a channel at the base of the monuments, was supposed to bring a god-king's blessing of fertility to the rice paddies downstream. Just beyond Tampaksiring is the famous watering place of **Tirta Empul**, with atmospherically mossy but rather recent bathing pools and temple. The water is holy, without having to be consecrated, and has magical and curative properties. On a hill overlooking the site is an "occasional palace" built in

Above: Entrance to the cave temple Goa Gajah.

1954 by Sukarno, who was always associated closely with his mother's native Bali.

UBUD

The village of **Ubud**, on the west bank of the Petanu, is the usual base for exploring the antiquities and legions of other attractions in south-central Bali. Ubud is the geographic and cultural hub of rural Bali, and the island's artistic capital. Yet it was never a royal capital, and the fact that it is now to Bali what Yogyakarta is to Java has to do with the 20th century infusion of European ideas and styles which has made Balinese art what it is today. At the beginning of the 20th century, the art of Bali was exclusively traditional in the truest sense of the word. It was an aspect of daily life and ritual, a way to beautify the environment and a means of honoring the gods. There was some slow innovation, but no emphasis on individual creativity; artists neither signed their work, nor experimented with new mediums and forms. It is often remarked that the Balinese language has no word for "art" as a category of activity in its own right. For better or for worse, the introduction of "art for art's sake" fell to a tiny band of European paradise-hunters who found their way to Ubud in the halcyon days between the Dutch conquest and the Japanese invasion.

Foremost among this lucky few was the remarkable Walter Spies, a romantic who had been a painter in the Ukraine and a musician in Batavia before ending his wanderings in Bali. In **Campuan**, west of the center of Ubud, Spies built a Europ-Balinese-style house which may be rented, for a price, from the **Tjampuan Hotel**. His major contributions were in the field of painting. Bali escaped the Islamic ban on human and animal representation, but knew little of perspective and possessed limited technical skills. Spies' instruction and his own flamboyant style inspired a generation of young Balinese artists, who combined this new insight with their own imagination and experience to produce lush, teeming tableaux of Balinese life, landscape and mythology.

Ubud's **Museum Puri Lukisan** displays many early works of the *Pita Maha* art society, which Spies founded, together with a Dutch artist, Rudolf Bonnet, and a local aristocrat, Gede Agung Sukawati. Sukawati went on to become a respected Indonesian statesman, whose funeral in 1979 was hailed as "the last great Balinese cremation." The greatest artist in the Pita Maha school was probably I Gusti Nyoman Lempad, whose drawings of cremation towers and *Ramayana* scenes can be seen in the **Neka Gallery**. In **Penestanan**, west of Campuan, a colony of young artists continues the Pita Maha tradition. There are scores of other studios and small galleries in and around Ubud, and despite the stultifying influence of the tourist market,

many continue to produce innovative work. Unfortunately, modern Ubud suffers from success. There are bars and even a supermarket; the local inhabitants, who won recognition in the early 1980s for their pioneer attempts to manage tourism by teaching visitors informed respect for the place and its culture, are being swamped again.

The invigorating European influence of the pre-war period was not limited to visual art. The dramatic, hypnotic *kecak* or "Monkey Dance," which every tourist usually sees, was choreographed in 1931 by Spies and a German film-maker. Nevertheless, the elements were Balinese; only the indigenous genius of Bali made the fusion possible. That this genius lives on in the heart and lives of the people is aptly demonstrated by the villages en route from Denpasar to Ubud, each of which seems to specialize in some particular craft or performance.

Batubulan, the birthplace of the *kecak* and now the site of Denpasar's music and dance academy, is also a center of stone-carving, where numerous teenage craftsmen liberate gods and demons from blocks of locally quarried soapstone. Eminently unsuitable as souvenirs, they have been little affected by tourism. Statues from Batubulan grace and guard temples all over Bali.

Celuk, a little further up the road, produces delicate gold and silver jewelry. As in most parts of Indonesia, metalsmiths in Bali are traditionally a closed and privileged group; even Brahmins must address them in high Balinese. In Celuk, however, almost every family cashes in on the trade. Nevertheless, traditional methods, using manual bellows and a metal spike knocked into a tree trunk for an anvil, have survived. The village of **Sukawati** is an important custodian of the Balinese *wayang kulit* tradition, of all the island's arts perhaps the one least influenced by the west. Bali almost certainly derived its shadow-plays from East

and musician who performs for big foreign crowds, there are those who reserve their skills for themselves, their families, their villages and their gods. Balinese culture is poised between life and art.

Klungkung (Semarapura), in the eastern wing of Bali's "amphitheater," is a good place to glimpse what the royal art of Bali looked like before the western infusion. This area was, for a long time, a center of Balinese civilization. The first Majapahit viceroys ruled from a site near the old capital of Pejeng, but after the fall of Majapahit in Java, Bali was reunited under the *Dewa Agung* or god-king of **Gelgel**, just south of Klungkung, on the seaward side. The state temple of **Pura Dasar** still stands there. The Gelgel dynasty sponsored a renaissance of Hindu culture in Bali just when it was being obliterated in Java, and built the so-called *Sad Kahyangan* or Holy Temples, of which everybody agrees there are six. Exactly which six temples they are continues to be a point of contention. Eventually, the Gelgel empire declined and lost its grip upon its vassals. As in Java, such misfortune called for a change of palace, and around the beginning of the 18th century the dynasty moved 3000 meters to the present capital of Klungkung, where it retained a residual spiritual authority over the other states until the Dutch conquest.

The **Kerta Gosa,** in the center of modern Klungkung, is a hall of justice, retained under the Dutch as the seat of the highest indigenous court on the island. Built in the mid-18th century, it is an open-sided *pendopo* pavilion of the type long favored for official buildings in Java. The inside of the roof is entirely covered by intricate concentric friezes depicting divine punishment and reward, perhaps intended to induce honesty in the witnesses. The paintings, last restored in 1948, are in drawn in the traditional-style and the figures in the flat, almost cartoon-

Java, but has developed its own style with small, robust puppets, less delicate and insect-like than those of Yogya.

Mas is a woodcarving center. In the past, wood carvings were always elaborately finished in brilliant colors, but the Western love of things "natural" got the better of the Balinese passion for decoration, and most are now left unpainted. Themes vary from traditional Vishnu and Sita figures to sleek realistic animals and psychoticly twisted heads.

Batuan and **Peliatan** both have famous dance groups, performing to the crashing, shimmering cascades of the Balinese *gamelan*, so different from the deep, drifting current of its Javanese counterpart. Dancers are the stars of Bali, from the pre-pubescent girls who alone may perform the delicate, vibrant *legong* to the sinewy athletes who execute the warlike *baris*. However, for every dancer

Above: A glimpse of the famous "monkey dance." Right: A wooden ceiling in Klungkung.

like *wayang*-style that was so typical of Balinese art before the advent of Spies. Also in this style, the ceiling of the **Bale Kambang** or "Floating Pavilion" in the nearby Klungkung Palace, depicts the holy Sutasoma converting animals to Buddhism. This style is sometimes also known by the name of a village near Gelgel, **Kamasan**, where it is still painted on cloth, as an art form in its own right. Kamasan also has silversmiths and goldsmiths. Another notable craft center near Klungkung is **Tihingan**, where *gamelan* gongs are forged.

With the disintegration of the Gelgel empire, Bali split into nine states; besides Gelgel's successor Klungkung, these were Badung, Bangli, Buleleng, Gianyar, Jembrana, Karangasem, Mengwi and Tabanan. **Bangli** is 26 kilometers northwest of Klungkung, on the threshold of the mountains proper; a vantage point nearby offers panoramic views of the entire lush cradle of southern Bali. Bangli's state temple, **Pura Kehen**, is one of the most beautiful on the island, and is almost always included among the six holy *Sad Kahyangan*. Kehen is built on three rising terraces, and the central courtyard contains an 11-tier *meru* tower. An inscription from 1204 proves that there has been a temple on this site since before Majapahit. **Gianyar,** also in the east of the natural amphitheater, between Klungkung and Pejeng, was the most vigoros and expansive of the kingdoms in the late 19th century, but its request for Dutch help in 1899 was the beginning of the end for all of the empires. The **Puri Dalem** palace at Gianyar is one of the few still inhabited by a royal family.

The capital of the kingdom of Badung stood – as already noted – on the site of present-day Denpasar. Two more of the nine kingdoms, Mengwi and Tabanan, were also in the core piedmont area, but west of Denpasar and Ubud. **Mengwi**, now a modest village 20 kilometers northwest of Denpasar, was snuffed out by internal war and divided among its neighbours in 1891, before the Dutch arrived. The state temple, **Pura Taman**

155

Ayun, is unusual because of its large size and lily-lined moat. This temple was founded in 1634, although most of the present structure dates from 1937. In the nearby village of **Kapal** is an older temple, **Pura Sada**, with a split gate from the time of Majapahit and a reconstructed *prasada* or *candi*-like sanctuary, which is rare in Bali.

The second royal site in this region, **Tabanan**, lies further west, amid some of the most fertile of Bali's bounteous rice lands. The cultural center here is called **Gedung Mario,** in memory of Bali's greatest 20th-century dancer and chore-ographer, I Nyoman Mario, a native of Tabanan. Other attractions of the western half of the piedmont include the **Tanah-lot Temple**, a cliff-top, sea temple like Ulu Watu, and the **Monkey Forest**, site of the **Bukit Sari Temple**, near Sangeh, which is worth visiting just to see the tame monkeys swarm through a grove of

Above: The Tanahlot temple. Right: A statue in the Monkey Forest.

nutmeg trees. Nutmeg, along with cloves, first brought Europeans to Indonesia, and, for that matter, Columbus to America. It is native only to the Mo-luccas, the Spice Islands proper, which lie some 1500 kilometers east, and the Monkey Forest is the only nutmeg stand on Bali, and who planted it remains a mystery.

THE MOUNTAINS

Mountains are central to Balinese cul-ture. Before the advent of Hinduism, their ancestors already lived there; that the Indian gods should have similar tastes surprised no-one. The direction in which the mountains lie, *kaja*, is naturally favorable, just as the seaward direction, *kelod*, is a source of evil influences. However, while there is no mountain without its own deity, the uplands are not so hospitable to human life and only a tiny fraction of Bali's people live there. When all travel still occurred on foot, the mountains were seen as a distant and sacred realm, visited only when religious festivals demanded it. They still feel a world away from the warm, rich airs of the lowlands. The mountains of the far west are almost completely uninhabited and have been designated as a vast nature reserve, the **West Bali National Park**. Until the last one was killed by a big-game hunter in the 1930s, the Balinese tiger had made this truly wild part of the island his refuge. The old state of Jembrana, near present-day **Negara**, clung to the narrow southern coast of the wilderness as a marginal, out of the way country. Substantially Muslim today, Negara is more an outpost of East Java than an appendage of Bali; in fact, it is best known for its Madurese-style water buffalo races. Balinese say that the west, the domain of the setting sun, is an inauspicious direction. Negara, being both in the west and by the sea, could hardly face worse prospects.

Mt. Batukau is the westernmost of the semicircle of very high mountains which rims the southern amphitheater. Like its antithesis, the sea, a great peak demands to be honored by a temple: hence the remote **Pura Luhur**, set among mossy forests on Batukau's southern flank. Access to this temple is via Tabanan. Further east, one of the island's two main roads skirts the serene mountaintop lake of **Bratan**, which is suspended in the dead crater of a volcano of the same name. The flimsy, thatched pavilions of the lowland Balinese houses would be of little use in this alpine country; instead, there are sturdy cottages of wood and tile. The lakeside temple of **Ulun Danu** is one of the most atmospheric in Bali. A little further up the road is an anomalous piece of worldly luxury, the **Bali Handaya Country Club** with its international class 18-hole golf course.

The most striking landscape feature of mountain Bali is the 12-kilometer wide caldera which contains the center of the volcano and **Lake Batur**. Bali's highest

temple, **Pura Tegeh Koripan** (also known as Pura Sukawana) is located 1745 meters up the windswept northwestern rim near **Penulisan** and grants superb views on a clear day. Inscriptions found here date back to the 11th century and it is thought that this was the mountain sanctuary of the Pejeng kings, the *kaja* counterpart of the temple of Penataran Sasih.

The village of **Batur**, also on the lip of the caldera, was located in the crater itself until 1926, when it was destroyed by a major eruption. The **Ulun Danu** temple was destroyed by the lava flows, but miraculously, its shrine to the lake-goddess in was swept to safety and was the only part of the original temple to survive. Small wonder that the Balinese, at the mercy of their mountains, are one of the most superstitious people on earth. Tempting fate for the sake of tourist dollars, some are still bold enough to make their homes by the foot of "the beast," in **Toya Bungkah**, where hot volcanic springs supply pools at the lakeside, where at night one can soak under a steamy canopy of stars.

On the far side of Lake Batur is the isolated village of **Trunyan**, one of the few inhabited by the people classified as "Bali Aga." They are distinguished from other (Majapahit) Balinese mainly by their willingness to concede that they are of indigenous rather than Javanese descent. To this day they retain a number of unique customs including that of leaving their dead to rot above ground in bamboo cages, a grisly tourist attraction. Not surprisingly, Trunyan, and the Batur area in general, is one part of Bali where visitors are tolerated rather than welcome.

Not content with the candidates in East Java, the Hindu dynasties of Bali sought to bring Mt. Meru, India's cosmic world-mountain, closer to home. **Mt. Agung**, at once the highest (3142 meters) and the most easterly (hence the most auspiciously located) of Bali's major peaks, was the natural choice. As the abode of the departed ancestors of pre-Hindu times, Mt. Agung served as an Olympus of sorts. The foundations of the great temple at **Besakih**, 950 meters up the southwest flank of Mt. Agung, were probably laid as a prehistoric terraced sanctuary for ancestor worship.

By the 11th century, Besakih was used by Hindu kings; in the 15th century, the Dewa Agung of Gelgel, descendant of Majapahit viceroys, made it his ancestral temple. Gelgel's successor, Klungkung, is still responsible for the upkeep of key parts of the monument, but every regency and many other groups maintain their own shrines. Besakih is the mother temple of Bali; the one truly pan-Balinese religious site. Through centuries of division after the decline of Gelgel, Besakih continued to represent the spiritual unity of Bali.

The size and beauty of the Besakih complex, containing around 30 temples

Right: Mt. Agung – the seat of the gods.

in all, reflect its unique status. The style is austere, relatively free from the excessive ornamentation of many other Balinese monuments. Its jagged split gate and black *meru* flowers silhouetted against the misty slopes of Mt. Agung are a haunting and unforgettable sight. The central shrine, in particular, expresses the humility beneath the often cheeky exuberance of Balinese religious art. It consists simply of three empty thrones, one each for Brahma, Vishnu and Shiva. Sculptors may parody lesser deities and demons, but are not allowed to depict the *Trisakti*, the highest gods, themselves.

Once every 100 years, Besakih is the focal point of the *Eka Dasa Rudra* ceremony, designed to stablilize and purify the entire cosmos, just as lesser rites ensure harmony in the family and village. *Eka Dasa Rudra* involves millions of man-hours of labor in the preparation of offerings and the execution of rituals. In March 1963, the great ceremony was actually in progress when Mt. Agung erupted, killing more than 2000 people and devastating the surrounding countryside. Lava streams reached the sea in some places, yet Besakih itself was unscathed. The catastrophe was clearly a bad omen of cosmic proportions and has often been linked to the communal violence which followed two years later, during which up to 100,000 communists are thought to have been killed in Bali. The carnage was seen partly as a purge of the evil influences which had displeased the gods.

THE NORTH COAST

The northern coast of Bali has been set apart from the rest of the island both by geography and history. Before the construction of the present road network in the 1920s and 30s, the east-west mountain spine was a formidable barrier to overland communication and the Balinese were reluctant seafarers. Drier and

less fertile than the south, the north is naturally poorer in food resources, although it has compensated over the centuries by exporting slaves, coffee, cattle and copra. North Bali had a respectable Hindu kingdom of its own, **Buleleng**, but it was defeated by the Dutch almost half a century before the fall of the south. A self-confident and aggressive power in the early 19th century, Buleleng invoked the wrath of the Dutch in 1846 by snubbing their ambassadors and plundering one of their ships. After two attempts, a punitive expedition finally took control of the kingdom in 1869. The Buleleng commander took poison and the Dutch set about building the town of **Singaraja** on the site of the old capital. Buleleng women were ordered to cover their naked breasts "to protect the morals of the Dutch soldiers;" that respectably brassièred Balinese now frown upon topless tourists is a wonderful historical irony.

As the main Dutch beachhead, Singaraja achieved significance as a port and administrative center. In 1882 it was placed under direct Dutch rule and elevated to residency capital for Bali and Lombok; in the first years of independence it controlled all of Nusa Tenggara, from Bali to Timor. Today, even sea traffic has, for the most part, deserted Singaraja for the new port of **Celukanbawang**, and the old capital is a rather pretty, little town with tree-lined streets and *dokar* horsecarts.

Hotel Singaraja once served as the Governor's mansion. The **Gedong Kertya** historical library, founded in 1928, is a repository for the precious *lontar* (palm leaf manuscripts) and the copper plate inscriptions that record Bali's indigenous history, mythology and traditional medicine.

The temples of North Bali show some surprising differences from those of the south. Meru towers, for instance, are much less common, and a soft pink sandstone is used instead of the usual grey stone and tiles. Most striking, however, are the carvings: perhaps due to some spiritually corrosive effect of the long

159

Dutch presence, those that adorn northern temples are often absurdly secular and playful. The temple at **Jagaraga**, where the army of Buleleng was defeated in 1849, sports big-nosed Dutchmen in a prewar-era motorcar and a steamship under attack by a sea monster. **Pura Meduwe Karang**, in **Kubutambahan,** has domestic scenes of lovers and a man on a bicycle. Domestic architecture in North Bali features corrugated iron roofs in place of the rustic thatch of the south, confirming the general impression that in scenery, there is no competition. The north coast does, however, have superb and relatively unspoiled black sand beaches around **Kalibukbuk** and **Yeh Sanih**.

KARANGASEM

Karangasem, located in a tight little coastal depression at the foot of Mt.

Above: Ritual food offerings to appease the gods.

Agung, was the easternmost of Bali's pre-colonial kingdoms. After the calamitous eruption of Mt. Agung in 1963, superstition caused the capital to be renamed **Amlapura**, signifying a break with the unhappy past. Like Buleleng, Karangasem was poor in local resources and hence open to foreign adventures. In the late 18th and early 19th centuries, it played a major role in the extraordinary Balinese enterprise of conquest and colonisation of the neighboring island of Lombok – a miniature Asian colonialism in the shadow of the bigger European one. In 1849, after siding with Buleleng in a losing war against the Dutch, the governor-general awarded Karangasem to its own former vassal Mataram, in Lombok.

Restored to independence in 1894, by the Dutch themselves, Karangasem became the kind of malleable native state of which Batavia could be proud. Its kings devoted themselves to architectural escapism in the style of their Javanese counterparts. Their traditional home is the **Puri Agung Karangasem**, which is a modest red brick compound, while their descendants live in the flamboyant, but dilapidated **Puri Kanginan**; an eclectic amalgam of European, Chinese and Balinese styles.

The last Raja also built two outlying follies: a pleasure palace on the coast (1921) and a neo-traditional bathing complex inland at **Tirta Gangga** (1946). Despite damage sustained from the eruption of 1963 and from political vandalism during the same period, the latter is still a pleasant place to swim under the gaze of bizarre statues from a romantic era.

Overseas expansion distracted Karangasem's attention from its own immediate hinterland. About seven kilometers from the capital, **Tenganan**, a community has survived which, like the far less accessible one in Trunyan, considers itself linked to Bali's pre-Majapahit civilisation. The cultural idiosyncracies are strikingly visible here. The entire village is walled and the houses are arranged symmetrically along two wide, stone lanes. Tenganan is the only place in Indonesia, and one of only three places in the world, where the fabulously difficult technique of "double *ikat*" weaving is still practiced. This technique involves dyeing both warp and weft threads before they are combined on the loom; tiny errors could ruin the pattern, yet the *kamben geringsing* produced often features intricate designs. The art of preparing and writing *lontar* (palm leaf manuscripts), in Bali's own Indic script, has also survived here.

Karangasem now has its own slice of the tourist action: **Candi Dasa**, on the main road from Karangasem to Klungkung, which has only recently come of age as a beach resort. Less expensive than Sanur and less frantic than Kuta, Candi Dasa is allegedly where the cognoscenti, and certainly the yuppies, stay.

The innocuous little ferry-port of **Padangbai**, on an unblemished tear-shaped bay, west of Candi Dasa, connects Bali to the neighbor which it once dominated, **Lombok**. South of the ferry's course, the arid island of **Nusa Penida**, once a penitentiary for exiles from Klungkung, is a premonition of the change of environment awaiting passengers in Lombok.

LOMBOK

Long regarded – not least by the Balinese themselves – as an ugly stepsister to her glamorous neighbour, Lombok is currently emerging from obscurity and becoming an eastern extension of the Bali tourist playground. In a sense, this is true to the history of the island, which for the last three centuries has been dominated by Bali. Lombok, however, is also the western threshold of the harsh and variegated natural and cultural world of Nusa Tenggara, utterly different from rich, homogeneous, introspective Bali.

The Lombok Strait is no trifling shelf like that which divides Bali from Java, but a huge cleft scoured by powerful currents, the route of nuclear submarines passing undetected between the Indian and Pacific Oceans. A formidable barrier for animal migration, it marks the zoogeographical Wallace Line which conventionally divides the Asian fauna of the western archipelago from the Australasian sphere of the east. The parrots and parakeets of Lombok, absent from Bali, portend the transition. Lombok also serves as a transition between the seasonal, but reliable climates of East Java and Bali, and the dangerous semi-aridity of the rest of the lesser Sundas. Lombok blooms like Bali only at high altitude and in areas of intensive irrigation; its population density is only half that of its neighbor, and some parts suffered a famine in 1966.

Mt. Rinjani, a volcano, dominates the entire Lombok landscape. The Balinese say that Mt. Agung and Mt. Rinjani are husband and wife, but the latter is larger, more central and at the same time more isolated. At 3726 meters, Mt. Rinjani is the second highest mountain in Indonesia, outside the snowcaps of Irian Jaya. A road to the crater has been planned, but for now the climb takes two days, there and back. It is suitable only for the fit and well-equipped, and should not be attempted in the wet season, when the paths turn into waterfalls. Only serious mountaineers aim for the peak itself; most climbers are content with the emerald, pine-ringed crater lake, **Segura Anak,** which fills the caldera.

Mt. Rinjani and its lake are sacred to the indigenous people of Lombok, the *Sasak.* They speak a language closely related to that of Bali, and like the Balinese they are farmers rather than seafarers, but for all intents and purposes, the similarities end there. Never deeply affected by the Indian and Javanese influences which transformed Bali, the Sasak have retained the thatched pile-houses, *ladang* agriculture and a good deal of the animist religion of virgin Indonesia. Back-strap hand-looms are in common use: **Sukarare** is the main rural weaving center, but almost every village has at least one family of weavers. Sasak basketware is also widely prized. The Sasak, who have remained truest to their *adat* (tradition), are those who class themselves as *Waktu Telu,* a term of obscure origin indicating incomplete compliance with the duties of Islam. Though self-professed and circumcised Muslims, the *Waktu Telu* do not find it necessary to pray the prescribed five times per day, or to observe the fasting month. Some even openly venerate ancestor shrines as well as the spirit of Lake Segura Anak. The homeland of the *Waktu Telu* lies on the isolated northern side of Mt. Rinjani, around **Bayan** and **Senaru**.

The majority of Sasak, however, are more orthodox Muslims inhabiting the mosque-studded lowland corridor which cuts across the island south of Rinjani.

These are the *Waktu Lima* Sasak, and they are even more antithetical to the Balinese in spirit. The number of *Waktu Lima* seems to be growing at the expense of the *Waktu Telu,* as state pressure and smoldering resentment against Lombok's resident Hindu-Balinese combine to make Islamic orthodoxy more attractive.

As in other parts of the archipelago, it is not clear exactly how Islam first came to Lombok. Local tradition suggests a connection to the legendary Muslim evangelist Sunan Giri, whose tomb is near Surabaya in East Java. Equally likely is the theory that the Macassarese of South Celebes, who dominated the Lesser Sundas in the 17th century, played a major role. In either case, Islam was well enough anchored to survive two centuries of Hindu Balinese rule. At the end of the 17th century, the Balinese state of Karangasem founded colonies in Lombok which subdued the Sasak and made their *datu,* or lords, into vassals. The most intensively colonized area was in the west of the island, around the foremost Balinese colonial state, **Mataram**, namesake of two historic Javanese dynasties. With the application of Balinese irrigation techniques, Mataram became a major rice producer and exporter; it is still the greenest part of Lombok and home to the majority of the Lombok Balinese, who make up about 20 percent of the island's population.

The town of Mataram is now the seat of the provincial government of Nusa Tenggara Barat (Lombok and Sumbawa) and home to an absurd number of civil servants and soldiers. The bureaucratic nature of Indonesian society is most evident in such places; fairly populous, but lacking major commerce and industry. Every second building seems to sport a government signboard, and every second person is a government employee.

Mataram's old port was **Ampenan**, once a major center of commerce, but now a broken-down jetty bypassed even

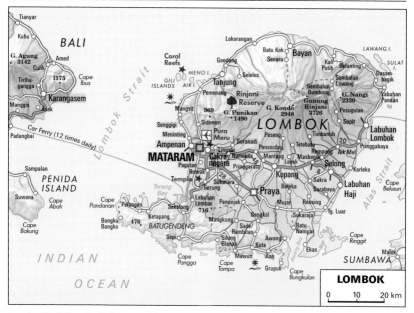

by the Bali-Lombok ferry, which docks further south at **Lembar**. **Cakranegara**, where the Mataram princes built their courts, has become a commercial extension of Mataram, with a large Chinese community. **Pura Meru**, in Cakaranegara, is Lombok's largest Balinese temple. Presumed to date from the early 18th century, it contains more than 30 shrines and was intended to symbolize the unity of the Balinese plantations in Lombok under Mataram's leadership – a function reminiscent of Besakih in Bali itself. The **Puri Mayura** royal garden is a last remnant of the *kraton* of Cakranegara. Its centerpiece is a *bale kambang* (floating pavilion) on an island in an ornamental lake. Nearby is a more recent palace building housing a collection of photographs and memorabilia from Dutch times. The rest of the old palace, including the high defensive walls which surrounded it, were razed in the Lombok War of 1894.

From 1849 until its fall, Mataram was a substantial power, ruling the whole of Lombok and eastern Bali (Karangasem) as well. But the Mataram Balinese were better soldiers and engineers than administrators, and their clumsy oppression provoked a series of Sasak uprisings. In 1894, a Sasak appeal for help gave the Dutch an excuse to clip Mataram's wings. Troops landed at Ampenan, and the old king was forced to accept an ultimatum, whereupon the Dutch marched to Cakranegara. However, the crown prince ambushed them as they camped within the *kraton* walls. Using modern rifles that were obtained from European traders, the Balinese wounded 272 and killed 113, including the second in command, P. P. H. van Ham, who is buried at **Karang Jankong**, between Cakranegara and Ampenan, where he died while trying to lead survivors back to the coast. The Indies press cried treachery and the otherwise sluggish Dutch national sentiment boiled over. Within three and months, and after a heavy artillery barrage, reinforcements had retaken Cakranegara. The Mataram dynasty was obliterated and the Dutch

163

In the irrigated country around the capital, the immigrant Balinese nobility recreated their native world of temples and bathing places. On **Mt. Pengsong**, five kilometers south of the town, a series of white shrines stands on a rocky outcrop. In the small town of **Narmada**, some ten kilometers east of Cakranegara, a modest hill has been transformed into a complex of tiered gardens, pools and pavilions. The design is said to be a symbolic replica of Mt. Rinjani and its crater lake; ceremonies held on the mountain itself are also held here simultaneously. **Suranadi**, above Narmada, is a place of pilgrimage on account of its holy springs that match those at Tampaksiring in Bali. The **Lingsar** temple complex combines Hindu and *Waktu Telu* shrines, and features a pond containing, of all things, holy albino eels which emerge from dark conduits when fed pieces of hard-boiled egg.

took direct colonial control of the entire island.

With the conquering army came a Dutch scholar, Dr. J. L. A. Brandes, who was anxious to save from destruction any literary treasures he might find in this most distant and vigorous offshoot of old Hindu Indonesia. In the village temple in **Pagutan,** he found the one and only manuscript of the 14th-century panegyric *Negarakrtagama*, the major source of information about Majapahit and arguably the most important single document of Indonesian history. It is impossible to know what other priceless material vanished; when Brandes arrived, many *lontar* manuscripts had already been burned to boil tea on Dutch campfires. For decades the *Negarakertagama* was kept in the Netherlands, but on the occasion of the Dutch royal visit in 1970, it was presented to the National Museum in Jakarta.

The art and ceremonial culture of Balinese Lombok duplicate those of the mother island. The Sasak arts, for their part, combine styles from many different sources, including the Hindu overlord. *Cupak Gerantang* is a dance popular all over the island; it recounts the story of the East Javanese cultural hero, Panji. In the east of the island, dancers wear masks like Balinese *topeng*. *Rudat* and *Oncer*, vigorous male dances, seem to be more indigenous in their inspiration. And the ubiquitous *gamelan* music is played everywhere.

The beaches of Lombok share the excellence of its mountains. **Senggigi Beach**, with a new and expensive luxury hotel, is beach being pushed by the local government, but there are miles of empty sand in the **Meninting** area north of Ampenan and at **Kuta** in the south. The offshore islands of **Gili Air**, **Gili Meno** and **Gili Terawangan**, in the northwest, are famous for their coral reefs. **Labuhan Lombok**, on the east coast, is the way to Sumbawa.

Above: Stick fighting – a popular sport and tourist attraction on Lombok.

DENPASAR (Area Code 0361)

LUXURY: **Natour Bali**, Jl. Veteran 2, tel: 225681-5.
MODERATE: **Denpasar**, Jl. Diponegoro 103, tel: 226336. **Elim**, Puri Oka, Jl. Kaliasem 3, tel: 222165. **Pemecutan Palace**, Jl. Thamrin 2, tel: 223491.
BUDGET: **Adi Yasa**, Jl. Nakula 23, tel: 222679. **Wisma Taruna Inn**, Jl. Gadung 31, tel: 226913.

Restaurants

FOOD STALLS: night markets at **Kereneng Terminal** & **Kumbasari Shopping Centre**.
INDONESIAN: **Restaurant Betty**, Jl. Sumatra 56. **Gajah Mada Restaurant**, Jl. Gajah Mada. **Rumah Makan Wardani**, Tapakgangsul. *CHINESE:* **Puri Selera**, Jl. Gajah Mada 16. **Atoom Baru**, Jl. Gajah Mada 106.

Shopping

Sanggraha Kriya Astra (State Handicrafts Center), Tophati, on road to Batubulan. Many smaller craft shops along Jl. Gajah Mada. Weaving factory at **Pertenunan Carma**, Jl. Letda Suci 2, south of Bali Museum.

Museums

Bali State Museum, Jl. Letnan Kolonel Wisnu, Tue-Thu & Sun 7 am-2 pm, Fri 7-11, Sat 7-12:30, closed Mon and holidays. **Art Museum**, Jl. Bayusuta. Daily 8 am-4:30 pm.

Cultural Events

Abiankapas arts center has *kecak* nightly from 6 to 7 pm. **Kokar** academy rehearsals may be open to public; timetables vary. In **Batubulan**, *barong* dance every morning from 9 to 10 am. **Ayoda Pura**, Tanjung Bungkak, on Sanur road, has *kecak* dances nightly from 6 to 7 pm. **Hotel Puri Pemecutan** stages regular *wayang kulit.*

Tourist Information / Post

Badung Tourist Office, Jl. Surapati 7, tel: 223602. Mon-Thu 7 am-2 pm, Fri 7-11, Sat 7-12. **Dinas Pariwisata**, near GPO in administration complex south of town, is the State Tourist Authority for whole island. **Denpasar Post Office**, administration complex; Kuta & Sanur branches generally more convenient. **DHL Courier Service** is at Jl. Tanjung Bungkak 92.

Arrival / Transportation

AIR: Ngurah Rai International Airport, 12 km S of town; counter for fixed-price, pre-paid taxis. *Bemos* to airport leave from **Stasiun Tegal**. Most people bound for Kuta or Sanur go straight there from airport. Airline Offices: **Garuda**, Jl. Melati 61, tel: 227825; **Merpati**, Jl. Melati 51, tel: 235556; **Bouraq**, Jl. Sudirman 7A, tel: 237420.
SEA: Harbor & **Pelni** agent at **Benoa**, 10 km S.
RAIL: No railways on Bali, but rail office at Jl. Diponegoro 172 sells tickets for Java plus Denpasar-Banyuwangi road/ferry connection.
BUS: Batabulan for buses to the N & E (Ubud, Bangli, Padang Bai, Singaraja). **Kereneng**: local destinations

(Sanur, Batubulan). **Ubung**: N & W (Tabanan, Mengwi, Gilimanuk, Java). **Suci**: to Benoa. **Kartini**: to Sangeh. **Tegal**: Kuta, Uluwatu, airport.
LOCAL: *Bemos* operate between the 6 bus stations.

SANUR (Area Code 0361)

LUXURY: **Alit's Beach Bungalows**, tel: 288567. **Bali Hyatt**, tel: 281234. **Baruna Beach Inn**, Jl. Sindhu, tel: 288546. **Bali Sanur Bungalows**, Jl. Tanjungsari, tel: 288423. **Sanur Beach**, tel: 288011. **Segara Village**, tel: 288407. **Sindhu Beach**, Jl. Sindhu, tel: 288351. **Tanjungsari**, Jl. Tanjungsari, tel: 288441. **La Taverna Bungalows**, Jl. Tanjungsari, tel: 288497.
MODERATE: **Diwangkara Beach Hotel**, Jl. Hang Tuab, tel: 288577. **Laghawa Beach Inn**, Jl. Tanjung Sari 51, tel: 288494. **Hotel Ramayana**, Jl. Tanjung Sari, tel: 288359. **Hotel Santai**, Jl. Tanjungsari, tel: 287314. **Taman Agung**, Jl. D. Tamblingan, tel: 288549.
BUDGET: On Jl. Danau Buyan: **Hotel Rani**, tel: 288578; **Hotel Sanur Indah**, tel: 288568; **Hotel Taman Sari**, tel: 288187.

Restaurants

FOOD STALLS: near the 3 budget guesthouses.
Hotels all have own restaurants: **Tanjung Sari Hotel Restaurant** & **Kuri Putih** in Bali Sanur Irama Bungalows are authentically Balinese. Independent restaurants include **Trattoria da Marco** (European), off Jl. Sanur and **Si Pino's**, Jl. Sanur (opp. Bali Beach entrance). Best Chinese restaurant: **Telaga Naga**, opp. Bali Hyatt. Near Kulkul you can find good seafood.

Museum

Museum Le Mayeur, Sanur Beach. Tue-Fri & Sun 8 am-4 pm, Sat 8-12:30, closed Mon.

Tourist Information / Post

Tourist information, in large hotels. **Post office**, Kantor Pos Sanur, Jl. D. Buyan.

NUSA DUA (Area Code 0361)

LUXURY: **Hotel Bualu**, tel: 771310. **Hotel Nusa Dua**, tel: 771210. **Bali Holiday Village** (Club Med). **Bali Sol Hotel**. Many offer on-site restaurants & cultural events.

KUTA AND LEGIAN
(Area Code 0361)

LUXURY: **Bali Mandira Cottage**, Jl. Padma, Legian, tel: 751381. **Bali Oberoi**, Kayu Aya (far N end) tel: 751061. **Kartika Plaza Beach**, Kuta, tel: 751067. **Hotel Jayakarta**, Legian, tel: 751433. **Legian Beach**, Jl. Melasti, Legian, tel: 751711. **Natour Kuta Beach**, Kuta, tel: 51361. **Pertamina Cottages**, far south, tel: 752651.
MODERATE: **Kuta Cottage**, Jl. Bakung Sari, tel: 751101. **Camplung Mas**, Legian, tel: 751580. **Poppies Cott.age**, Poppies Lane 1, Kuta, tel: 751059. **Ocean**

Blue Resort, Legian, tel: 751964. **Legian Village**, Jl. Padma, Legian, tel: 751182.

BUDGET: More than 300 *losmen* & home-stays. A selection: **Arena Bungalows**, near Poppies Lane 1. **Kedin Inn**, tel: 752935. **Rita's House**, tel: 751760. **Berlian Inn**, tel: 751501. **Sari Jaya**, tel: 756909. **Ayu Beach Inn**, near Poppies Lane 2. **Taman Mekar**, **Taman Indah**, **Taman Ayu**, Poppies Lane 1. **Puspa Beach Inn**, Jl. Bakungsari, tel: 751988. **Ady's Inn**, Jl. Melasti, Legian, tel: 753445.

Restaurants

Most restaurants serve whole east-west spectrum, from Balinese & Chinese, to hamburgers.

Recommended: **Made's Warung**, (Balinese and International) Jl. Pantai Kuta, classic traveler hang-out. **Poppies Restaruant**, off Poppies Lane. **TJ's** (Mexican!), Poppies Gang. **Swiss Restaurant**, Jl. Pura Bagus Taruna, Legian. **Bali Indah**, Jl. Buni Sari. **Lenny's**, Jl. Pantai Kuta. **Mini Restaurant**, Jl. Legian. **Gosha Seafood**, Jl. Melasti, Legian.

Shopping

Kuta & Legian are major fashion centers in Southeast Asia. Boutiques: **Pasar Seni**, Jl. Bakung Sari; beach end of Jl. Melasti, Legian.

Cultural Events

Banjar Pengaretan, **Banjar Tegal** & **Indra Prasta** in Kuta, & **Banjar Legian Kelod** & **Banjar Seminyak** in Legian, give Balinese dance performances. Real native entertainment is pubs, discos & nightclubs: **Peanuts Club**, **The Jaya Pub** & **Double Six** are the European hang-outs.

Tourist Information

Government Tourist Office, Jl. Benesari, tel: 753540.

Post Office

Post office, Kuta Postal Agent, Jl. Legian, sells stamps, stationery etc, also poste restante. **Main office**, **Kantor Pos**, off Jl. Ngurah Rai.

Medical

The next **hospital** is in Denpassar: R. S. U. Sanglah, tel: 227911.

Arrival / Transportation

Main *bemo* stand: Jl. Legian/Jl. Pantai Kuta intersection, but *bemo* also travel down Jl. Legian. *Bemo* go to Tegal station, Denpasar, also S to Ngurah Rai airport. Bicycles, motorcycles & jeeps can be rented from many hotels and *losmen*. **Garuda Airline Office**: Kuta Beach Hotel, Jl. Pantai Kuta, tel: 751361.

UBUD AND SURROUNDINGS
(Area Code 0361)
Accommodaton

LUXURY: **Hotel Tjampuhan**, Campuan, tel: 975368. **Padmah Indah Cottage**, Penestanan, tel: 975719. **Pringga Juwita**, Ubud, tel: 975734. **Kupu Kupu Barong**, Kedewatan, tel: 975478.

MODERATE: **Oka Kartini's**, Padangtegal. **Oka Wati's Bungalows**, Ubud, tel: 975063. **Puri Saraswati**, Ubud. **Hotel Puri Saren**, Ubud. **Ubud Inn**, Ubud. **Fibra Inn**, Ubud, tel: 975451.

BUDGET: **Arjuna Inn**, Campuan. **Munut Bungalows**, Campuan. **Oka Homestay**, Pengosekan. **Guci Homestay**, Pengosekan. **Negara Homestay**, Peliatan. **Mandala Homestay**, Peliatan. **Mudita Inn**, Peliatan. **Puri Agung**, Peliatan. **Agus Pension**, Ubud. **Artini**, Ubud. **Frog Pond Inn**, Ubud. **I Made Sadia** homestay, Ubud. **Karyawan**, Ubud. **Hotel Mendra**, Ubud. **Monkey Forest Hideaway**, Ubud. **Warsi's House**, Ubud. **Pondok Indah**, Ubud. **Bendi's**, Ubud.

Restaurants

Restaurants in hotels & many *losmen*, often open to non-residents. Also: **Cafe Lotus**, Puri Saraswati, Ubud. **Cafe Wayan**, Ubud. **Griya**, Ubud. **Murni's Warung**, Campuan. **Nomad Restaurant**, Ubud.

Shopping

Main street lined with kiosks selling carvings, basketry, antiques, *batik*, paintings. Most can be bought more cheaply direct from makers in Ubud & surrounding villages. Concentrations of artists' workshops in **Penestenan** & **Padangtegal**.

Museums / Galleries

Museum Purbakala Gedung Arca, (archaeology), Pejeng, tel: 26101. Tue-Sat 7:30 am-1:30 pm, closed Sun & Mon. **Galleries: Museum Lempad**, former home of late I Gusti Nyoman Lempad, Ubud. **Puri Lukisan Museum**, Ubud. Daily 8 am-4 pm. **Neka Gallery**, Padangtegal. **Museum Neka**, Campuan. **Agung Rai Gallery** & **ARMA (Agung Rai Museum of Art)**, Peliatan.

Cultural Events

Details of day's events at **Tourist Office**.

DANCE: **Banjar Padangtegal**, Padangtegal. *Kecak*-dance, Wed & Sun 7-8 pm. **Pura Dalem Puri**, Peliatan. *Legong* dance, Sat 7:30-8:30 pm. *WAYANG KULIT:* **Oka Kartini**, Peliatan. Wed & Sun 8-9 pm.

Tourist Information

Tourist Office is on the main street, next to the market.

Post

Post office in Padangtegal, near Gallery Neka.

Arrival / Transportation

Bemo leave from marketplace for Denpasar and elsewhere. Bicycle/motorcycle rentals can be arranged through most *losmen*. **Surya International**, opp. Puri Lukisan Museum, tel: 51673/51786, confirms international flight reservations.

BATUR CRATER
(Area Code 0366)

PENELOKAN: not really recommended as place to stay. **KINTAMANI: Losmen Miranda** & **Losmen Superman** are budget-priced, **Puri Astina** and **Sasaka Inn** are more comfortable.

TOYAH BUNGKAH (Tirtha): *MODERATE:* **Hotel Puri Bening Hayato**, tel: 51234. *BUDGET:* **Awangga Bungalows, Nyoman Mawa Homestay, Arlina's Bungalows**, tel: 51165.

Arrival / Transportation
Bemo run between Kintamani, Penelokan, Kedisan & Toyabungkah. Boats between Kedisan, Toyabungkah & Trunyan.

SINGARAJA
(Area Code 0362)

Most people prefer Lovina Beach, 10 km further W. But plenty of accommodations in town: *MODERATE:* **Hotel Wijaya**, Jl. Jen. Sudirman 74, tel: 21915. *BUDGET:* **Hotel Sedana Yoga**, Jl. G. Dada 136, tel: 21715. All others on Jl. Jen. A. Yani: **Sentral**, no. 48, tel:21896; **Niaga**, no. 8, tel: 21907; **Gelar Sari**, no. 87, tel: 21495.

Museum
Museum Gedong Kirtya (manuscripts museum), Jl. Veteran 20, tel: 41645. Mon-Thu 8 am-2 pm, Fri 8-11, Sat 8-12.

Post
Post office, E end of Jl. Jen. A Yani.

Arrival / Transportation
Minibus terminals at W end of town for Denpasar & the W, at E end for Kintamani & Amlapura. Bus cos near Yani/ Diponegoro junction run direct to Java from Singaraja.

LOVINA BEACH
(Area Code 0362)

Reached by *bemo* from Singaraja's westerly bus station. Many *losmen,* bungalows & small restaurants. Tourist zone stretches 10 km, encompassing **Anturan, Kalibukbuk, Lovina** & **Temukus**. *MODERATE:* **Aditya Hotel**, Temukus, tel: 41059. BUDGET: **Agung Homestay**, Anturan, **Baruna Beach Cottage**, Anturan. **Lila Cita Beach Inn**, Anturan. **Banyualit**, Kalibukbuk. **Ayodya**, Kalibukbuk.

AMLAPURA AND SURROUNDINGS
(Area Code 0363)

Amlapura itself has **Lahar Mas Inn** at W end of town & **Sidha Karya** on Jl. Hasannudin, but most visitors prefer **Homestay Lila** in Abian Soan, 5 km W of town. Six budget *losmen* at scenic **Tirtagganga** to the N.

CANDIDASA (Area Code 0363)

More than 40 *losmen* on this stretch of road & beach, all in budget price range, simple lodgings and luxury hotels: **Puri Bagus Candidasa**, tel: 41131. **The Watergarden**, tel: 41540.

Restaurants
Hawaii Restaurant, Sumber Rasa (Chinese) & **Lotus Seaview** are up-market eateries.

LOMBOK
MATARAM & SURROUNDINGS
(Area Code 0370)

BEACH HOTELS: **MENINTING: Sasaka Beach** (moderate). **SENGGIGI: Senggigi Beach Sheraton**, tel: 93333 (luxury). **Pondok Senggigi** & **Mascot Cottage**, tel: 93365 (budget);
IN-LAND: *MODERATE:* **Granada**, Jl. bung Karno, Mataram, tel: 32660. **Nitour Hotel**, Jl. Yos Sudarso 4, Ampenan, tel: 23780. **Hotel Paradiso**, Jl. Angsoka 3, Mataram, tel: 32675.
BUDGET: **Hotel Shanti Puri**, Jl. Maktal 15, Cakra, tel: 32649. **Pusaka**, Jl. Hasanuddin 23, tel: 33119. **Hotel Wisata**, Jl. Koperasi 19, Ampenan, tel: 26971. **Wisma Triguna**, Jl. Koperasi 76, Ampenan, tel: 31705.

Restaurants
INDONESIAN: **Garden House Restaurant**, Mataram Shopping Centre, Jl. Pejanggik, Mataram. **Jasmin**, Jl. Kebudayaan 3, Cakranegara. **Madya**, Jl. Hasanuddin, Cakranegara. **Minang**, Jl. Hasanuddin, Cakranegara. **Mulia**, Jl. Pabean, Ampenan. **Taliwang**, Jl. Pejanggik, Mataram. *CHINESE:* **Aroma**, Jl. Palapa 2, Cakranegara. **Asia**, Jl. Selaparang, Cakranegara. **Pabean**, Jl. Yos Sudarso, Ampenan. **Tjirebon**, Jl. Yos Sudarso, Ampenan.

Shopping
Textiles: **Slamet Riadi**, Jl. Tenun 10, Cakranegara, tel: 31196. *Antiques:* **Wayan Wika**, Jl. Bangau 12, Cakranegara. **Sudirman**, Jl. Yos Sudarso 88, Ampenan, tel: 32553.

Museum
Nusa Tenggara Barat State Museum, Jl. Panji Tilar Negara, Mataram, tel: 32159. Tue-Thu & Sun 8 am-2 pm, Fri 8-11, Sat 8 am-1 pm.

Tourist Information / Post
Tourist information, Jl. Langko 70, Ampenan, tel: 31730. Mon-Thu 7 am-2 pm, Fri 7-11, Sat 7 am-1 pm.
Post office, Jl. Sriwijaya, Mataram.

Arrival / Transportation
AIR: Selaparang Airport, a short distance N of Mataram. **Merpati**, Jl. Yos Sudarso 6, Ampenan, tel: 23762.
SEA: 12 ferries each direction daily between Padangbai (Bali) & Lembar (a few km S of Mataram by *bemo*). Hourly boats to Sumbawa from Labuhan Lombok on E coast.
LOCAL: *Bemo* station – **Sweta**, at crossroads 2 km E of Cakranegara, on main road.

MT. RINJANI
There are two approaches: from the north via **Senaru** (normal route), or from the east via **Sapit** and **Sembalun** (more difficult). Both routes are arduous, require tents and supplies, and take 3-4 days up and down. Guides recommended – can be found at *losmen* in Batu Kok and Senaru.

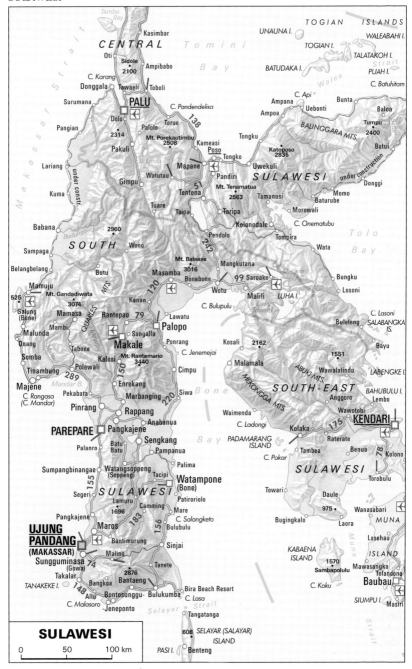

SULAWESI

0   50   100 km

SULAWESI

UJUNG PANDANG

THE TORAJA HIGHLANDS

AROUND RANTEPAO

It wasn't until Indonesian independence in 1949 that this island with the distinctive orchid shape, which lies on the Equator, is inhabited by only 16 million people and measures 189,000 square kilometers, received the name Sulawesi (from *sula besi*, or ironsmith). The Dutch colonial masters who had controlled the island since 1667 had called it *Celebes*, after the term *Ponto dos Celebres*, meaning "Place of the notorious," which was used by16th-century Portuguese explorers. The "notorious" in question were local seafarers: Muslim Bugis and Macassarese who engaged in fishing, trade and piracy.

Not until the 20th century were the Dutch able to "pacify" the Toraja, the Malayan people who inhabited the highlands. Since then, these erstwhile headhunters, with their spectacular funerary rites, archaic rituals of buffalo sacrifice and striking clan houses, have become ethnologic and tourist attractions of the first order.

As early as 1858, the English scientist A. R. Wallace ("Wallace Line") had recongnized the exceptional character of the fauna of Sulawesi. The island is surrounded by deep waters and as a result, has been isolated for most of the earth's history; 98 percent of the indigenous mammals (apart from the bats) are endemic, only to be found here. Among these are the *babirusa*, a wild pig who has two extra, powerful tusks growing out of his upper jaw through the back of his nose; the wild dwarf buffalo *anoa*; the herbivorous *cuscus* bear, who uses his muscular tail to help in climbing; the tailless macaque; and the *tarsier*, tiny dwarf apes, which weigh only 100 grams. An exceptionally rare bird, the *maleo*, buries its eggs (which weigh about 225 grams each) in warm sand like a crocodile, and forgets about them. Wallace himself discovered the *papilio androcles*, one of the largest swallowtail butterflies in the world, in South Sulawesi. (Please think about endangered species; don't buy specimens of any kind.)

UJUNG PANDANG

Since the 16th century, the Macassar capital **Ujung Pandang**, once a fortress of the mighty Sultan of Gowa, has been a city of traders and sailors. Today, the 1.5 million inhabitants of this predominantly Muslim port include Buginese, Chinese, Mandarese, Toraja, Minahasa, Javanese, Balinese, Minang, Batak and other peoples of the Pacific islands.

Half a day is enough time to see the city. One highlight is **Fort Rotterdam**, which Admiral Speelman expanded and

named after his native city, after the Dutch victory over the Makassar Sultan Hasanuddin in 1667. This victory gave the VOC a firm foothold from which to dominate its competition, the Portuguese, English, Maccassars and Buginese, in the growing spice trade. To the left of the entrance is **Speelman's House**, the oldest building in the fortress, dating from 1686. The Dutch chapel at the center of the courtyard dates from the 18th century. The **La Galigo Museum** has been set up in the former storehouses of the East India Company to display *lepa lepa* (outrigger boats), fishing and farming equipment, wedding gowns of silk woven with gold threads, as well as *kris* (knives) and jewelry from the age of the Sultans. A **silk manufacturer's** on Jl. Ontah continues to weave traditional pat-

Above: Tautau figures, carved from wood, serve as repositories for the souls of the deceased. Right: The deceased should be escorted into the Hereafter by as many buffalo as possible.

terns. About three kilometers north of the fort, in the harbor of **Pelabuhan Paotere**, one can watch Bugis and Maccassar schooners loading and unloading. Traditional wooden, one-masted vessels, called *prahu pinisi*, bring wood from Kalimantan and industrial goods from Java into the country.

Indonesians of Chinese descent pray to the "Divine Goddess" for their welfare in the **Tian Hou Hong Temple** (Jl. Sulawesi/Jl. Serui). These Chinese, or *orang cina*, dominate trade and business in Ujung Pandang. On the main shopping street of **Jl. Somba Opu** they operate a remarkable number of goldsmith's and jeweler's shops, catering to the Muslim tradition that a groom give gold to his bride on the morning after their wedding. **Antique shops**, offering a range of ethnic souvenirs from, are concentrated at the north end of Jl. Somba Opu. (**Note:** old Toraja *tautaus* may not legally be purchased or taken out of the country.)

When the tropical sun finally sinks into the red-stained sea at the end of the day,

countless food stalls turn the **shore promenade** of **Jl. Penhibur**, near the Hotel Makassar Golden, into a kind of giant, improvised open-air restaurant. The choices are endless; everything from grilled fish (*Ikan Batar*) to *Coto Makassar*, a local soup made from the organs of buffalo, to skewers of grilled goat meat (*Sate Kambing*).

THE TORAJA HIGHLANDS

The eight-hour, 328 kilometer bus ride from Ujung Pandang into Toraja country passes through a rich and varied landscape. There are coastal stretches with Bugis boats, crab-ponds, broad rice paddies, bizarre, tower-like limestone cliff formations, a traditional shipyard and then the broad bay of **Pare-Pare** with its fish restaurants (specialties are *udang* and red snapper). After this, the route follows the Sadang River before passing through a hilly, Muslim region. Next, one traverses the well-known coffee-growing territory of **Kalosi** and crosses a 1100

meter pass with marvelous views before finally arriving at *tanah toraja*, the picturesque **Toraja Highlands**.

In the region around the administrative center **Makale,** and the tourist center **Rantepao**, live the partly Christianized Sadang-Toraja, who were feared as headhunters as recently as 100 years ago. Their animistic religion (*aluk todolo*), which placess strong emphasis on blood sacrifice, and revolves around a higher being called *puang matua*, is officially regarded as a variation of Hinduism. The tourist office in Rantepao provides tourists with information about impending Torajan funeral ceremonies and their ritual status: the higher the caste of the deceased, the longer the ceremony (up to two weeks), the more splendid the "burial village" that will be specially erected for the occasion, and the more numerous the guests and the number of sacrificial pigs and water buffalo that will be consumed. In the well-heeled class of rajahs, up to 100 buffalo can lose their lives for such a service; those from the unpropertied

caste of former slaves sometimes has to make do with a single chicken.

The deceased, who has usually been kept at home for some time, as an embalmed corpse, is finally officially buried in a carved wooden coffin in a cliff near the village, or laid to rest in a tomb, burial house, or limestone cave. The famous *tautaus*, effigies of the dead which are thought to be the repository of their souls, are placed in front of the coffin. These reminder the living to give proper reverence to their ancestors and to continue the ritual re-clothing of their bones.

Characteristic of the *tongkonan*, the traditional clan houses of the Toraja, is the sharply curved ridge-pole, low in the middle and pointing to the heavens at either end. Seen from the side, this roof reminds some ethnologists of Polynesian sails; others think of the sterns of ships or buffalo horns. Affixed to clan pillars at the front of the house are the pick of the

Above: Toraja-kopi, babirusa teeth, bamboo flutes: everything's for sale except the head!

horn trophies from past funerals. Accross from the rows of houses are rice storehouses made of wood and bamboo; the rice harvest is protected by artfully carved and painted images of suns, chickens and buffalo heads.

AROUND RANTEPAO

Every six days, a big cattle market is held in **Rantepao**. Honored as sacrificial animals, water buffalo with symmetrical markings and blue eyes go for prices above one million rupiahs. As well as pot-bellied pigs of all sizes, bamboo stalks filled with foaming *tuak*, the ubiquitous palm wine, are also for sale.

In a limestone cliff formation near the Torajan village of **Marante,** you can see impressive galleries of ancestors with *tautaus*, caves full of skulls and weathered *erong* (wooden coffins). Nearby, the well-run **Marante Highland Resort** presents folklore evenings that are well worth experiencing, as well as opulent buffets.

172

Nanggala features an imposing row of 14 rice storehouses and *tongkonan*, as well as a bat tree.

The venerable Torajan village of **Kete Kesu** lies amidst vivid green rice fields; the *tongkonan* here are among the oldest in the region. The *tautaus* in the nearby burial-clifff have long since been looted by art thieves. The ancient wooden coffins in the walls, however, have been well preserved.

Londa has a much-visited burial-cliff that is 70-meters high with deep limestone caves full of bones (bring a flashlight) and galleries guarded by countless *tautaus*. The graves of the aristocracy are located at a dizzying height. Somewhat further east, in **Pabaisenan**, is a holy tree with an infant's grave in its trunk.

Next to the old village of **Lemo** is one of the most impressive Toraja burial-cliffs around. The local Raja clan had burial chambers hewn into the rock face; these are closed with ornamental wooden doors and are "guarded" by larger-than-life *tautaus*.

In **Bori**, massive menhirs have been arranged in a circle to form a *rante* (buffalo sacrificing ground) for the artistocracy. This serves as a reminder of the Neolithic origins of Torajan culture.

One of the loveliest rice-paddy landscapes in the world is that of the *sawah* fields and steep cliffs between **Lempo** and **Batutumonga**. From the panorama restaurant in Batutumonga, a path with spectacular views leads to nearby **Lokomata**. There, you can watch stone-cutters engaged in the tedious and difficult task of hewing burial chambers from the hard, dark volcanic rock.

Palawa is worth a visit for its clan houses decorated with carved buffalo heads, as well as its wide selection of traditional woven textiles. Decorative fabrics which make wonderful bedspreads and tablecloths, these are the work of women from the neighboring villages of **Sadan** and **Tobarana**.

UJUNG PANDANG (Area Code 0411)
Accommodation

LUXURY: **Marannu City**, Jl. Hasanuddin 3, tel: 315087. **Marannu Tower**, Jl. Kajaolalido 1, tel: 327051. **Victoria**, Jl. Sudirman 24, tel: 328888. **Makassar Golden**, Jl. Pasar Ikan 52, tel: 314408. *MODERATE:* **Kota Makassar**, Jl. Chairil Anwar 28, tel: 317055. **Pondok Suada Indah**, Jl. Hasanuddin 12, tel: 317179. **Venus Kencana**, Jl. Botolempangan 17, tel: 324995. **Widhana**, Jl. Botolempangan 53, tel: 21393. *BUDGET:* **Erik's Homestay**, Jl. Karunrung 9A, tel: 321998. **Wisma Tiatira**, Jl. Sutomo 25, **Hotel Delta**, Jl. Hasanuddin 43, tel: 312711.

Restaurants

Surya Super Crab, Jl. Nusakambangan 16 (specialties: lobster, crab and octopus). **Rumah Makan Labbakang**, Jl. Chairil Anwar. **Bamboo Den**, Jl. Gunung Latimojong 55. **Restaurant Ujung Padang**, Jl. Irian 42.

Tourist Information / Post

Tourist information, Kantor Gubernur, Jl. Urip Sumoharjo, km 5.5, tel: 320616. **General Post Office**, Jl. Slamet Riyadi 10. **Telephone/telex**, Jl. Veteran Utara 206.

RANTEPAO (Area Code 0423)
Accommodation

LUXURY: **Marante Highland Resort**, Jl. Jurusan Palopo, tel: 21616, fax: 21122 (the island's best food and service). **Toraja Cottages** (old-style buildings) and **Toraja Prince** (new building), Jl. Pakubalasalu, tel: 21430. **Misiliana**, 3 km from Rantepao, toward Makale, tel: 21212. **Novotel Toraja**, Rantepao, tel: 21192. *MODERATE:* **Rantepao Lodge**, Jl. Pao Rura (2 km S of Rantepao). **Wisma Maria II**, Jl. Pong (1 km S of marketplace, toward Makale). **Hotel Pison**, Jl. Pong Tiku 8, tel: 21344. *BUDGET:* **Wisma Rosa**, Jl. Sa'adan 28, tel: 21075. **Wisma Irama**: Jl. Abdul gani 16, tel: 21371. **Wisma Imanuel**, Jl. W. Monginsidi 16, tel: 21416. **Wisma Monton**, Jl. Abdul Gani 14A, tel: 21675.

Restaurants

CHINESE: **Rahmat**, Jl. J. A. Yani, tel: 21175 (lunch buffet) *TORAJAN:* **Indra**, Jl. Landorundun 63. Pia's & Poppies, Jl. J. A. Yani 117, tel: 21362, next to the post office. *INTERNATIONAL:* **Takumande Opa** (in Hotel Misiliana), 3 km out of town, toward Makale. *INDONESIAN:* **Panorama Restaurant**, in Batutumonga, above the rice terraces.

Tourist Information

Tourist information, Jl. A. Yani 62, has information about funeral ceremonies.

ACEH / NORTH SUMATRA

BANDA ACEH
ISLANDS & COASTS
THE MOUNTAINS
MEDAN & THE PLANTATIONS
THE BATAKLANDS
PADANG LAWAS / NIAS ISLAND

ACEH

The Special District of Aceh is some 1500 kilometers closer to Mecca than is Jakarta, and it views itself as the proud and pure Islamic antithesis to Java's syncretism. The Christians of Northern Sumatra look at Aceh with suspicion. Here, public drunkenness and displays of affection, and indecent clothing are taboo. Yet, as long as these simple rules are observed, visitors are more than welcome.

Not only are the cities here quiet and clean; they are also of considerable historic and architectural interest. The interior is marked by a varied landscape: pine woods give way to broad, dry plains of grass. In the mountains, the tribes of Alas and Gayo are clearly distinct from the ethnic group of the Acehnese. The rain forest in the south is a huge national park, with a world-renowned whitewater river, the Alas.

The people of Aceh are of varied origin. Many of them could pass for Indians or Arabs; in Lanno, on the west coast, people tend to look more European (the heritage, some say, of Portuguese castaways). In the interior, the descendants of slaves from Nias and the Batak country add another ethnic twist.

Left: Transporting bananas in Aceh.

BANDA ACEH

In the 15th century, the province's capital **Banda Aceh** was already the most important harbor at the tip of Sumatra. It was from here that Ali Mughayat Syah, the first Sultan of Aceh, set out, around 1520, to conquer the surrounding lands with their wealth of pepper and gold. In the mid-16th century, Aceh was one of the three main powers controlling the Straits of Malacca, entangled in endless three-way warfare with the Sultanate of Johor and the Portuguese of Malacca, it fought its, mostly naval, battles just off the coast of the Malay peninsula. Aceh was also the most distant vassal state of the Ottoman Empire. The region reached its peak during the reign of Sultan Iskandar Muda (1607-36), who elevated it to the leading power of the Western archipelago. Aceh developed into a center of Malayan literature and Islamic science.

Little is left today of the opulent 17th-century capital. The *kraton* complex of yore was located at the bend in the Krueng-Daroy river south of the current city center. The **Pintu Khop Gate** linked the now-vanished palace with the pleasure park of **Taman Sari**. Known as *Pintu Aceh*, this gate is a favorite theme of the gold- and silversmiths in Aceh. In 1880,

175

it served as the model for **Pendopo Gubernor**, the residence of the Dutch governor located upriver, which is still in use today as the Indonesian governor's residence. In the garden of Taman Sari, there is an unusual and mysterious sculpture, **Gunungan**; made from countless large gravestones which are arranged in size order around a pillar. The name means "like a mountain," and it is said that Iskandar Muda had this structure built to please his wife, who came from the mountains.

The central building of Aceh's **State Museum**, not far from Taman Sari, is a reconstruction of an Acehnic *adat* house from 1914. In Aceh, houses tend to be roomy, elegant versions of Malay pile houses. Men's and women's rooms are separate. The arched grating of the roof gable, which points toward Mecca, aids ventilation. Houses like this can still be found outside the city, particularly on the

Right: The Baiturrahman Mosque is the hallmark of Banda Aceh.

west coast. The museum displays jewelry, ceremonial garments and weapons, including the famous *rencong* knife. A special source of pride is the grave of Iskandar Muda. In spite of the fact that he once had an unsuccessful military commander castrated and even murdered his own son, he is still honored as a national hero.

In 1820, Aceh produced more than half of the world's pepper. After 1830, a new, strong and able leader, Tuanku Ibrahim, began a path of conquest which culminated in a confrontation with the Dutch, who had again built up economic and military strength. At first, the British compelled the Dutch to respect Aceh's independence. In 1871, however, an imperial deal led to one of the longest and most bitter colonial wars ever; in return for letting them have a free hand in Aceh, the Dutch turned the African Gold Coast over to England.

Some 2000 Dutch soldiers who died because the Dutch had a "free hand" in Aceh are buried in the **Dutch Cemetery**

west of Taman Sari. For more than 30 years, Aceh was the Sahara of the Netherlands; their Indian army was the Dutch answer to the Foreign Legion. Most of the people buried here, however, weren't Dutch, rather Javanese, Amboinese or Minahasa – who served as loyal slaves to a distant European royal house. Today, Dutch money pays for the upkeep of the cemetery.

Another monument to the war is the **Baiturrahman Mosque**, which the Dutch built in 1878 as a peace offering to the guerillas of the region. Not until 1904 were Aceh's residents truly able to come to terms with this expensive gift from the unbelievers. In 1935, the original dome was joined by two others; two more domes were added after independence.

The Dakota airplane on the square in front of the cemetery was donated by the people of Aceh as an **RI 100 Monument** to the besieged republic during the revolution of 1945-1949.

When Jakarta began to exercise its long-awaited power, general disappoint-ment was followed by quickly spreading resistance. Eventually, the government recognized Aceh's autonomy in religion, education and Islamic law: the precondi- tions for a still-uncertain peace.

ISLANDS AND COASTS

Indonesia's northernmost outpost is **We**, which lies 12 kilometers north of Banda Aceh, in the middle of the sea. The most important settlement on this lovely, hilly island is **Sabang**. The rise of the diesel engine and competition with the harbor of Belawan, near Medan, led to a decrease in Sabang's importance. Today, the harbor, surrounded by beautiful green hills, is reminiscent of a Carribbean island. The military has, however, settled in here. Today, the one-time defensive fortress, protecting against Japan and Malaysia, has its weapons aimed to the north, at the Nicobar Islands, base of the powerful Indian navy.

Paradoxically, Aceh's self-imposed religious fanaticism is based on an *adat*

177

society which, even by Indonesian standards, is rather pro-feminist. Newly-married couples move into the woman's house, not the man's. A married woman not only owns her house, but often the rice paddies, as well. Inheritance is passed on matrilinearly, as well as patrilineally. The 17th century even saw the succession of four queens ruling one after the other. Aceh's most famous daughter, however, is Cut Nyak Dhien, a guerilla heroine of the war of 1899. Today, there is a **Cut Nyak Dhien Museum** in Banda Aceh devoted to her. On a lonely beach on the west coast, near Meulaboh, a monument stands on the spot where her husband, Umar, died.

The well-maintained road running along Aceh's west coast is often called one of the most beautiful in the world because of the foaming mountain brooks that empty into the tumult of waves that crash onto the rocky beaches. It is be-

cause of its powerful surf during the West Monsoon, that the bay near **Calang** is known as the "Witch's Cauldron."

The plain of the east coast, between Banda Aceh and Medan, is both the cradle of early history and a center for the region's industrial future. When Marco Polo, the first European in Indonesia, stopped off on this coast on his way home from China in 1292, the inhabitants of *Ferlec* – known today as **Peureulak**, near **Langsa** – had already been converted to Islam by Saracen traders.

The earliest Indonesian testimony to Islam, the **Malik-as-Salih Gravestone** (1297), is located in a village 18 kilometers east of Lhokseumawe. The stone is a memorial to a ruler of the kingdom of Samudra, which bequeathed its name, in slightly altered form, to modern Sumatra. **Sigli**, near Banda Aceh, was the harbor of Pedir, from which Indonesian pilgrims embarked on their *hajj* to Mecca.

From an economic viewpoint, Aceh's new "gold mine," liquid natural gas, puts

Above: Dry rice cultivation in the mountains of Aceh.

all of its previous sources of revenue to shame. In 1971, near the small city of **Lhokseumawe**, prospectors discovered one of the largest oil fields in the world. The income from the export of gas is subject to strict central control, which is a continual source of irritation to the Acehners themselves, has undeniably contributed to the economic upswing the area experienced under the New Order. Hordes of foreign engineers and countless Indonesian laborers have converted Lhokseumawe into a high-tech economic center with a huge liquefaction plant and two fertilizer factories.

THE MOUNTAINS

The difference between Lhokseumawe and the highlands directly adjacent to it is breathtaking. Gayo settlements, such as **Tangse** and **Geumpang**, are scattered throughout the north, but the "capital" of **Takengon** is located on the bank of the deep, blue mountain lake **Tawar**. The Gayo own the best-irrigated rice paddies in Sumatra. They also cultivate coffee, tobacco, cloves and cinnamon, and are famous for their beautiful embroidery and ceramics.

In **Blangkejeren,** one can see some of the traditional houses which, like Borneo's longhouses, are home to several families at once.

The most fascinating sight in the south of Aceh, is the river **Alas**, whose source is on **Mt. Leuser** (3404 m). The course of the river drops more than 100 kilometers as it roars through a wild gorge that runs parallel to both coasts. Because of its natural beauty, this area has been made into a national park, home to elephants, rhinocerous, orangutans and tigers. At the **Bohorok Rehabilitation Center**, illegally captured orangutans are cared for and prepared for their return to the wild (see p. 183). **Kutacane** is the last outpost of farmers from the Batak country.

BANDA ACEH (Area Code 0651)
Accommodation
LUXURY: **Kuala Tripa**, Jl. Abd. Ujong Rimba 24, tel/fax: 24535. *MODERATE:* **Medan**, Jl. A Yani 19, tel: 21501. **Prapat**, Jl. A Yani 7, tel: 22159. **Rasa Sayang**, Jl. Teuku Umar 439, tel: 41983. **Pavilliun Seulawah**, Jl. Jl. Prof. A. M. Ibrahim II 3, tel: 22872. **Sultan**, Jl. Polem 1, tel: 22469. **Hotel Yusri**, Jl. KHA Dahlan 74, tel: 23543. *BUDGET:* **Losmen Aceh barat**, Jl. Khairil Anwar 16, tel: 23250. **Losmen Sri Budaya**, Jl. Prof A.M. Ibrahim III 5E, tel: 21751. **Lading**, Jl. Cut Meutia 8, tel: 21359. **Wisma Lampriek**, Jl. T. Daud Beureu-eh 153, tel: 23995.

Restaurants
ACEHNESE: **Asia Baru**, Jl. Cut Nyak Dhien. **Ujong Batee**, by beach on road to Krueng Raya, is a famous Acehnese seafood restaurant. Another is **Braden**, 9 km from town on road to Lhoknga. *CHINESE:* **New Tropicana**, Jl. A. Yani 90. **Aroma Restaurant**, Jl. TWK Muh. Daudsyah. *INDONESIAN:* **Dian**, Jl. A Yani. **Sinar Surya** (Padang), Jl. Safiatuddin 10.

Museums
Aceh State Museum, Jl. Sultan Alauddin Mahmudsyah, tel: 21033/2335. Tue-Thu & Sun 8:30 am-2 pm, Fri & Sat 8:30-12, closed Mon and holidays.

Tourist Information / Post
Jl. T. Chik Kuta Karang 3, tel: 23692. **Post office**: Jl. T. Angkasa. **Telephone:** Jl. T. Daud Beureu-eh 92.

Arrival / Transportation
AIR: **Blang Bintang Airport**, 17 km E of town. Flights to Sabang, Meulaboh & Tapaktuan, Medan & other big Sumatran cities. *Airline offices:* **Garuda** & **Merpati** in Hotel Sultan, Jl. T. Panglima Polem 1, tel: 32523 / 31811.

SEA: Local boats leave from Uleh Lheu harbor, long-distance ships from **Krueng Raya**. **Pelni office**: Jl. J. A. Yani 49, tel: 23976.

BUS: Terminal Teuku Umar (in front of Rasa Sayang hotel) for long-distance buses; most bus offices on Jl. Mohammed Jam. **Stasiun Kota**, in town center, Jl. Diponegoro for local services.

RURAL ACEH
Accommodation
TAKENGON: *(Area Code 0643) MODERATE:* **Renggali**, Jl. Bintang, tel: 21144. *BUDGET:* **Batang Ruang**, Jl. Mahkamah 7, tel: 21524. **Motel Triarga**, Jl. Pasar Inpres, tel: 21073. **Hotel Danau Laut Tawar**, Jl. Lebekader 402.

Museums
Museum Malikussaleh, Jl. May Jen T Hamzah Bendahara, Lhokseumawe. Mon/Wed/Thu 8 am-2 pm, Sun 8-10, closed Tue & Fri. **Museum Sepakat Segenep**, Kutacane. Tue-Thu & Sun 8-11, Fri 8-11, closed Sat & Mon.

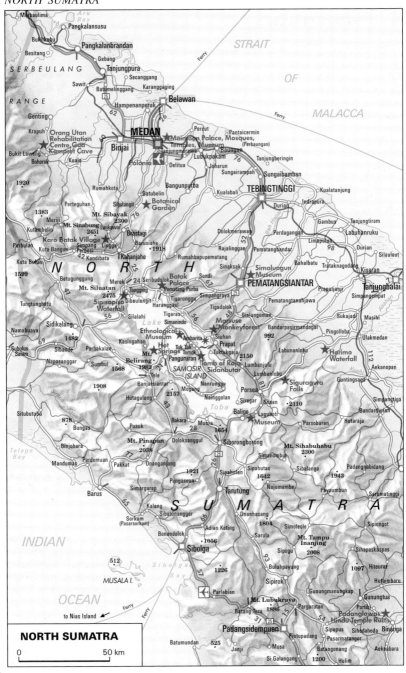

NORTH SUMATRA

0   50 km

NORTH SUMATRA

This province is the most populous, most fertile, most diverse, most spectacular, most visited and best known part of the island of Sumatra. Its capital, Medan, is one of the great export ports of Southeast Asia; its crowning landmark, the vast blue halo of Lake Toba, is known the world over as a symbol of Indonesia's natural beauty.

However, the rise of North Sumatra has been a relatively recent and rapid one. Less than 150 years ago, when Java was already a market garden, keeping sugar and coffee on the tables of Europe, interior North Sumatra was an unmapped wilderness inhabited by warring cannibals. More than 3500 years before, various tribes, today known collectively as *Batak*, left their settlements at the foot of the Himalayas and moved to this rough mountain landscape. Medan was an insignificant village amid alluvial swamps; part of a minor sultanate disputed between the Acehnese and the Dutch.

The first European to set his eyes on Lake Toba did so in 1853; the first tobacco in all of North Sumatra was planted near Medan in 1863. Not surprisingly, therefore, North Sumatra retains many clear reminders both of its unique indigenous cultural heritage and of its late colonial heyday.

MEDAN AND THE PLANTATIONS

Medan, Indonesia's third largest city, is a monument to capitalism: its power and creativity, but also its harshness and ugliness. Great wealth passes through, and air-conditioned cars, shopping centers and clubs testify to the affluence of those who control the flow of money. Medan is a place of cruel contrasts, almost untempered by the civic pride and facelifting operations that have been lavished upon the nation's capital and tourist towns; Medan has long ceased to be anybody's showcase. Broken pavements and zinc-roofed shacks line the dirty streets, and swarms of *becak* circulate aimlessly. However, it has vigor and life and an energy as intoxicating as its exhaust fumes. It is not too gigantic to overwhelm the visitor and boasts a number of architectural jewels from the time when it had not yet been engulfed by the shadier side of its success.

Medan rose on the tide of the economic *laissez-faire* which transformed the Dutch colonies in the late 19th century. The modern town's founding and spiritual father was the pioneer tobacco planter Jacob Nienhuys. The name of this commercial imperialist has survived better than those of his military counterparts – he is still honored by the **Nienhuys Fountain** outside the post office.

Tobacco was the beginning of the miracle, and Sumatran cigars are still a byword for those who understand such things, but other Midas crops followed: oil palms, tea and, above all, rubber, riding not at the heels, but on the wheels of the young automobile industry. The land which grew all this wealth was known as the Deli *cultuurgebied* (Deli plantation zone), after the sultanate which had nominal sovereignty over it, and Medan was its metropolis.

The Sultan's unholy alliance with Dutch capitalism was very profitable. As a result, **Maimoon Palace**, built for him by an Italian architect in 1888, is the most impressive royal residence anywhere in Indonesia. With its imposing arches and colonnades and stately grounds, the Maimoon Palace remains the symbol of Medan. Care was also taken to pander to native religious sensibilities; the **Grand Mosque**, built in 1906, is the finest in Sumatra. Dutch props, however, could only prolong the downfall of the old social order; in 1945 and 1946 most of the aristocracy were overthrown by revolutionaries.

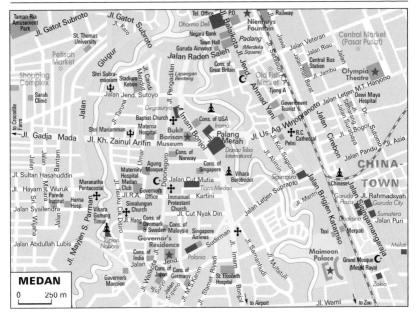

The assorted foreigners who made Medan – British, Americans, Dutch and Chinese – also built some interesting buildings for their own use. Most of them are found along **Jl. A. Yani** and around **Merdeka Square**. The **Witte Societeit,** once the exclusive European club, is now the Bank Negara. The old **Hotel de Boer**, once to Medan what Raffles Hotel was to Singapore, is the **Hotel Dharma Deli**. The lofty estate offices of **Harrison & Crossfield** are, appropriately enough, the headquarters of P. T. London Sumatra Indonesia; and the offices of Nienhuys' own company, the **Deli Maatschappij,** now belong to **PTP Tobacco**. The old **Governor's Residence,** on Jl. Jen. Sudirman, is still in use. The art-deco **Immanuel Church,** from 1921, still vibrates with the power of Batak hymns.

During the occupation, the Japanese built a Shinto temple in Medan, one of only two in their short-lived Southeast Asian empire. When British troops reoc-cupied the city in 1945, they stifled their urge to burn it when they realized that it would make a comfortable and stylish officers' mess. Today it is the private **Medan Club**, on Jl. Kartini.

As in Indonesia's other centers of commerce, the Chinese community has been the principal heir to the Dutch business power. **Vihara Gunung Timur** on Jl. Hang Tuah, is Sumatra's biggest Chinese temple; Chinatown is on the east side of the city, around Jl. Pandu. On Jl. A. Yani is the **Tjong A. Fie Mansion**, a lavish pre-war mansion named after its Chinese who owner did not live to see the succession. The unfortunate millionaire died of malnutrition in a Japanese prison camp; his mausoleum is in the **Pulau Brayan Cemetery**. Sukarno forced the last foreign capitalists out of Medan when he nationalized their enterprises in 1957, but today the foreigners are back; Medan has foreign consulates, an international school, even a Japanese club and restaurants. Medan's port is **Belawan**, 28 kilometers from the city center. In 1914,

Right: Enjoying a boat trip on Lake Toba.

it was already handling more than 3000 ships a year; now it is a grim giant's playground of silos, warehouses and storage tanks, eternally under repair and expansion.

What the Europeans called Deli is the entire strip of land east of the central mountains, from Aceh in the north to the Asahan river in the south. Here indentured Chinese and Javanese coolies, fed with opium to complete their dependency, were bought and sold like slaves by landlords whose decadent lifestyle gave the word Deli a taste of scandal as well as gold. The scientific side of the plantation racket was handled by the first branch of the Buitenzorg botanical gardens, in **Sibolangit**. Since 1973, Sibolangit has been joined by a more altruistic biological institution, the **Orangutan Rehabilitation Center** in **Bohorok**, in the Gunung Leuser National Park, 90 kilomters west of Medan (feedings at: 8:00 am and 3:00 pm). On weekends, the wild jungle river near Bohorok and **Bukit Lawang** becomes a playground for Medan's teen-agers; rafting in truck tires is a favorite pastime. New, simple hotels are sprouting along the river bank like mushrooms.

Pematang Siantar lies at the core of what is the most productive plantation area of all, at the foot of the mountains. In the Colonial-style **Siantar Hotel**, one can still "eat like a settler." In **Pangkalan Brandan**, northwest of Medan, the company which became Royal Dutch Shell built the area's first refinery, after a commercial oilfield was opened up in the 1880s. These were the first stirrings of what would develop into Indonesia's vast oil industry.

Since 1957, most of North Sumatra's plantations have been run as state enterprises, an unglamorous, but reliable export machine in the growing shadows of oil and gas refineries. The Deli strip is more than ever a plantation landscape, harshly geometric with its ordered ranks and squares of oil palms, rubber trees and tea bushes. Dusty access roads slice up the green blocks like long yellow wounds in the eroding earth.

THE BATAKLANDS

As the *cultuurgebied* expanded, it encroached upon the territory of tribal peoples over whom the old sultanates had never established firm control. These original inhabitants of North Sumatra are known collectively as *Batak*, and their homeland is that section of Sumatra's mountain backbone between the Alas valley in Aceh and the Minangkabau highlands of West Sumatra. At the widest point in the chain, the pine-covered peaks surround the extraordinary **Lake Toba**; at more than 1000 square kilometers, the biggest lake in Southeast Asia. In turn, the lake encircles the large island of **Samosir**. Batak country is one of the most productive and hospitable natural environments in Sumatra, and might have been expected to become a mighty state, like Java. Instead, it remained a decentralized society of fortified villages

Above: Hotel bungalows in Tuk-Tuk. Right: Batak musicians in Simanindo.

without kings or sultans, constantly torn by war, but reintegrated by trade, kinship and religious ritual.

Heathens and cannibals, the Batak awakened the disgust of European visitors from Marco Polo to Stamford Raffles. Today, they take a tongue-in-cheek pride in their gory past, playing on their primitive image not only to attract tourists, but also to intimidate other Indonesians. The Batak are among the most visible and dynamic ethnic groups in modern Many writers, generals and two prime ministers have come fron among their ranks. The stereotypical Batak is of an honest, blunt and volatile character; indeed, if a non-Batak Indonesian is compelled to speak less circuitously than the mores of his own ethnic group allow, he may apologize first for his "Batak-like" behavior.

In keeping with the fragmented nature of their old society, Bataks speak a number of different dialects and their in customs and religions vary. Conventionally, the Bataks are divided into six categories: Karo, Pakpak, Simelungun, Toba, Angkola and Mandailing. Closest to Medan are the *Karo Batak*, who inhabit the valleys around the new administrative town of **Kabanjahe**. Despite their relative accessibility, the Karo are often described as the most traditional of all the Batak. Most Karo are nominally Christian, but missionaries have always had an uphill struggle here; ancestor worship is still practiced, and sorcery and witchcraft are taken seriously. Many "conversions" have been matters of political expediency. Kinship and the clan system, which governs choice of marriage partners, still dominate all social relations.

The Dutch built an agricultural college in **Brastagi**, 11 kilometers north of Kabanjahe. In 1912, thousands of seed potatoes were distributed among local Batak farmers; they and many other temperate crops caught on, and the area now supplies avocados, cabbage, carrots and

flowers to Singapore, as well as Medan. Brastagi was and is, also a popular holiday resort – the **Bukit Kubu** is one of the most faithfully preserved colonial hotels in Indonesia.

In the Karo village of **Lingga** (eight kilometers southwest), one can see tombs, rice storehouses and an original old clan house that is still inhabited by several families. Another of the area's attractions is climbing the imposing volcano **Mt. Sibayuk**, which dominates the town. Another natural spectacle is the 120-meter waterfall **Sipisopiso**, near **Tongging** overlooking Lake Toba.

West of Tongging is the country of the *Pakpak Batak*, a small and obscure group whose main claim to faim is that they were implicated in the last reported incident of cannibalism in North Sumatra, which took place in 1906.

Related to the Karo are the *Simalungun Batak*, who occupy the northeast bank of the lake. In **Pematang Purba**, the house of a Simalungun chief has been preserved as a museum. The prime exhibit is the building itself; more than 100 years old and a beautiful example of Batak architecture. The all-wood construction is secured by notches and pegs, without a single nail; the roof covering is *ijuk*, thatch from the sugar palm. The gables and supporting piles are carved and painted in abstract patterns. A larger collection of Simalungun ethnographic exhibits is on display at the **Museum Simalungun** in **Pematang Siantar**, on the road down to the coast.

The largest and best-known Batak tribe are the *Toba Batak,* from **Samosir Island** and the lands on three sides of their eponymous lake. With their megaliths, buffalo horns and songs, this is the group people tend to think of as typically Batak. In the late 19th and early 20th centuries, the Toba Batak managed to make the leap from notorious, but respected savages, to proud and even more highly regarded Christians, without losing their own culture in the process. They were converted by German missionaries who placed a stronger emphasis upon the rapid cre-

185

ation of an independent church than their Dutch colleagues. Today, the Toba Batak are the largest coherent Christian community in Indonesia.

As the conventional first stop after Medan, on the overland route through western Indonesia, Lake Toba has become quite a tourist trap. The original resort, the one still favored by domestic visitors, is flashy **Prapat**, on the eastern shore, at the ethnic boundary between the Simalungun and the Toba. International visitors seem to prefer the earthier pleasures of Samosir Island, parts of which, notably the **Tuktuk Peninsula** directly opposite Prapat, are now an almost Kuta-like warren of *losmen*. Many locals have converted their picturesque traditional houses into lucrative tourist accommodations and have, themselves, retreated into simple bungalows to count their cash.

Tomok, the usual port of entry from Prapat, is a good place to see Toba Batak

Above: Ulos of the Karo Batak. Right: Karo clan house in Lingga.

handicrafts and arts. Twenty years of tourism have almost exhausted the supply of actual Toba antiques, but dozens of families sell lengths of beautiful dark *ulos,* the handwoven cloth of the Batak, to visitors. Despite its present commercial role, this cloth is still an important item of ritual exchange in Batak wedding ceremonies.

Under a sacred *harihara* tree in Tomok, one can see the stone sarcophagi of the Sidabutar Rajahs. Though they look like coffins, these normally contained not a prostrate skeleton, but the collected skulls of a whole family or clan, dug up and ceremonially re-interred after a year or so underground. Other such skull-coffins are shaped like round stone urns. A different style of megalith can be found in **Ambarita**, where chairs and tables have been hewn out of single boulders – massive, squat and lichen-covered, like some oversophisticated artistic joke. The villagers revel in their graphic explanation of the part played by this ponderous furniture in gruesome cannibalistic rituals.

Samosir is famous for its striking *adat* houses, distinguished by rakishly curved roofs which their inhabitants compare to the horns of a buffalo. In **Simanindo,** on the northern tip of the island, a particularly fine specimen has been restored to its original state. This was once the home of Raja Dapoton – not a real rajah with kingly powers, but the head of a *bius* or sacrifice-community, a quasi-religious federation of villages which celebrated its spiritual unity with an annual buffalo sacrifice. Buffalo were also slaughtered at the death of a *raja*, and the ten sets of horns attached to one of the main uprights indicates that ten generations of the same dynasty inhabited this house, which became a museum in 1968.

In the mornings, *sigalegale* puppets dance in Simanindo. *Sigalegale* are remarkably life-like human figures made of wood, without any of the comfortably stylized features of the *wayang golek* puppets. The puppets are animated by a complicated mechanism of strings and rollers; their dance is supposed to help diffuse the curse brought about by the death of a childless person, by bringing the spirit of the deceased into the puppet. A sponge in the puppets head's even allow the figures to weep real tears.

Simanindo as a whole is also a good example of a fortified *huta* (village). The stone and earth rampart, with its narrow tunnel gate, is still visible. This was originally augmented by a formidable palisade of sharpened bamboo stakes. The *ruma* (houses) were built in a single row on the lower side of the enclosure; opposite were the smaller *sopo* (rice barns), which also served as sleeping quarters for unmarried boys. A banyan tree also stood in the courtyard, the condition and health of which were supposed to be intimately related with the welfare of the *huta* and its leading family.

The forsaken ruins of more spectacularly fortified *huta* are scattered across several peaks and clifftops in the interior of the island. The landscape here is a wide, dry highland of lava rock, pierced by narrow gorges with vertical, daunting walls embracing streams which become dangerous torrents after heavy rains. There are coffee and clove plantations between stretches of grassland and low forest. A popular two-day trek crosses the island from Tomok or Ambarita, to **Panguru** on the west coast. Pangururan, which has an open-air market on Wednesdays, was the Dutch administrative center for Samosir and the western shores of Lake Toba. From there it is just two kilometers to **air panas**, the hot sulfer springs in **Bukit Pusuk**, which has a few simple *losmen*.

Three kilometers outside **Balige**, an attractive market town on the southern shore of the lake, is the grave of the most famous figure in Batak history: the twelfth and final bearer of the title of

Singamanaraja. Often described as god-kings or priest-kings, the *Singamanaraja* exercised little actual day-to-day power, but were held in religious awe by all Toba Batak. This particular *Singamanaraja* was a serious obstacle both to the German mission and the Dutch government. In 1883, he burned down two mission stations and a church, prompting military intervention in the Toba area. In 1907, the army finally tracked him down, captured and killed him. However, the ancestral home of the *Singamanaraja*, located in **Bakara,** is currently being reconstructed.

To the south of **Tarutung** is part of the more obscure areas which are the domain of the Muslim *Angkola* and *Mandailing Batak*. Not long before Christianity began to tighten its grip on the Toba area, the southern Bataklands were caught in the powerful shock waves of Islamic fervor generated by the Padri wars in Minangkabau, West Sumatra. Today, though far from being the most devout of Sumatra's Muslims, these southerners are re-

187

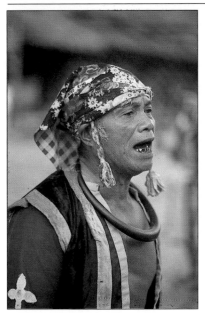

The Batak even wrote using their own modification of an Indian alphabet; museums and souvenir shops in the Toba area display calendars and magical texts in this script, inscribed on bamboo and bark. As knowledge both of Batak anthropology and Sumatran history has increased, the Batak have come to seem more like a fragment of Indic Sumatra, hemmed in by Islam, and defined by the absence of it, than a lost world of ancient tribes. As a source of the medicinal plant product camphor, the Bataklands participated very early in world trade. However, the most tangible evidence North Sumatra's past importance is the startling collection of temple ruins at **Padang Lawas**. Located south of **Gunungtua**, where tributaries of the Barumun river meet, on the eastern flanks of the Barisan mountain range, they are in what is today a very-out-of-the-way area.

Padang Lawas is among the outstanding mysteries of Indonesian archaeology. It constitutes the largest complex of antiquities in Sumatra, yet even the identity of the state which built it is unknown. There are no traces of urban settlement nearby, so it was probably an isolated religious sanctuary, like the Dieng plateau in Java. But for whom? Dated inscriptions here range from the 11th to 14th centuries, but none of them mentions a builder; one appears to be written in a Batak language. There are also no rich basreliefs of everyday life, as there are in Java, to provide clues. Some have associated Padang Lawas with the lost empire of Sriwijaya, but so far this is only supposition.

The Padang Lawas antiquities were discovered in 1845, by the German doctor and naturalist Franz W. Junghuhn, but remained obscure until another German, the eccentric freelance archaeologist Friedrich Schnitger, excavated here in 1935. Schnitger's methods left much to be desired – his accounts, for instance, refer casually to emptying temples of

volted by the dog-eating habits of their Toba neighbours, and are often reluctant to call themselves Batak at all. Of the two groups, the Mandailing are the more southerly, occupying the narrow neck of mountains along the Trans-Sumatran Highway between **Padangsidempuan** and the border with West Sumatra. Traditional Mandailing houses are built on the same principle as those of the Toba, but are far bigger and sometimes have multiple gables that are reminiscent of the Minangkabau style.

PADANG LAWAS

In the past, the Batak were often characterized as textbook "Proto-Malays" and were placed firmly at the bottom of the conventional evolutionary ladder of Indonesian cultures. Yet they were clearly influenced by Indian civilization.

Above: A Nias man wearing a headhunter ring. Right: Performing a war spirit dance in Nias.

their "rubbish," but he did succeed in saving some of the most important statues and inscriptions, which can now be seen in the National Museum in Jakarta, and he recorded the state of the monuments before they deteriorated still further. Many of the twenty-odd temples are little more than rubble today; some, however, have retained their form and decoration. The largest, known as **Biara Bahal I**, has recently been restored. At 13 meters tall, it consists of a hollow *candi* rising above a two-stage terrace and roofed by a hemispherical *stupa*.

Rather more is known about the iconography of these monuments than about their history. Almost all were Buddhist temples, but the Tantric Buddhism practiced here was of a mythical and organic nature. As with all great faiths, time and distance corrupted even this most elegant and intellectual of religions. In medieval Indonesia, it became a royal cult existing alongside Hinduism and stressing various high-pressure mystical shortcuts to enlightenment. One of these shortcuts involved mastering the dark forces in the world by making direct contact with evil and this was the technique celebrated at Padang Lawas. The dancing warriors and half-men on the temple walls are nothing less than demonic images. The ceremonies of the Bhairawa sect included mass human sacrifice; an old text compares the stench of the burning corpses to "the scent of ten thousand flowers." Priests, drunk on human blood, cackled, raved and danced into the night. Some see today's folk traditions as remnants of this Tantric barbarism; the magic wand, for example, which is a Tantric wand that is used as natural healer in Tibetan cloisters, is a *mantri*. Others consider these traditions to be innocent savagery. If the former are correct, even the cannibalism among the Bataks may be a relic of Indic "civilization."

NIAS ISLAND

Some 120 kilometers off the west coast of North Sumatra is one of Indonesia's

189

NIAS ISLAND

0   10   20 km

most spectacular freaks of cultural evolution, the island of **Nias**. It is the largest in a chain of islands that run parallel to the long axis of Sumatra, a half-submerged echo of the mighty Barisan mountain range.

Nias is Indonesia's most striking and most recent specimen of what used to be called a "megalithic culture;" one in which the regular creation of huge stone monuments fulfills important social functions. Although elements of this style and aesthetic can be found elsewhere in the archipelago, the overall effect of the monuments seems somehow "un-Indonesian." A *behu*, for instance, is a stone obelisk, often topped by a statue of a bird, like something out of imperial Rome. A *niogaji* is like a giant stone mushroom decorated, perplexingly, on the underside but not on the top. These and other megaliths were erected either at funeral celebrations or in connection with

the great "feasts of merit" whereby chiefs distributed their wealth to buy the right to increased rank and status. Less easily found today are the carvings which depict Nias warriors in strange, flared, sleeveless tunics and Norman helmets.

Most of what Nias has to offer, by way of art and spectacle, is concentrated in the southern part of the island, where around 30 traditional villages are still inhabited and many other groups of megaliths occur at abandoned settlement sites in the scrubby countryside. Southern Nias was fiercely resistant both to military and spiritual conquest. Dutch military expeditions burned villages here in 1847 and 1863, but it was not until 1908 that colonial power was respected. The Rhineland Missionary Society had to withdraw from its post here in 1886, and Christianity made little headway until after 1920. **Gomo**, an inaccessible place a roadless 15 kilometers from the southeastern coast, is regarded as the cradle of the Nias race, but the most interesting village is **Bawomataluwo**, a short drive from the main southern port, **Teluk Dalam**.

The **Chief's House** in Bawomataluwo is the biggest in Nias and must rank as one of the finest pieces of architecture in Indonesia. The graceful curving roof sweeps up to a majestic height of 16 meters at the ridge; the body is supported on a powerful lattice of wooden piles, each three-quarters of a meter thick. Even the unfortunate replacement of thatch by corrugated iron roofing does not destroy the effect. Inside, complex beamwork under the roof has eliminated the need for large numbers of uprights passing down through the living area, which is consequently as spacious as a castle. Shafts of light from open battens in the roof, illuminate superior woodcarving on walls and beams.

The rest of Bawomataluwo is, correspondingly, the epitome of a traditional southern Nias village. In front of the chief's house are two upended stones;

Right: The crystal-clear waters around Nias lure prospective snorkelers.

one of them, an eight-ton slab, was dragged four kilometers uphill from its quarry, to be erected here in 1914.

These megaliths stand at one end of a skilfully paved stone "runway," formerly used for dancing and ritual. One performance from the old repertoire is still available for tourists, at a price; the famous stone-jumping spectacle, in which athletic youths jump the two-meter stone pyramids to prove their manhood. In the past, this feat was made even more formidable by attatching bamboo blades and stakes to the obstacles. According to one story, the jumping-stone was originally intended as a simulation of the fortifications a warrior would have to face when trying to enter an enemy village.

Ancient Nias was a violent place, even by Indonesian standards. Its tribes were constantly at war with each other, mainly with the intent of procuring slaves for service, sale or ritual sacrifice. Foreigners bought, as well as kidnapped, many Nias slaves; one of the principal consumers in the 18th century was Dutch

Batavia. Small wonder that an important village like Bawomataluwo was built in a matchless defensive location; on a steep prominence approached by a narrow switchback pathway of more than 400 steps. There are fine views of the surrounding countryside, which contains many other interesting villages; a visit to **Hilisimaetano** is particularly recommended.

Despite its relatively recent "discovery" in the 1980s, Nias is no longer *outré* as a tourist destination. However, its eccentric location, destitute middle-class hotels and limited facilities keep it off most standard itineraries. What development there is, is unevenly distributed. The local government has done its best to concentrate accommodation facilities in the administrative capital, **Gunungsitoli**. The center for tours, performances and special events in **Bawomataluwo**, which is almost as worldly as Samosir. From Bawomataluwo, you can see the blue waters of the surfers' Mecca and snorkelers' paradise, **Lagundi Bay**.

MEDAN
(Area Code 061)
Accommodation
LUXURY: **Danau Toba International**, Jl. Imam Bonjol 17, tel: 557000. **Garuda Plaza**, Jl. Sisingamanaraja 18, tel: 716255. **Polonia**, Jl. Jen Sudirman 14, tel: 535111. **Tiara Medan**, Jl. Cut Mutiah, tel: 674000.
MODERATE: **Labana Inn**, Jl. Abd. Lubis 67, tel: 557997. **Garuda City**, Jl. Sisingamangaraja 27, tel: 717733. **Dharma Deli**, Jl. Balai Kota 2, tel: 557744. **Dirgasurya**, Jl. Imam Bonjol 6, tel: 552662. **Pardede International**, Jl. Ir H Juanda 14, tel: 543866. **Sumatera**, Jl. Sisingamangaraja 35, tel: 721551.
BUDGET: **Irama**, Jl. Palang Merah 112, tel: 326416. **Petisah**, Jl. Nibung 22, tel: 522942. **Zakia Hotel**, Jl. Sipisopiso 10, tel: 722413. **Sarah Guesthouse**, Jl. Pertama 10, tel: 719460. **Wisma Yuli**, Jl. Sisingamangaraja, Gg. Pagaruyung, tel: 722413.
Restaurants
INDONESIAN: **De Boer**, in Hotel Dharma Deli. **Bukit Kubu**, Jl. Padang Bulan (7 km from city center). **Garuda**, Jl. Pemuda 20C/D, tel: 717692. **Vegetarian Indonesia**, Jl. Gandhi 63A (next to Bioskop Benteng), tel: 526812.
CHINESE: **Bali Plaza**, Jl. Kumango 1A, tel: 515505/14852. **Hawa Mandarin**, Jl. Mangkubumi 18. **Polonia**, Polonia Hotel, Jl. Sudirman.
WESTERN: **Lyn's**, Jl. Jen A. Yani. **Tip Top**, Jl. A. Yani.
Shopping
ANTIQUES & CURIOS: The specialty street is Jl. Jen. A. Yani. **Indonesia Art Shop**, no. 1A. **Borobudur Art Shop**, no. 32. **Toko Yulida**, no. 33. **Toko Selatan**, no. 44. **Toko Masrilusa**, no.61. **Toko Bali**, no. 68.
ART: **ABC Art Gallery**, Jl. Jen. A. Yani 50. **Nu Chou** (Chinese brush painting), Jl. Thamrin 74 (above Phoenix photo studio). **Simpassri** (local artists' display), Jl. Jen Suprapto, off Jl. Teratai.
Museums
North Sumatra State Museum, Jl. H. M. Joni, tel: 715799. Tue-Sun 8:30 am-5 pm, closed Mon. **Museum Juang 45** (revolutionary history), Jl. Pemuda 17. Mon-Thu & Sat 8:30 am-1 pm, Fri 8:30-12, closed Sun. **Museum Perjuangan 'Bukit Barisan'** (military), Jl. Palang Merah, tel: 716972. Mon-Thu 8 am-3 pm, Fri 8-11, Sat 8-12, closed Sun.
Zoos
Medan Zoo, Jl. Brigjen Katamso, Desa Baru. Daily 8 am-4 pm. **Crocodile Farm**, 8 km NW, in Asam Kumbang, open daily 9 am-5 pm, feedings 4:30 pm.
Cultural Events
Bina Budaya, Jl. Perintis Kemerdekaan (opp. Angkasa Hotel). Twice-weekly cultural events. **Taman Ria Amusement Park**. Permanent cultural exhibits and occasional performances. **Tapian Daya Cultural Centre**, Jl. Binjai.

Tourist Information
North Sumatra Tourist Office, Jl. J. A. Yani 107, tel: 538101. Mon-Thu 7:30 am -4 pm, Fri 7:30-12, closed Sat & Sun.
Post / Telecommunications
At the intersection of Jl. Balai Kota and Jl. Prof. H. M. Yamin.
Hospitals
Rumah Sakit Umum Dr. Pirngadi (General Hospital), Jl. Prof. H. M. Yamin 47, tel: 713332. Private hospitals: **St. Elizabeth**, Jl. Imam Bonjol 38, tel: 322455. **Herna**, Jl. Mojopahit 118, tel: 510766.
Consulates
United Kingdom, Jl. Jen. A. Yani 2, tel: 518699. **USA**, Jl. Imam Bonjol 13, tel: 712200/712463.
Arrival / Transportation
AIR: Regular flights from Medan's **Polonia Airport** to Penang, Singapore, Jakarta as well as Frankfurt and Vienna. *Airline offices:* **Garuda**, Jl. Balai Kota 2 Dharma Deli Hotel), tel: 516400. **Merpati**, Jl. Brig. Jen. Katamso 72, tel: 514057. **Mandala**, Jl. Brig. Jen. Katamso 37E, tel: 56379. **MAS** (Malaysia), in Hotel Danau Toba International, Jl. Imam Bonjol 17, tel: 519333. **Singapore Airlines**, Jl. Sudirman 14 (in Polonia Hotel), tel: 325300. **SMAC**, Jl. Imam Bonjol 59, tel: 537760. **Thai Airways**, Jl. Balai Kota 2 (Dharma Deli Hotel), tel: 510541.
SEA: Passenger boats connect Medan and Penang once daily; tickets from **Trophy Tours**, Jl. Brig. Jen. Katamso 33D, tel: 514888, or **Eka Sukma Wisata**, Jl. Sisingamangaraja 92A, tel: 720421. *Damri* busses to the port (Belawan) leave from Stasiun Sambu, Jl. Sutomo (city center). **Pelni** operates services to Tanjung Pinang (Riau) & Jakarta. **Pelni office**, Jl. Kol. Sugiono 5, tel: 518899, or Jl. Palang Merah, Belawan.
BUS: **Pinang Bari** bus station, 10 km NW of center, for all destinations N of Medan (Brastagi, Binjai, Banda Aceh). **Amplas** bus station, 7 km SE, for all southern cities (Prapat, Padang, Jakarta).
LOCAL: **Sambu terminal**, near market, is main *bemo* station; *becak* are often easier to find. Taxis with meters and air-conditioning: **Metax**, tel: 550711, **KARSA**, tel: 520952. Main taxi stands: Polonia Hotel & Danau Toba International Hotel.

BOHOROK
90 km from Medan. Orangutan feeding at 8 am and 3 pm. Permit in WWF Visitor Center in Bukit Lawang; passport necessary. Departure 45 minutes before feedings. Guides only necessary for longer tours. Lodging in 16 simple hotels along the river.

BRASTAGI
(Area Code 0628)
LUXURY: **Sibayak International**, Jl. Merdeka, tel: 91301. *MODERATE:* **Brastagi Cottage**, Jl. Gundal-

ing, tel: 91345. **Bukit Kubu**, Jl. Sempurna 2, tel: 91524. **Rose Garden**, Jl. Peceren, tel: 91777. **Rudang Hotel**, Jl. Sempurna 3, tel: 91579. *BUDGET:* **Wisma Dieng**, Jl. Udara 27. **Ginsata Hotel**, Jl. Veteran 27, tel: 91441. **Wisma Sibayak**, Jl. Udara 1, tel: 91104. Inexpensive bungalows just out of town, including: **Karo Hill**, Jl. Pendidikan.

PRAPAT
(Area Code 0625)

LUXURY: **Danau Toba International**, Jl. Kol. Tpr. Sinaga 17, tel: 41583. **Natour Hotel Prapat**, Jl. B. Jamin Purba 1, tel: 41012. **Niagara**, Jl. Pembangunan 1, tel: 41028. *MODERATE:* **Atsari**, Jl. Kol. Tpr. Sinaga. **Budi Mulya**, Jl. Kol. Tpr. Sinaga 17, tel: 41216, tel: 41216. *BUDGET:* **Pago Pago Inn**, Jl. Haranggaol. **Soloh Jaya**, Jl. Haranggaol. On Jl. Sisingamanaraja: **Singgalang**. On the market: **Charlie Guesthouse**.

Cultural Events
Batak Cultural Centre, Jl. Josef Sinaga 19. Music and dance events Sat nights. **Prapat Hotel** also stages cultural performances. Week-long Danau Toba festival held every June.

Shopping
Jl. Sisingamangaraja for souvenirs; **Saturday market** (Tigaraja ferry dock). **Labuhan Graha**, 25 km from Prapat, specializes in *ulos* cloth.

Tourist Information / Post
Pusat Informasi, Jl. Kol. Tpr. Sinaga (at entrance to Prapat). **Post office**, Jl. Sisingamangaraja.

Arrival / Transportation
PT Andilo Nancy & other agencies on Jl. Sisingamangaraja sell long-distance bus tickets. Ferries for Samosir from **Tigaraja dock**, near the market.

SAMOSIR
(Area Code 0625)

MODERATE: **Silinton Hotel**, Tuktuk, tel: 41345. **Carolina**, Tuktuk. **Toledo Inn**, Tuktuk. **Pulau Tao Cottage**, on island off Simanindo.
BUDGET: Concentrated on Tuktuk peninsula, with more than 40 lakeside *losmen*. **Tuktuk Timbul**, the Siallagan Family's bungalow hotel, is a quiet enclave between Tuktuk & Ambarita, tel: 41374.

Shopping
Tomok's main street is permanent market for Toba Batak crafts and souvenirs.

Museum
Museum Huta Bolon, Simanindo, Samosir. Open daily 9 am-5 pm.

Cultural Events
Inquire at **Golden Tourist Information Service**, Tomok, & **Museum Huta Bolon**, Simanindo.

Arrival / Transportation
Regular ferries between Prapat & Tomok, and between Tigaras & Simanindo. Road bridge approach via Tele on W side of lake. Buses drive almost the entire circumference of island, and from the W drive inland as far as Roonggurni. Motorcycles can be rented on Tuktuk.

AROUND LAKE TOBA

Museum Pemda, Jl. Pasanggrahan 1, Balige. **Museum Rumah Bolon Pematang Purba**, Pematang Purba. Mon-Sat 7:30 am-4:30 pm, closed Sun.

PEMATANG SIANTAR
(Area Code 0622)

Museum Simalungun, Jl. Jen. Sudirman 10, tel: 21054. Mon-Sat 8 am-3 pm, closed Sun. **Pematang Siantar Zoo**, Jl. Kapt. M. H. Sitorus 10, tel: 21511. Mon-Thu 8 am-3 pm, Fri 8-11:30, Sat 8 am-2 pm, Sun 8 am-6 pm.

SIBOLGA
(Area Code 0631)

MODERATE: **Hotel Tapianauli**, Jl. S. Parman 5, tel: 21816 (N of city). **Nauli Hotel**, Jl. Dr. Sutomo 17 (E of city), tel: 22326. *BUDGET:* **Indah Sari Hotel**, Jl. A Yani 29, tel: 22208. **Pasar Baru Hotel**, Jl. Suprapto 41, tel: 22167.

NIAS
(Area Code 0639)
Accommodation

GUNUNGSITOLI: In town center: **Hotel Hawaii**, Jl. Sirao, tel: 21021. 4 km out of town: **Wisma Soliga**, Jl. Diponegoro 432, tel: 21815.

TELUKDALAM: Sabar Menanti, **Wisma Jamburae**, **Effendi**, all near waterfront.

LAGUNDI BAY: A dozen *losmen* with attached eating places in **Jamburai**.

OTHER: Most villages, incl. Bawomataluo, can arrange overnight accommodation for courteous visitors, usually in the mayor's home.

Arrival / Transportation
AIR: SMAC has scheduled flights Medan-Gunungsitoli (**Binaka Airport**, 19 km from town).
SEA: Jumping-off point for Nias is **Sibolga**, 107 km from Prapat. One boat daily to Gunungsitoli (N Nias); Daily except Sun, 1 boat to Telukdalam (S Nias), from harbor (Pelabuhan) 2 km S of town. Tickets from **P.T. Simeulue**, Jl. Pelabuhan 9, at old harbor near center of town.
LOCAL: Regular daily buses from Gunungsitoli to Telukdalam (120 km, 6-hour trip), but roads elsewhere are often only suitable for motorcycles or walking.

PADANG LAWAS

From **Padangsidempuan**, buses leave for **Gunungtua**, which has *oplet* services to **Portibi**, access point for the ruins.

MALAY SUMATRA

THE RIAU ARCHIPELAGO
MAINLAND RIAU
SOUTH SUMATRA PROVINCE
JAMBI

Colonialism and commerce may have made Medan, in many ways, the heart of Sumatra, but it is a very eccentric heart. The plantation zone is a freak of fertility at the northern extremity of a great band of malarial lowland jungle and acid mangrove swamp, which stretches down two-thirds of the length of Sumatra, east of the Barisan range. The dominant element in this, perhaps the most quintessentially Sumatran landscape, is water.

Huge brown rivers wind ponderously across the wide, wet, olive-drab plain to discharge themselves into branching, brackish deltas. At the coast, the mangrove-lined tidal channels interlock with each other until the divide between land and sea is unclear; the coastline seems to crumble gradually eastwards into a maze of islands.

The dominant people of this watery country are the *Malays*; historically the most influential and the best known of all Indonesia's ethnic groups. Not without reason did English writers, before the rise of modern national terminology, refer to the whole of island Southeast Asia as the "Malay Archipelago."

The Malay language was the *lingua franca* for traders from Aceh to the Phil-

ippines long before it became, in slightly different forms, the national languages of both Indonesia and Malaysia. "Malay" was a synonym for the Muslim, maritime culture which united the trading ports of the island world; a flexible category which almost anyone could join by converting to the Islamic faith and speaking the Malay language. People calling themselves Malays were found everywhere in the archipelago, and even today members of interior tribes in Kalimantan still *masuk Melayu* ("enter Malay-ness") to become respectable in the cosmopolitan coastal towns. However, the accepted homelands of the Malay people are eastern Sumatra and the Malay peninsula, on opposite sides of the Strait of Malacca.

Modern political geography has thus split the Malay world down the middle. In the space of a few decades, Sumatran Malays have learned to regard their cousins in Malaysia as foreigners, and Christians from Ambon as compatriots. Within Indonesia, however, the Malays still perceive themselves as a distinct ethnic group. In Sumatra they dominate the three east-coast provinces of **Riau**, **Jambi** and **South Sumatra**, with a combined population of some eight million people; about a quarter the entire Sumatran population on less than half of its overall the land area.

Left: Women selling fruits and vegetables on Riau Island.

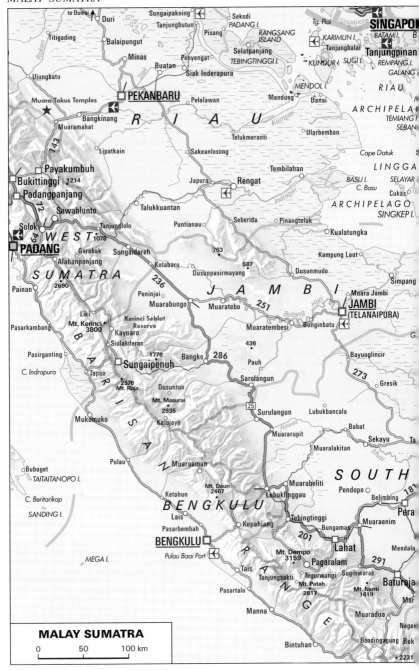

MALAY SUMATRA

0   50   100 km

to Dumai · Duri · Sungaipakning · Sekodi · PADANG I. · Tg. Piai · Singapore Strait · SINGAPORE · BATAM I. · B

Titigading · Balaipungut · Tanjungbutun · Pisang · RANGSANG ISLAND · KARIMUN I. · Tanjungbalar · BATAM I. · Tanjungpinan

Ujungbatu · Minas · Buatan · Penyengat · Selatpanjang · TEBINGTINGGI I. · KUNDUR I. · SUGI I. · REMPANG I. · GALANG

Muara Takus Temples · Bangkinang · Siak Inderapura · Pelalawan · MENDOL I. · Mendung · Danai · RIAU ARCHIPELAGO

Muaramahat · R I A U · Telukmeranti · Ularbemban · TEMIANG I. · SEBAN

143 · Lipatkain · Sakeanlosong · Cape Datuk · L I N G G A

Payakumbuh · Japura · Rengat · Tembilahan · BASU I. · C. Basu · SELAYAR · Cukas

Bukittinggi 1214 · Padangpanjang · Talukkuantan · Seberida · Pinangteluk · A R C H I P E L A G O SINGKEP I.

Sawahlunto · 72 · W E S T · Tanjunglolo · Puntianau · Kualatungka · Simpang

Solok · 1078 · Garabak · Sungaidareh · 763 · Kampung Laut

PADANG · Alahanpanjang · S U M A T R A · Kotabaru · 587 · Dusunmudo

Painan · 2690 · Peninjai · Dusunpasirmayang · J A M B I · Muara Jambi · G.

Muarabungo · Muaratebo · 251 · JAMBI (TELANAIPURA) · Batang Hari

Liki · Mt. Kerinci 3800 · Kayuaro · 236 · Muaratembesi · Bunginbatu · Bayunglincir

Pasarkambang · Siulakderas · 436 · 273 · Gresik

Pasirganting · Kerinci Seblat Reserve · 1778 · Bangko · 286 · Pauh

C. Indrapura · Tapan · Sungaipenuh · Sarolangun · B A R I S A N

2576 Mt. Raja · Dusuntuo · 25 · Surulangun · Lubukbancala · Babat

Mukomuko · Mt. Masurai 2935 · Katojayo · Muararupit · Sekayu · Ta

Pulau · Rawas · Muaralakitan · Musi

Bububget · Muaraaman · S O U T H

TAITAITANOPO I. · Ketahun · Mt. Daun 2467 · Muarabeliti · Pendopo · Belimbing · 181

C. Beritarikap · SANDING I. · B E N G K U L U · Lubuklinggau · Pera

Lais · Tebingtinggi · Muaraenim · Mendala

MEGA I. · Pasarbembah · Kepahiang · Bungamas · 291

BENGKULU · Mt. Dempo 3159 · 201 · Lahat · Baturaja

Pulau Baai Port · Tais · Tegurwangi · Pagaralam · Sugihwaras · Mar

Pasartalo · Tanjungsakti · Mt. Patah 2817 · Mt. Nanti 1619 · Muaradua

Manna · R A N G E · Bandingagung · Buk

Bintuhan · Negeri · 2231

APUR I.

BESAR I.

NGGA ISLAND

Tengkis

C. Samak

Belinyu BANGKA

Bakit

Sungailiat

Kelapa 705

Tanjungniur

Muntok □PANGKALPINANG

Carat

ungsang *Bangka* C. Selokan Pangkol

Koba

Berikat

Airgegas 654

Saleh *Strait*

LEPAR I.

LEMBANG

aju Toboali Sadai

C. Baginda

U M A T R A C. Kait

graja *Lumpur*

uagung

Talang Rimbo

Talangjauh C. Lumut

Musi

Talangbatu

ratu

ngratu Menggala C. Serdang

MPUNG

bumi Surabaya

Seputih

25 Bandar Jaya

THE RIAU ARCHIPELAGO

As befits a maritime people, the Malays centerd their culture not on the mainland, but in the **Riau Archipelago** which is scattered across the narrow southern end of the Strait of Malacca, just off the tip of the Malay peninsula. This critical strategic location astride the most important shipping lane in the world has made Riau a historic focus of power and piracy, wealth and war. The cultural and historical interest of insular Riau combines with its accessibility and the desert-island beauty of its coasts and islets – almost uniqe in eastern Sumatra – to make this, for many foreigners, the most immediately attractive and favored part of Malay Sumatra.

After the fateful fall of Malacca to the Portuguese in 1511, the descendants of the Malaccan sultans established a new kingdom, Johor, further south. At various times the royal seat of Johor was not in present-day Johor, on the Malay peninsula opposite Singapore, but in Riau. As in Java, the repeated changes of capital were usually caused by succession quarrels and civil wars. In 1819, Raffles took advantage of one of these to snatch one of the Riau islands from under the noses of the Dutch; his prize was to become the city-state of Singapore, whose skyscrapers now gaze distainfully across the water. British intervention saw the old state of Johor permanently divided into two kingdoms: Johor proper, on the British (now Malaysian) side of the strait, and **Riau-Lingga** on the Dutch (Indonesian) side.

Riau-Lingga was itself the uneasy union of two distinct courts: that of the native Malay sultan and that of a Bugis viceroy. Early Indonesian politics favored such two-headed states, but the ethnic division was unusual. The Bugis aristocrats descended from interlopers from the east who, dispersing from their South Sulawesi homeland during the

197

wars of the 17th and 18th centuries, insinuated themselves into the ruling elites of many Malay states. The Bugis court was based on the tiny island of **Penyengat**, across the harbor from **Tanjung Pinang**, on the south side of the Riau archipelago's largest island, **Bintan**. When the position of viceroy was abolished under Dutch pressure, at the beginning of the 20th century, Penyengat became the true capital of a united kingdom; but in 1911 the refractory sultan was dismissed by the Dutch and replaced by direct Dutch administration.

Penyengat is well worth a visit because of its historic remains, which are now being progressively restored. The palace buildings themselves have been destroyed or have vanished, but several royal tombs and an attractive, old, yellow mosque are in good condition. The mosque contains a unique library which includes some hand-scripted korans. Riau has an old reputation as a literary center for the Malay language, and when the Dutch decided, in the 1890s, to standardize the Malay language used in their administration and school system, it was the Riau variant which they selected as the official model.

Long known as a den of smugglers, the fast-growing port of **Tanjung Pinang** bustles with the business, shady and otherwise, of three countries. The goldsmiths accept Singapore dollars, the televisions in coffee shops and restaurants are more likely to be showing ads from Kuala Lumpur than Jakartan propaganda. There are some parks, supermarkets and pre-fab concrete suburbs, but at its heart Tanjung Pinang is still a raw Malay trading town of wood and water. Houses are built on long piles, over the sea which serves as both street and sewer. Local travel is by boat or along rickety wooden walkways which are suspended over

Right: A market trader selling her wares in Riau.

slicks of waterborne garbage. Watercraft of all descriptions fuss bewilderingly to and fro while an amplified call to prayer floats across th harbour from a tin-roofed mosque. These are images that repeat throughout the Malay areas of Sumatra. The **Riau Kandil Museum**, about two kilometers outside Tanjung Pinang, is an informative tribute to the way of life which they symbolize.

The commercial dynamism of Tanjung Pinang is mainly parasitic, or exploitive. Since the foundation of Singapore, Indonesian Riau has been forced into the economic shadow of its northern neighbors, picking up crumbs by providing odd services unavailable or prohibitively expensive across the water. There is, for instance, no direct surface link from Singapore to mainland Sumatra; sea passengers must transfer in Tanjung Pinang. Just outside the town, the twin villages that are simply known as **Kampung 12** and **Kampung 16**, meet the demands of another type of visitor; those who come looking for regulated, cheap prostitution. Even nature is exploited; a giant development project is transforming a large part of **Batam Island** into an industrial zone.

Beyond Batam and Bintan, Riau quickly becomes wilder. Most settlements are just tiny pile-top fishing villages, sometimes perched out on fringing reefs, hundreds of meters from land and fresh water. Hundreds of islands are completely uninhabited, but at night, the straits between them are sprinkled with the man-made stars of pressure lanterns, used by fishermen to lure dazzled fish to *prahu* and stilt-houses on the dark water. The warm, shallow seas of the Riau archipelago are as clear as gin and contain a spectacular marine life; divers also come here for to explore the wrecks which the wars and storms of the centuries have left among the coral.

Near **Tanjungbalai**, on **Karimun Island** west of Batam, a Buddhist religious inscription has been cut in Indic charac-

ters into a flat rock. This utterly isolated antiquity is one of the earliest pieces of evidence of Indian culture in Indonesia. The island of **Lingga**, which lies due south of Bintan, was the seat of the Malay half of the Riau-Lingga state in the 19th century. The jungle-beleaguered remains of the royal palace and mosque, together with the graves of the Malay sultans, lie within walking distance of the little port of **Daik**. **Dabo**. The adjacent island of **Singkep**, is the center of a small, tin mining industry. In the days of the sultanate, Singkep paid its annual tribute in this metal. The province of Riau also includes the much more remote islands that are thinly scattered across the South China Sea; as far east as Borneo and as far north as the nature reserve of **Pulau Laut**, on the same latitude as Brunei. Driving a wedge of Indonesian territorial water between the two halves of Malaysia, these otherwise insignificant outposts of the *merah putih* are jealously guarded because of their strategic importance and suspected oil wealth.

MAINLAND RIAU

Ancient Riau was a sea kingdom with dependencies on mainland Sumatra, but the modern province of Riau includes a huge slice of the mother island, known as **Riau Daratan** or Mainland Riau. The capital is no longer Tanjung Pinang, but **Pekanbaru**, a new town about 160 km inland on the **Siak river**. Like every big river in eastern Sumatra, the Siak once supported a trading kingdom of its own – **Siak Sri Indrapura**, now an obscure little place half-way between Pekanbaru and the sea. The last palace of the defunct sultanate has been preserved there as the **Museum Asserajah El Hasyimiah**. Built between 1886 and 1889, it is an interesting piece of architecture from the beginning of the golden age of Dutch imperialism, a solid castle-like construction with Islamic styling, set in elegant gardens. The building was renovated and the museum established with financial aid from the new lord of the Siak, the oil giant Caltex.

Caltex has also sponsored the meteoric growth of Pekanbaru itself. Until the discovery, on the eve of the Pacific war, of major oil deposits to its north, Pekanbaru was just a lively but small river-port at the highest navigable point on the Siak. Today it is a booming oil town with an international airport. Pekanbaru's roads, power, education and health services are all well above usual Indonesian standards. The oil wells themselves are scattered over a huge tract of forest, but the very earliest, which first flowed in March 1941, can be seen, complete with commemorative plaque, on the main road three kilometers north of the **Minas** camp. The Siak river is navigable, but not for tankers, so the oil is pumped through a prodigious surface pipeline directly to the purpose-built port and refinery in **Dumai**, one of the biggest oil terminals in the world.

The forests surrounding these oilfields are the home of one of lowland Sumatra's enigmatic tribal populations, known by local Malays as the *Sakai*. It is not really known whether they represent a pre-Malay "remnant," like the upland Bataks, or an isolated splinter of later migrations – fugitive slaves, perhaps. The Malays regard them with the customary mixture of contempt and fear, despising their lack of civilization, but being half-animist themselves, they often fear the spiritual power of the tribesmen. Oil drilling, as such, is relatively friendly to the environment, and has not destroyed the rain forest habitat of the Sakai, nor its rich fauna; which includes tapirs, rhinos and even tigers. However, the logging industry, which eagerly makes use of the jungle roads constructed by the oilmen, poses an ever increasing threat. The government is trying to resettle the Sakai in permanent villages, where they can be educated and controlled. Some have voluntarily moved to the Rumbai-Dumai road, where their thatched bamboo huts stand in jarring contrast to the shining oil

pipeline which has brought so much change to Sumatra.

Apart from the Siak, other important rivers of mainland Riau include the **Rokan** and the **Kampar**, which are renowned for the spectacular and dangerous tidal bores which surge along them during the spring tides. River-dwelling Malays have made a sport of "surfing" the advancing wave in small canoes; on the Kampar, this forms the core of an annual festival.

High on the clear upper reaches of the Kampar, near the border with West Sumatra and at the foot of the Barisan range, is the only well-known antiquity of Riau province: a small but striking group of Buddhist temples known as **Muara Takus**. Of the several buildings that are visible, **Maligai Stupa** is the best preserved. The slender, waisted, uncluttered profile of this *stupa* reveals a gentler aesthetic at work than that which produced Padang Lawas.

Beneath its crumbling brick skin, Maligai has a core of hard sandstone which has saved its graceful form from the ravages of time. The temples at Muara Takus probably date from the 11th and 12th centuries. Like those at Padang Lawas, they have been associated with the shadowy empire of Srivijaya, which Chinese sources depict rising from nowhere in the late 7th century to dominate the whole of the western archipelago for 600 years. In 1937, a Dutch scholar suggested that Muara Takus was the site of the Srivijaya capital itself, thus giving Riau its own stake in a mystery which has been hotly debated ever since.

SOUTH SUMATRA PROVINCE

Much evidence suggests that Srivijaya was based not at a remote interior citadel, but at a great trading port, and the conventional favorite has always been **Palembang**. The southern-most of the large Malay towns, modern Palembang is

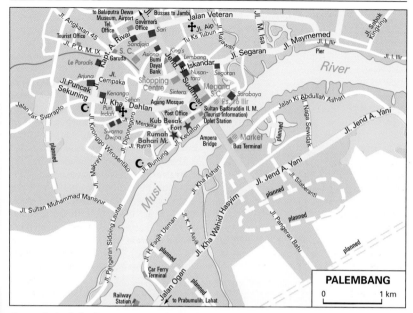

PALEMBANG

0   1 km

the capital of the important province of South Sumatra, and the largest city on the island, after Medan. Palembang is not a coastal harbor, but a river port some 100 kilometers from the mouth of the **Musi river**. The Musi is Sumatra's largest river, draining an area of rain forest almost as big as Ireland; by the time it reaches Palembang it is already hundreds of meters wide and navigable for ships of 10,000 tons. Salt and fresh water are all the same to the amphibian culture of the Malays, who have reproduced the waterborne lifestyle of the Riau archipelago here in the heart of Sumatra. The banks are lined with the pile-top settlements of the Musi, from Palembang to the sea, with the piles increasing in length with the tidal range. In **Sungsang**, the floors stand a dizzy five meters above the river at low water, and visitors can walk for kilometers along high *nipah*-trunk boulevards. There used to be countless dwellings which literally floated on rafts, but these are beginning to disappear. Many Palembang Malays prefer to build their homes over water even when roads and building land are available. A thousand years ago, the situation was probably not very different. One account of the Srivijayan capital indicates that the king lived on dry land, but his subjects made their homes on the water, where they were exempt from paying taxes.

That the city was composed mainly of wooden pile-buildings helps to explain why so few relics of Srivijaya's greatness have survived. Of the moderate haul of inscriptions and Buddhist images collected here over the years, many have long since been removed to the National Museum in Jakarta. The remainder are on display in Palembang's **Balaputra Dewa (Provincial) Museum**. One of the finest is a serene Buddha carved in granite, a rock which does not occur near Palembang and must have been imported. Other exhibits include Chinese pottery which was excavated in the city. **Bukit Seguntang**, in the southern end of the city, is supposed to have been the site of a religious sanctuary. Local legend has it

201

ing one of the most powerful sultanates in Sumatra and a wily and resilient opponent of both Javanese and European expansion. The VOC defeated Palembang and established a fort there in 1659, but the sultanate retained considerable autonomy. The **Grand Mosque** in the center of town was founded in 1740, at a time of renewed wealth and expansion. Most of Palembang's sultans are buried in the **Royal Cemetery**. The best-known today, is Mahmud Badaruddin, whose slaughter of the resident Dutch garrison in 1811, led to his eventual exile in 1821, and to the end of real independence for Palembang. Under Dutch rule, Palembang increased in commercial importance and in 1900 it was the largest city in Sumatra. The presence of Chinese also grew accordingly. On **Kemaro Island**, at the confluence of the Musi and two of its tributaries, there is a picturesque Chinese temple that is about 100 years old.

that a descendant of Alexander the Great came down to this hill, from heaven, to become the first king of Srivijaya. Even allowing for tropical rates of decay, the absence of temple ruins is surprising given that when a Chinese pilgrim visited Srivijaya in A.D. 671, there were reportedly a thousand monks there, studying Buddhist texts. So, enough doubt remains for speculation as to the location of Srivijaya to continue.

After the demise of Srivijaya in the 14th century, Palembang seems to have come under the rule of Javanese kings. Strong Javanese cultural influence is still evident. For instance, Palembang is one of only two places outside Java which have traditionally produced *batik* cloth. The traditional house of the Palembang elite, with its two-tier *limasan* roof, also clearly demonstrates Javanese elements.

Despite the Javanese influx, Palembang regained its independence, becom-

The standard symbol of modern Palembang is the monumental **Ampera Bridge**, the only road link between the two halves of the city. It stretches across the brown depths of the Musi and when it was built in 1964, the central span could be raised to the top of its high pillars, allowing big ships to pass underneath; but ambitious mechanisms tend to have short working lives in Indonesia, and it has been out of order for a long time.

The source of Palembang's wealth has changed repeatedly over its long history. It is often said that Srivijaya, in contrast to the great Javanese kingdoms, possessed no agricultural hinterland, drawing its power instead from gold, luxury forest products, transit trade and military might. However, skilful land management has made the drier parts of Palembang's hinterland a valuable garden of rice, rubber, coffee, cotton and fruit.

In the 17th century, pepper, native to the foothills of the Himalayas, was the main trade crop. Howeverk, minerals have been just as important to the area as

Above: Chinese inhabitant of Tanjung Pinang. Right: Everyday life on muddy waters.

the agricultural products. In the 18th century, Palembang had the good fortune to gain control of the newly discovered sources of valuable tin on the islands of **Bangka** and **Belitung**, opposite the mouth of the Musi. Tin is still mined on these islands, where much of the population descends from the Chinese contract-coolies once shipped from Canton to work the same mines.

In the 20th century, oil overshadowed all other exports. The first drilling concession in the Palembang area was issued in 1899, not long after the first finds in North Sumatra and long before the opening of the Riau fields. The South Sumatra Basin is now the biggest and most productive oilfield in Indonesia, exploited by the state oil giant Pertamina, which has given Palembang its television station, sports stadium and clock tower. The Pertamina headquarters is in **Plaju**, just east of Palembang, where the cracking towers and gantries of a huge refinery and petrochemicals plant stand like a floodlit space platform in the jungle.

On the western margin of South Sumatra is a set of monuments dating from the opposite end of Indonesian history; the **Pasemah Megaliths**. These mysterious carved stones lie scattered throughout the valley beyond **Lahat**, where a tributary of the Musi cuts into the Barisan mountain range near the border with Bengkulu province. Some of the most striking megaliths, including the magnificent elephant sculpture known as *Batu Gajah*, have been removed to the museum in Palembang, but many remain, including an impressive concentration in **Tegurwangi**, between **Pagaralam** and **Tanjungsakti**.

Though they are conventionally described as "prehistoric," recent research indicates that at least somr are from the 7th century or later, contemporary with Srivijaya. At any rate, these are no "stone age" monuments; many of the sculptures depict figures with metal swords and rings, and even bronze kettledrums of the Dong Son pattern known to have come to Indonesia at the beginning of the Chris-

203

tian era. They must, therefore, represent a sustained megalithic tradition, comparable to those of Nias and Samosir. The monuments at Pasemah include avenues of upright stones, troughs with human heads at each end, giant rice-pounding blocks, stone terraces, hollow chests and statues, and basrelief carvings which utilize the natural curves of their parent boulders so skilfully that they resemble three-dimensional sculptures. Even the sparse local population, which claims descent from Javanese Majapahit, is at a loss to explain the purpose of most of the imagery, and nothing suggests that this remote valley will ever divulge the secrets of its past.

The desolate, riverine wilderness north of the Musi is home to the *Kubu* tribesmen, a marginal forest people comparable to the Sakai of mainland Riau. Malays make much of the story that despite living their lives surrounded by rivers and swamps, their superstitious fear of water is so great that they never bathe. The ancestral hearth of the Kubu is supposed to lie on the **Lalang river**, one of the emptiest parts of Sumatra.

JAMBI

Sandwiched between the giants of South Sumatra and Riau is the smaller province of **Jambi**. The central artery of Jambi, the **Batang Hari river**, springs from the mountains of West Sumatra and meanders for almost 800 kilometers across the eastern plain, making it even longer than the mighty Musi, though not as broad or powerful. Like the Musi, the Batang Hari is an historic highway of Malay commerce, and Melayu, the ancient kingdom of the Batang Hari, gave its name to the entire Malay race.

This Melayu seems to have pre-existed even Srivijaya, sending tribute to imperial China as early as the 5th century. In the late 7th century, Melayu seems to have become a Srivijayan vassal, but it maintained an autonomous existence of sorts until 600 years later, when it freed itself from Srivijayan influence with the help of Javanese allies, and ultimately inherited some of the fading luster of Srivijaya for itself.

The capital is thought to have been **Muara Jambi**, a short distance down the Batang Hari from the present provincial capital, which bears the same name as the province. The ruins of seven temples can be made out on the riverside, but the standard of preservation is disappointing. Like Srivijaya, Melayu has left nothing photogenic for the sightseer. Nor does modern Jambi have much to offer after Palembang, except some *batik* workshops and fine 19th-century Malay houses with carved gables and shutters.

From Jambi, the most interesting road runs west towards the mountains, following the current of Sumatran history after the demise of Srivijaya. In 1347, a prince called Adityavarman was sent from East Java to govern Sumatra, now known generally as Melayu, in the name of the kingdom of Majapahit. Born of a mixed marriage between a Melayu princess and a Javanese noble, Adityavarman was a member of the same Bhairawa sect that built the grim shrines at Padang Lawas; a huge statue found on the upper Batang Hari, and now on display in the National Museum in Jakarta, depicts him as a demonic, snake-draped figure standing on a corpse, which in turn rests on a pedestal of human skulls.

Adityavarman did not stay in Jambi long, but moved upriver to the Barisan mountains, taking with him both the historic luster of Srivijaya and Melayu, and the dark aura of his sect. By the time the first European ships arrived in the Malacca Strait, Islamic sultanates were the masters of coastal and riverine Sumatra. However, the natives continued to live in awe of a vague and mysterious king, who held court somewhere in the remote mountains of West Sumatra.

TANJUNG PINANG (Area Code 0771)
Accommodation
LUXURY: **Bintan Beach Resort**, Jl. Pantai Impian 1, tel: 23661. **Paradise**, Jl. Potong Lembu 58B, tel: 21831. *MODERATE:* **Wisma Riau**, Jl. Yusuf Kahar 8, tel: 21023. **Rainbow**, Jl. D. I. Panjaitan, km 6, tel: 21982. **Garden Hotel**, Jl. G. Subroto 282, km 5, tel: 22344. *BUDGET:* **Johnny's Guest House**, Jl. Lorong Bintan II 22, tel: 23996. **Bong's Homestay**, Jl. Lorong Bintan II 20, tel: 25624.

Museum
Riau Kandil Museum, Jl. Bakarbatu, 2 km outside town on road to Kijang.

Telecommunications / Post
Telecom, Jl. Hang Tuah 11, open 24-hours. **Post office**, Jl. Merdeka 17, Mon-Sat 8 am-8 pm, Sun 8 am-1 pm.

Arrival / Transportation
AIR: Kijang Airport, 12 km SE of Tanjung Pinang. Daily flights to Pekanbaru & Jakarta. **Merpati**, Jl. Bintan 44, tel: 21267. **SMAC**, Jl. J.A. Yani km 5, tel: 22798.

SEA: Frequent launches to Batam Island & Singapore. Boats leave at least 3 times weekly for Pekanbaru, via Siak Sri Indrapura; boats to Island Riau. **Pelni ships** go to Jakarta & distant destinations from **Kijang** harbor. **Pelni office** in Tanjung Pinang: Jl. J. A. Yani km 5, tel: 21513. Boats to Penyengat leave from main jetty.

BATAM ISLAND (Area Code 0778)
Sekupang is arrival point for launches from Singapore. **Nagoya** is Batam's developing new town, with restaurants & souvenir shops. **Hang Nadim Airport** has at least 3 daily flights to Jakarta, and service to Bandung as well as most important Sumatran towns. Many *LUXURY* hotels, incl. **Turi Beach Resort**, Nongsa, tel: 761080.

PEKANBARU (Area Code 0761)
Accommodation
LUXURY: **Indrapura**, Jl. Dr. Sutomo 86, tel: 36233. **Mutiara Merdeka**, Jl. Yos Sudarso 12, tel: 31272. *MODERATE:* **Anom**, Jl. Gatot Subroto 3, tel: 22636. **Badarussamsi**, Jl. Sisingamangaraja 71, tel: 22475. **Hotel Bunda**, Jl. Prof. Moh Yamin 104, tel: 21728. *BUDGET:* Concentration of cheap *losmen* on Jl. Nangka near bus station, incl. **Hotel Linda**, no. 133. Additional *losmen* near harbor, incl. **Nirmala**, Jl. Yatim, tel: 21314. Elsewhere: **Gemini Guesthouse**, Jl. Taskurun 44, tel: 32916.

Tourist Information / Post
Dinas Pariwisata, Jl. Gajah Mada 200, tel: 31562. **Post office**, Jl. Jen. Sudirman.

Hospital
Rumah Sakit Umum Pekanbaru, Jl. Diponegoro 2.

Arrival / Transportation
AIR: Simpang Tiga Airport, 10 km S of town, connection by taxi only. Daily direct flights to and from Singapore. *Airline offices:* **Garuda/Merpati**, Jl. Jen. Sudirman 343, tel: 41555. **SMAC**, Jl. Jen. Sudirman 106, tel: 32622. **Silk Air**, Jl. Yos Sudarso 12A (in Hotel Mutiara Derdeka), tel: 28175.

SEA: Boats leave daily down Siak river for Batam & Tanjung Pinang. Tickets from **Asia Restaurant** near harbor entrance.

BUS: Long-distance bus terminal on Jl. Nangka in S of town; most bus company offices nearby.

MUARA TAKUS
Ruins are near **Pongkai** village, 26 km from main Pekanbaru-Bukittinggi highway. Side-road to ruins turns off at **Muaramahat**, where *bemo* are available. Accommodation: **Losmen Arga Sonya**, Muaramahat.

PALEMBANG (Area Code 0711)
Accommodation
LUXURY: **Lembang**, Jl. Kol. Atmo 16, tel: 363333. **Sandjaja**, Jl. Kapt. A. Rivai 35, tel: 310675. **Swarna Dwipa**, Jl. Tasik 2, tel: 313322. *MODERATE:* **Le Paradis**, Jl. Kapt A. Rivai 58, tel: 356707. **Sari**, Jl. Jen. Sudirman 1301, tel: 313320. *BUDGET:* **Kenanga Inn**, Jl. Bukit Kecil 76, tel: 358166. **Hotel Purnama**, Jl. Mayor Ruslan 7, tel: 351400.

Museums
Museum Budaya Sultan Mahmud Badaruddin, Jl. Benteng (near Ampera bridge). Mon-Thu 8 am-4 pm, Fri 8-12 & 2-4 pm, Sat 8 -12, closed Sun. **Balaputra Dewa Museum**, Jl. Sudirman, km 6 (on road to airport). Tue-Thu 8 am-2 pm, Fri 8 am-1 pm, Sat & Sun 8-12, closed Mon.

Tourist Information / Hospital
Dinas Pariwisata, Jl. P.O. M. IX, tel: 357348, Mon-Thu 8 am-2 pm, Fri 8-11, Sat 8-12, closed Sun. **Pertamina Hospital**, Pertamina Complex, Plaju.

Telecommunication / Post
Post office, Jl. Merdeka 3. **Telecom**, Jl. Merdeka 5.

Arrival / Transportation
AIR: Talang Betutu Airport, 17 km N of the city. *Airline offices:* **Merpati**, Jl. Jl. Sudirman 75, tel: 360003.

SEA: Ferries leave from **Boom Baru** harbor for Bangka Island & Bayungelincir (near Jambi). Smaller boats travel upriver as far as one day's journey.

RAIL: Train station on Jl. Ogan, 8 km from city center on S side of river. 3 trains daily to Tanjungkarang and Java; 3rd-class trains also run to Lubuklinggau on the Bengkulu line, one of the N routes.

BUS: Bus & *bemo* terminal, **Tuju Ulu**, for buses N to Jambi & Padang, W to Lahat & Bengkulu, & S to Lampung & Java.

LOCAL: Ampera, by bridge. Motorboats for charter W of bridge off Jl. Kraton.

WEST SUMATRA

MINANGKABAU HIGHLANDS
BUKITTINGGI
PADANG & THE LOWLANDS
THE MENTAWAI ISLANDS

MINANGKABAU HIGHLANDS

If Sumatra has ever had a single heart, it beats in the maze of green peaks and switchback ravines that make up West Sumatra's **Minangkabau highlands**. Appropriately situated at the center of the island's mountain backbone, mid-way between Aceh and Lampung, this area has been both a sanctuary of tradition and an epicenter of change for all of Sumatra. It is the dynamic contradiction between these two roles that has made West Sumatra a key contributor to the history and culture of modern Indonesia as a whole. The name Minangkabau conjures up diverse and apparently ill-assorted images: on the one hand, a colorful antique culture of picture-perfect architecture, quaint costumes and dances; on the other, a dynamic, educated, enterprising, outward-looking society of traders, teachers, soldiers and leaders.

The traditional cradle and cultural heartland of the Minangkabau people is the area known as **Tanah Datar**, around the small town of **Batusangkar** in the southern shadow of the 2891 meter-high volcano **Mt. Merapi**, the dominant peak of the highlands. Legend has it that the

Left: A Minangkabau woman in traditional costume.

earliest ancestors of the Minangkabau lived in **Pariangan**, a village southwest of Batusangkar, on the slopes of Mt. Merapi. Tanah Datar was the seat of the mysterious "Kings of Minangkabau," whose strange, half-mystical authority radiated outwards from these hidden hills for four centuries. In terms of practical power, the *Raja Yang Dipertuan Sakti* of Tanah Datar seem to have had little control, even over their own homeland.

The Minangkabau believed their kings were descendants of, alongside the emperors of China and Constantinople, Alexander the Great. The truth is almost as impressive: the Minangkabau dynasty has been traced to Adityavarman, the half-Javanese demon-worshipper who was dispatched from the court of Majapahit in 1347, to govern Malayu (Sumatra) as a vassal ruler. For some unknown reason, the dynasty gradually retreated up the Batang Hari river to settle in Tanah Datar. The only tangible remnants of its first years in Minangkabau are the **Adityavarman Stones**, gravestone-like rock tablets inscribed in Sanskrit-based scripts. Examples can be seen by the side of the road near **Limakaum** and at several other sites in the Batusankar area. Some of the inscriptions are in an indigenous Indian-derived script related to that found in Java, others in an alphabet

207

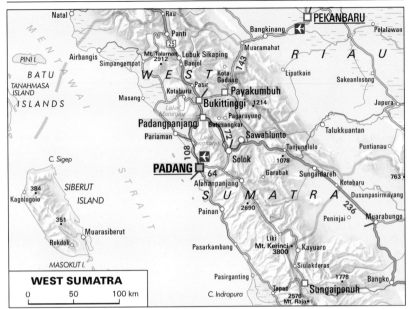

WEST SUMATRA

0   50   100 km

imported directly from India; most remain undeciphered.

The first European to reach Tanah Datar and set eyes upon a Minangkabau king was Tomas Dias, a renegade Portuguese in the service of the Dutch East India Company. Dias marched over the mountains from eastern Sumatra in 1684. At the end of this astonishing journey, executed at a time when the interior of Sumatra was utterly unknown to Europeans, he was greeted by an escort 4000 strong, bearing golden umbrellas and gift-laden trays. Passing through three gates into a palace guarded by 100 musketeers, he was presented with a silver-inlaid musket, a halberd, a thoroughbred horse and a set of pornographic pictures as royal gifts, together with the right to enslave and sentence to death in the king's name.

Like most of their counterparts in Java, the ceremonial buildings of Minangkabau were built of timber, and have not survived. Again as in Java, royal centers tended to change location at the slightest

provocation, and are difficult to trace. To make things still more complex, there was not one king but three: after the arrival of Islam in the 16th century, the old autocratic Indic kingdom was replaced by a peculiar triple monarchy in which a *Raja Ibadat* ("King of Religion") and a *Raja Adat* ("King of Custom"), reigned alongside the *Raja Alam* ("King of the World") himself.

Historians have come to believe that the last capital of the *Raja Alam* was located in **Pagaruyung**, five kilometers east of Batusangkar. Just outside this village, a replica of the old palace, **Istana Pagaruyung**, has been built by the government. The new building is far larger than it should be, but it embodies the dramatic lines of traditional Minangkabau architecture, and is being established to serve as an informative museum about the Pagaruyung dynasty.

The Minangkabau house is the most striking and distinctive in Indonesia, and many have called it the most beautiful. Like the Batak, the Minangkabau have made a long-redundant structural feature, the saddleback roof formed by a load-bearing ridge-beam, into an art form. Each roof section ends in a graceful horn which sweeps upwards to a narrow point, sometimes twice as high as the center of the ridge; with two telescoping extension roofs protruding from each end of the main central section, a large Minangkabau house cuts the skyline with a dramatic saw of curved spires. Many of them are very big; designed to shelter an entire matrilineal clan, the largest cover areas of up to 450 square meters. The wooden foundation piles continue upwards through the living area to support the roof, providing a framework of uprights between which partitions can be hung to create separate compartments for individual families.

Externally, these houses are decorated with rectangular panels that are covered with floral motifs, which hide the abutments of the beams supporting the floor. A short distance from each house are square rice barns, which are styled to match. A surprisingly large number of old *rumah gadang* still stand in Tanah Datar, notably in the villages of **Balimbing**, **Limakaum** and **Pariangan**, as well as in Batusangkar and Pagaruyung; most, however, have surrendered their rustic palm-fiber thatch to the shining advance of corrugated iron. Additional works that are of architectural interest in the Minangkabau uplands are provided by mosques, many of which display the multi-tiered *meru* roof pattern inherited from the Hindu period. One mosque near **Solok**, in the far south of the area, combines a three-layer *meru* with the more modern Middle Eastern *qubbah* dome to create a remarkable pagoda-like strucure.

Islam and Tradition

West Sumatra is generally thought to be a "serious" Muslim area, where sincere faith is an important part of life; the surviving animist traditions are weaker here than in the Bataklands. However, the dominant *adat* of West Sumatra, which involves matrilineal descent and inheritance, is also taken seriously, while the patriarchal wisdom of Mohammed and his interpreters is usually passed over. Some of the implications of Minangkabau *adat* may be a bit unusual by Western norms. A dead man's wealth, for instance, is inherited by his sister's children in preference to his own.

The present balance between Islam and Minangkabau tradition has not been achieved without friction. In the early 19th century, the greatest of all slips along the fault line between the two caused a tremor which both destroyed the ancient Minangkabau monarchy and initiated the conquest of West Sumatra by the Dutch. In 1803, far-off Mecca was conquered by a puritanical Muslim sect called the Wahhabites, whose bloody zeal inspired a handful of Minangkabau pilgrims, then present in the holy city, to plan a similar venture in their own country. Upon their homecoming, the "Padri," as they were known, launched a civil war aimed at purifying Minangkabau society of such evils as gambling, betel-chewing and matrilineal inheritance. The reformers gained steady ground in their struggle against conservative chiefs, and around 1815 the Minangkabau royal line was all but exterminated. In 1821, surviving aristocrats signed the Minangkabau highlands over to the Dutch, whereupon the Padri quickly found themselves on the receiving end of someone else's crusade. The "Padri wars" engaged colonial armies intermittently for 17 years. The first stronghold founded by the Dutch in the uplands was **Fort van der Capellen** in Batusangkar, long used as a school and now as a police station. The permanent center of colonial power was **Fort de Kock**, the foreign irritant around which the pearl of modern **Bukittinggi** has grown.

BUKITTINGGI

Like Bandung, Bukittinggi is a colonial foundation which, for want of a local rival, has become the region's cultural capital. This, together with its fine climate and setting, makes Bukittingi the most attractive town in West Sumatra as well as the usual base for exploring the Minangkabau highlands. The town is 930 meters above sea level, on the edge of the **Ngarai Sianok Gorge**, a sheer canyon carved from the white pumice of the surrounding plateau. The Mediterranean climate allows the cultivation of European flowers and vegetables. The name means "High Hill," a reference to the defensible rise which forms the core of the old settlement. When the fort was first built in 1825, it was called *Sterrenschans*, the Fort of the Stars. Only later was it renamed Fort de Kock, after the army commander who presided over the defeat of

Above: The rebuilt palace of King Adit-yawarman in Batusangkar.

Diponegoro's revolt on Java, in 1830. Until the Pacific war, Fort de Kock was the only name by which anyone except local natives knew what is now Bukittinggi. On the surviving ramparts of the fort, a Dutch cannon still watches over the countryside it once terrorized.

The very highest point in town is occupied not by the fort, but by **Taman Bundo Kanduang**. Part of the park is a sad, barred-cage-style zoo, but it is also home to the **Rumah Adat Baandjuang Museum**, which is worth visiting. The centerpiece of the museum, which was opened in 1935, is a fine Minangkabau house that was built in 1844. Displays also include local wedding and dance costumes, musical instruments and historic weaponry. The other museum in town is the **Army Museum**, next to the **Panorama Park**, which overlooks the Ngarai canyon. The most interesting exhibits date from the regional rebellion of 1958, when Bukittinggi briefly became the capital of the "Revolutionary Government of the Indonesian Republic." The rebels aimed to free the outer islands from the economic centralism and political leftism of Java. However, Sukarno had Bukittinggi bombed and eventually captured by government troops, causing lasting bitterness. Later, Suharto's regime rehabilitated the rebellion as an anti-Communist crusade, a sort of premonition of the birth of the New Order.

Modern Bukittinggi is a relatively clean, orderly place whose charm has not been drowned in poverty and petrol fumes. Sedate horsedrawn carts, rather than shameful *becak* or snarling *bajaj*, are used to transport small loads of passengers. The town's best-known landmark is its **Jam Gadang**, or Big Clock. This is a European-style public clock-tower fitted with a decorative little roof in the horned Minangkabau style. So great is the renown of this unlikely timepiece that the whole town is occasionally known as "Kota Jam Gadang" after it. The clock stands at the central intersection, close to the lively main market. Bukittinggi owed its initial growth spurt to its central location within the network of roads which the Dutch built throughout the uplands, to facilitate their military pacification and economic exploitation. By 1915, Bukittinggi's market was visited by some 40,000 people on fine Saturdays; it is still a dizzying experience, a uniqe opportunity to watch the Minangkabau in one of their favorite and most characteristic environments, and a good place to buy their distinctive food and crafts.

The Minangkabau are opportunists, taking advantage of the opportunity to make a deal in any field; from petty trade, to cash crops, to Western schooling. Long before the Padri wars, the Minangkabau had developed coffee, introduced to Indonesia by the Dutch, into a major source of wealth; once defeated on the battlefield, they wasted no time making a new sort of victory out of the educational opportunities provided by their enemies.

Bukittinggi, blessed in colonial times with the only teacher training college in Sumatra, was at the heart of a Minangkabau intellectual boom which produced a crop of writers and politicians completely out of proportion to the population and the economic importance of the area.

Many of the distinguished Minangkabau figures came from tiny villages near Bukittinggi. **Kota Gadang**, within walking distance, on the opposite side of the Ngarai gorge, has produced no less than two Indonesian prime ministers. Yet, it is indicative of the Minangkabau enigma that this illustrious little place also gives every impression of conservatism; priding itself, for instance, on its beautiful filigree silverwork and on its hand-embroidered cloth. Other villages in the area have other craft specialities of their own: brass dishes and betel boxes in **Desa Sunga**, silk weaving and wood-carving in **Pandai Sikat**, blacksmithing in **Sungaipuar**, and basketwork in **Payakumbuh**.

The most characteristic Minangkabau handicraft is *songket*, heavy cotton cloth highlighted with (now mostly ersatz) gold and silver threads. **Silungkang** village, in the far southeast of Tanah Datar, is one of the best-known sources of high quality *songket*. Traditional entertainment can also be seen in the villages. Minangkabau bullfights (bull versus bull), are staged in **Kotobaru** and **Buta-palano**, near Bukittinggi. Another big social event for male villagers is a wild pig hunt. More sophisticated entertainment can be seen at the state-sponsored Academy of Minangkabau Performing Arts in **Padangpanjang**. Traditional dance genres include the *Randai*, a vigorous all-male form incorporating movements derived from the martial arts, and the *Tari Lilin*, a dance for lithe women who must keep hold of saucers bearing lighted candles. The Minangkabau folk orchestra is a combination of gongs, xylophones, drums and flutes.

211

The Minangkabau highlands are also rich in natural spectacles. Stately **Mt. Merapi** makes a spectacular and popular climb, starting from Kotobaru. **Lake Maninjau** is a huge, icey-still crater lake between Bukittinggi and the sea; further south, and in the process of developing into a tourist destination, is the equally large **Lake Singkarak**.

For those interested in wild flora and fauna, there are several nature reserves. **Batang Palupuh** is one of the few places where a living specimen of *Rafflesia arnoldi* (see p. 218) can easily be found. In the **Anai Valley**, near Padangpanjang and the dramatic **Harau Canyon**, north of Payakumbuh, protected refuges have been created for the wild pigs, tapirs, leopards and tigers, which are hunted with such passion elsewhere in Minangkabau. A much larger reserve, **Rimba Panti**, is in the far north of the province.

The old heart of Minangkabau country consisted of three fertile core territories or *luhak* – Tanah Datar, Agam (the Bukittinggi area) and Limapuluh Kota (the "fifty towns," near Payakumbuh). Together, these three comprised the *darat* — literally just "the land," meaning the ethnic homeland, the birthplace of the Minangkabau people and their culture. Roughly speaking, the *darat* covers the mountains and valleys between **Bonjol** in the north, where today's trans-Sumatran highway crosses the equator, to the attractive traditional village of **Cupak** in the south.

The antithesis of *darat* is *rantau*, a term which, in Minangkabau thought, covers not only the remainder of the province, but also the rest of Sumatra, Indonesia and the world. The mountains are fertility, antiquity, security, purity and home – the mother country, the high womb and cradle of the race. The sea is vast and capricious, the obscure and dangerous outer world. Yet the Minangkabau have not been an insular or xenophobic people; the *rantau* is as important a part in their lives as the *darat*.

The cultural institution of *merantau* urges young men to leave home for a finite time, to seek knowledge, wealth and maturity in the wider world. During the *merantau*, a traveler is expected to support himself by means of enterprise and guile, considered the quintessential Minangkabau qualities. That they like to think of themselves as a savvy race is nicely illustrated by their own explanation of the origin of their ethnic name. A conflict between a group of Sumatrans and Javanese, runs the story, was to be decided by a bullfight. Java's champion was a monster of an animal, but the wily Sumatrans brought on a half-starved calf. Mistaking the bull for its mother, the calf ran to suckle and ripped open the belly of the giant with a knife that had been attached to its nose.

PADANG AND THE LOWLANDS

The Minangkabau people have certainly shown more enthusiasm and aptitude for the wiles of business than have most Indonesians. Nowhere is this more apparent than in the provincial capital of **Padang**, where even wholesale businesses are in the hands of *pribumi* traders rather than the familiar Chinese. Historically, European and indigenous commerce have combined to make Padang an important business center, and the third largest city in Sumatra. In the 17th century, it was already a VOC outstation, where Indian cloth was hawked to the Minangkabau; in the 18th, the native merchants got the upper hand, and foreigners were tolerated more or less at their pleasure. Between 1795 and 1819, the town was in British hands, whereafter the Dutch returned with renewed vigor and used Padang as a base for their campaigns against the Padri, developing it at

Right: The pawprint of a rare Sumatran tiger.

the same time into a collection and export point for rice, coffee, tobacco and spices from Minangkabau, which the Dutch came to know as the "Padang Uplands." Since independence, the regional capital has been definitively reclaimed by the Minangkabau; traditionally part of the *rantau,* Padang is being absorbed into the *darat,* and now rivals Bukittinggi as a cultural as well as a political focus. Padang has a university and an arts center, and its **Adityawarman Museum** is the most important museum for Minangkabau anthropology, history and art.

Padang has also given its name to the remarkable style of cookery which has become the trademark of Minangkabau in the *rantau*. The Padang restaurant is as familiar throughout urban Indonesia as the fish and chip shop in Britain, but the best place to sample Padang food is, of course, Padang itself. At a decent *rumah makan Padang,* the waiter brings a selection of a dozen dishes, balanced precariously along the length of his arm. The ingredients range from beef and chicken

to tripe, but what almost all recipes have in common is a quantity of chilli and other fiery spices which can be downright dangerous to the unprepared diner.

Low, flat and exposed to drenching sea winds, Padang is an appallingly hot and wet place, especially during the west monsoon. It is not unusual for 17 centimeters of rain to fall on a single November night. Old-style Padang houses were fortified against the elements, resting on tall piles to surmount floodwaters, and with wide, overhanging roofs to combat the onslaught of sun and rain; the current trend towards the pan-Indonesian, concrete blockhouse-style is far less practical and much uglier. South of Padang, the coastline is rugged and scenic, with fine beaches at **Bungus** and **Pasir Putih**.

Of special interest in **Pariaman**, a seaside town 36 kilometers north of Padang, is the *Tabut* festival which is celebrated there at the beginning of the first month of the Muslim calendar. *Tabut* commemorates the martyrdom in battle of two of Mohammad's grandsons. Although it is associated with the Shiite sect, considered to be heretics by most Indonesian Muslims, this festival is held in many parts of the archipelago – but nowhere as dramatically as in Pariaman. In a communal ritual of almost Balinese color and extravagance, the Pariaman Minangkabau construct and destroy huge effigies of the Bouraq, a mythical flying animal supposed to have borne the souls of the heroes to heaven. Vibrantly painted, the images are danced through the streets only to be tossed into the sea, whereupon Minangkabau thrift suddenly resurges as spectators dive in to recover valuable pieces of decoration.

The railway connecting Padang to its mountain hinterland was completed in 1892. It was essentially built to serve the big coalfield at **Sawahlunto**, which supplied fuel for the steam-driven sea and rail arteries of the Dutch East Indies. There is a branch line that goes to Bukittinggi, but only freight trains operate on it now. Train buffs, however, may just be lucky enough to cadge a ride on the footplate of one of the last commercial steam locomotives in Indonesia and the world.

West Sumatra is not one of the largest provinces of Sumatra, but at almost 50,000 square kilometers, it is still bigger than any Javan provinces. And with a population of only 3.8 million, heavily concentrated around Padang and the central *darat*, there are large tracts of wilderness. The greatest of these is in the south, some ten hours' drive from Padang. It forms the northern extremity of the huge new **Kerinci Seblat Reserve**. This magnificent sanctuary is one of the Indonesian government's greatest conservation gestures. Covering 1.5 million hectares of high-altitude forest and marsh, it includes segments of three separate provinces. **Sungaipenuh**, the administrative center for the park, lies in a high valley on the western fringe of Jambi. **Mt. Kerinci**, at 3806 meters the tallest peak in Sumatra, and a tough two-day climb for experienced hikers, stands close to the border between Jambi and West Sumatra. However, the wildest part of the reserve is further south, in the heart of the province of Bengkulu.

THE MENTAWAI ISLANDS

About 130 kilometers from the West Sumatran coast, in what Indonesians call the "Indonesian Ocean," lie the extraordinary **Mentawai Islands**. In the 19th and early 20th centuries, European explorers and writers valued the Mentawais as a source of stories about noble savages and tribal utopias. Ritual war and a diet of sago, tubers and the occasional banana, probably made life there less than paradisical in practice, but the Mentawais are certainly a world apart. Their culture is even more singular than that of Nias, part of the same long island chain. The people of the Mentawais pose some interesting challenges to modern historians studying early Indonesia. Until late colonial times, they seem to have lacked not only such technological innovations as metalworking, but also such Javan basics as pottery use, rice-growing and betel-chewing.

Christian missionary work began in the Mentawais in 1901, but large-scale conversions did not occur until after the Pacific war, and the overall process of change was probably retarded rather than advanced by the guerilla campaign for souls that was fought by the Muslims and Catholics against the Protestant pioneers. Loincloths made of stamped tree-bark may have been preached and laughed into history, but the islanders' beautiful body tattoos are not so easy to cast off. Traditional houses can also still be seen in several remote villages, including **Sakelot** and **Rokdok** on the northernmost and largest island, **Siberut**. However, it is the least tangible remnants of heathendom – like beliefs in spirits, possessions and taboos – that may well prove to be the most durable of all.

BUKITTINGGI
(Area Code 0752)
Accommodation
LUXURY: **Pusako**, Jl. Soekarno-Hatta 7, tel: 22111; **Denai**, Jl. Rivai 26, tel: 21511.
MODERATE: **Benteng**, Jl. Benteng 1, tel: 21115. **Dymen's**, Jl. Nawawi 1-5, tel: 21015. **Lima's**, Jl. Kesehatan 34, tel: 22641. **Minang International**, Jl. Panorama 20, tel: 21120.
BUDGET: on Jl. A. Yani: **Yusuf Hotel**, no. 111, tel: 21133; **Murni**, no. 115, tel: 21824; **Singgalang**, no. 130, tel: 21576; **Srikandi**, no. 117, tel: 22984. Elsewhere: **Pemandangan**, Jl. Yos Sudarso 3, tel: 21621. **Surya**, Jl. A. Karim 7, tel: 22587.
Restaurants
INDONESIAN (Padang): **Ria Sari**, Ngarai Sianok Shopping Center, Jl. Jen. Sudirman 1, tel: 21503. **Roda Group Restaurant**, Pasar Atas, Block C-155. **Selamat**, Jl. A. Yani 19, tel: 22959. **Simpang Raya**, Muka Jam Gadang, tel: 22585.
CHINESE: **Mona Lisa**, Jl. A. Yani 58, tel: 22644.
EUROPEAN: Traditional hangout for western travelers is **Stars Cafe**, Jl. A. Yani 109.
Shopping
Many craft & antique shops along Jl. Minangkabau, esp. near Gloria Cinema: **Tiga Putra** (no. 19), **Nuraini** (no. 25), **H. Muchtar** (no. 90). Also: **Aishachalik**, Jl. Cindur Mato 94 (extension of Jl. Minangkabau); **Basrida**, Jl. Yos Sudarso 2. Daily **Central Market** down the street from the clocktower.
Cultural Events
Randai dancing at zoo, Wed, Sat & Sun at 11 am. Traditional dance and *pencak silat*, daily at 8:30 pm, at Jl. Lengogeni 1, belown Jam Gadang.
Museum / Zoo
Taman Bundo Kanduang park contains both **Rumah Adat Baandjuang Museum** and **Bukittinggi Zoo**.
Tourist Information
Pasar Atas (main market), tel: 22403.
Arrival / Transportation
BUS: Bus station on Jl. Aur Kuning, 3 km SE of town. Most bus company offices here. **LOCAL:** Horsecarts are one of Bukittinggi's trademarks.

PADANG
(Area Code 0751)
Accommodation
LUXURY: **Pangeran Beach Hotel** (Istana Pangeran), Jl. Juanda 79, tel: 51333, in the N of city.
MODERATE: **Hang Tuah**, Jl. Pemuda 1, tel: 26556. **Machudum's Hotel**, Jl. Hiligoo 43, tel: 22333. **Mariani International**, Jl. Bundo Kanduang 35, tel: 25466. **Natour Muara**, Jl. Gereja 34, tel: 35600. **Pangeran Hotel**, Jl. Dobi 3-5, tel: 31233.
BUDGET: **Cendrawasih**, Jl. Pemuda 27, tel: 22894. **Tiga Tiga**, Jl. Pemuda 31, tel: 22633.

Restaurants
INDONESIAN: **Alima**, Jl. Pasar Baru 29, tel: 21794. **Simpang Raya**, Jl. Bundo Kanduag 3, tel: 26430. *CHINESE:* **Apollo Mandarin**, Jl. Cokroaminoto 36A. **King's**, Jl. Pondok 86B, tel: 21701.
Shopping
Pasar Raya (main market), Jl. Pasar Raya (next to city hall).
TEXTILES: **Batik Semar**, Jl. Hiligoo, tel: 21215. **Songket Silungkang**, Jl. Imam Bonjol, tel: 23711. **Toko Batik Arjuna**, Jl. Pasar Raya, tel: 23253. *OTHER HANDICRAFTS & ANTIQUES:* **Abu Nawas**, Tabing Airport. **Mochtar**, Jl. Pondok 85, tel: 25615. **Panay**, Jl. Iman Bonjol 5/IV, tel: 21259. **Toko Sartika**, Jl. Jen. Sudirman 5, tel: 22101.
Museum
Adityawarman Museum, Jl. Diponegoro, tel: 22316. Tue-Sun 6 am-4 pm, closed Mon.
Cultural Events
Taman Budaya, Jl. Diponegoro (opposite museum): Dancing and *pencak silat*, daily 9 am-2 pm.
Tourist Information
Tourist office for W. Sumatra in **Dina's Pariwisata**, Jl. J. Sudirman 43, tel: 25080. Mon-Thu 7:30 am-2 pm, Fri 7:30-11, Sat 7:30-12:30.
Post Offices
Padang Tourist Office, Jl. Hayam Wuruk 51, tel: 34186. **Post office**, Jl. Bagindo Aziz Chan 7.
Government Offices
PHPA Office (permits for Mentawais & reserves), Jl. Raden Saleh 8A, Padang Baru, tel: 25136. **Police station**, Jl. M. Yamin.
Arrival / Transportation
AIR: Tabing Airport, 6 km by taxi. *Airline offices:* **Garuda**, Jl. Jen. Sudirman 2, tel:30737. **Merpati**, Jl. Gereja 34 (in Natour Muara Hotel), tel: 36501. **Mandala**, Jl. Pemuda 29A, tel: 32773. **Silk Air**, Jl. Bundo Kanduang 20 (in Desona Hotel), tel: 38120. **Pelangi Air**, Jl. Gereja 34 (in Natour Muara Hotel), tel: 38103.
SEA: Teluk Bayur harbor, 6 km S of town center. **Pelni office**, Jl. Tanjung Priok 32, Teluk Bayur, tel: 33624.
BUS: Bus station **Lintas Andalas**, Jl. Pemuda. Frequent buses to and from Bukittinggi; long-distance services to other Sumatran towns and Jakarta. **LOCAL:** *Bemo* terminal off Jl. M. H. Yamin, between bus station and market. Main taxi stand in front of market.

MENTAWAI ISLANDS
No hotels or homestays, but a **PHPA Guesthouse** in **Muarasiberut**. Permission from police in Padang necessary to visit **Mentawais**.
Boats leave Padang harbor regularly; **SMAC** flies once a week (Wed) from Padang to **Rokot Airstrip**, Sipora Island.

BENGKULU

SOUTH SUMATRA

BENGKULU
LAMPUNG

BENGKULU

Bengkulu is the modern Indonesian rendition of Bencoolen, a name that was once famous because of its association with the long British presence in what ultimately became the Dutch East Indies. In 1685, the British East India Company, expelled from the Moluccas and Java by the Dutch and their allies, set up shop in a friendly pepper-growing area on the southwest coast of Sumatra. Disease and intrigue thrived in the Bencoolen "factory," as the British called their overseas trading stations, but so, on the whole, did trade; thirty years later the company could afford to build the formidable **Fort Marlborough** a short distance along the coast from the original settlement. The modern town of Bengkulu has grown up around the fort, which still has commanding views of the market, the Chinese quarter and the harbor it was built to guard. Indeed, it is still occupied by the modern military. Unfortunately, the army has recently seen fit to encase most of the fort's venerable walls in white concrete, giving it all the charm of a nuclear bunker. Nevertheless, the imposing main gateway, and the old gravestones in the

Left: A fierce-looking war-dancer from South Sumatra.

courtyard, with their interesting English inscriptions, have been preserved. The **Parr Monument**, opposite the fort, commemorates a British resident who was stabbed in his bed by native assassins, in 1807.

The most illustrious Englishman to live in Bencoolen was also that greatest of all colonial-heroes, Thomas Stamford Raffles. A reformer and a scholar, Raffles continues to evoke admiration long after figures like Cortez, Coen, Clive and Rhodes have become distasteful. Unfortunately, the time he spent in what was then a quite shabby Bencoolen, forms a rather sad epilogue to his years as the British ruler of Java.

In 1818, after the Java was returned to the Dutch at the end of the Napoleonic wars, a despondent Raffles was posted to this last remaining British colony in the archipelago. In Bencoolen he remained indefatiguable, banning slavery, introducing coffee and sugar cultivation, and opening schools; during expeditions to other parts of Sumatra, he documented new species, languages and archaeological remains, and – almost incidentally – founded Singapore. However, it was a time of unhappiness and misfortune. Four of Raffles's five children died of tropical fevers, and he was constantly tortured by frustration at the greater prizes which had slipped from his grasp. In 1823, as he set sail to return to England, his ship caught fire and sank. Raffles escaped with his life, but little else. Among other things, he lost the notes and drawings which would have enabled him to write half a dozen standard works on Southeast Asia. Two years later, imperial diplomats returned Bencoolen to the Dutch, in exchange for the old port of Malacca on the Malay peninsula, ending the possibility of British settlement in the islands. An appropriately sad monument to Raffles is the **British Governor's Residence** in Bengkule; a sorry, banyan-strangled ruin just a five minutes' walk from the fort. The large, stone house has been uninhabited since a great earthquake in 1914.

The town of Bengkulu has certainly improved since Raffles described it in 1818, as, "without exception the most wretched place I have ever beheld." Today it is a peaceful, friendly, not unattractive town, with the newly appreciated advantage of fine sandy beaches. However, it has not lost its insular, backwater atmosphere. Ironically, it was the very marginality and irrelevance of Bengkulu which made it, in the last years before the Pacific war, the involuntary home of another great figure of Indonesian history – Sukarno. The future president lived here in rather comfortable political exile between 1938 and 1942, in the house that today is marked by a flag, just off Jl. Sukarno-Hatta.

Bengkulu is the capital of a long, narrow, sparsely populated province of the same name. Despite the fact that almost half of its perimeter is seacoast, Bengkulu is so long that it borders no less than four other Sumatran provinces. The interior is just a strip of the Barisan mountain range. Much of the north forms part of the **Kerinci Seblat Reserve**, which also sprawls into West Sumatra, South Sumatra and Jambi. **Mt. Seblat** itself is an impressive 2383 meter-high mountain on

the eastern border. Bengkulu's is the wildest section of the park, where rhinos, tigers, tapirs, clouded leopards and sun bears are as plentiful as they get in modern Sumatra. Outside the reserve, such spectacular game may still be shot, and Bengkulu has become a mecca for Indonesian hunters. In the center and south, one item of flora enjoys better protection than the fauna: the *Rafflesia arnoldi*, the largest flower in the world. The pungent, visceral bloom of the parasitic rafflesia can also be viewed elsewhere in Sumatra, but Bengkulu is the area most closely associated with the plant as it was here that Raffles and the naturalist Arnold became the first Europeans to discover it, in 1818. Catching a *Rafflesia* in bloom is always a tricky business, but specimens do exist in a reserve at **Tabah Penanjung**, on the road inland from Bengkulu. Clinging to the flank of the Barisan range, Tabah Penanjung also offers superb views of the Indian Ocean.

The central interior of Bengkulu province consists essentially of a double row of peaks separated by a dramatic valley. The main settlements here are **Kepahiang** and **Curup**, on the headwaters of the Musi river, which eventually escapes from this trench into the eastern lowlands and becomes the great brown traveling sea which rolls through Palembang. The upper reaches of the Musi are the home of Bengkulu's best-known native people, the *Rejang*.

The Rejang were once accomplished miners, extracting and exporting gold from the rich deposits northwest of Curup. At the end of the 19th century, however, the Dutch took over themselves in a frenzied goldrush which quickly made Bengkulu Indonesia's largest gold-producing area. Today, most of the mines in **Lebong Tandai**, on the **Ketahun river** have been closed.

Enggano is Bengkulu's lone link in the chain of maverick islands running parallel to Sumatra's west coast. A cen-

tury ago, Enggano was an even greater anthropological curiosity than Nias or the Mentawais, lacking even weaving as well as metal, pottery and rice. Its culture is exceptionally fragile under foreign pressures, and the health of its people even more so. The native population fell from about 3000 in 1862, to 329 in 1914, and 162 in 1928. Numbers have since recovered, but immigration of Javanese, Chinese and other Sumatrans has all but submerged the island's indigenous identity. Tourist literature still displays drawings of the weird, beehive-like traditional houses of Enggano, but neglects to add that the last of these disappeared before the 1914. Real adventurers who can speak Indonesian will enjoy checking out what is left, though, especially since the island is so tantalisingly inaccessible. The name "Enggano" is rather inauspicious, deriving from a Portuguese word meaning "deceit" or "disappointment;" in the 16th century, Portuguese ships avoiding the pirate-infested Strait of Malacca must have made landfall here on the way to Java. Enggano is also where the first Dutchman stepped ashore in Indonesia, in 1596.

LAMPUNG

The southernmost province of Sumatra is **Lampung**. At the closest point on the Sunda Strait, Lampung is less than 30 kilometers from Java. As a result, it is the only part of modern-day Sumatra to have maintained greater Javan influences than Maylay. In a little wooden museum in the village of **Pugung**, not far from the provincial captial of **Tanjungkarang**, a Buddhist statue in East Javanese style stands as a reminder of this connection. With the fall of Majapahit and the rise of the coastal sultanates in the 16th century, Lampong, alone in Sumatra, fell under the power of Banten, which was just over the water in West Java. Banten exploited Lampung because it was a source of valuable pepper, and installed its own vassal chiefs in order to secure and cement its authority.

After the demise of the Banten sultanate in 1809, it took the Dutch a long time to bring Lampung under their own direct control – near **Kalianda**, on Lampung Bay, is the ruined fort that belonged to one of the warlords of the time. Meanwhile, the area became a refuge for fugitives and criminals; the landless and the lawless fleeing from a desperate, *cultuurstelsel*-burdened Java. The peasant hero Saijah and heroine Adinda, of Multatuli's mid-19th century political novel *Max Havelaar*, ended their stories in Lampung, on the bayonets of a colonial expedition. When, at the beginning of the 20th century, the Dutch began to consider the increasing problem of Javan overpopulation, it seemed appropriate to formalize Lampung's long-standing function as a safety valve. The first "transmigrants" from Java arrived in Lampung in 1905, and they have continued to come ever since. While *transmigrasi* now extends to all the main outer

islands of Indonesia, its effect is still most dramatic where it started, in Lampung. Half of this province's six million inhabitants speak Javanese or Sundanese; whole towns – like **Metro**, inland from Tanjungkarang – give the impression of having been transplanted, virtually intact, from Java.

The indigenous people of Lampung have never been very numerous and still number less than a million. They and the province take their name from a legendary ancestor, who was supposedly a brother of the kings of Sunda and Majapahit, and who lived in what is now Bengkulu. Certainly Lampung culture seems closely related to that of the Rejang in Bengkulu. The Indic script they used for example, was almost identical; in Lampung, it was still universally known among young people as late as 1920, and was used in the romantic and scurrilous verses exchanged between lovers during courtship. Thanks to such folk applications of writing, popular literacy in many parts of Indianized, pre-

Above: A beautiful sunset in South Sumatra.

Islamic, pre-colonial Indonesia was probably higher than in the Europe of the day. Lampung was one of the last places to lose this art, just after the written word re-entered the culture as a European "innovation." Unfortunately, Lampung's script disappeared with remarkable completeness in a very short time, and specimens are now extremely difficult to find.

The area above **Krui**, on the rugged west coast, is one of the purest remaining in Lampung. To the west is the tail end of the Barisan range, a band of quite impressive mountains, including the 2231 meter-high **Mt. Pesagi**. **Lake Ranau**, on the border with South Sumatra, is a beautiful mountain lake, complete with hot springs, and is one of the area's most popular attractions

The remainder of Lampung is the flat green purgatory typical of eastern Sumatra, inlaid with a shining brown tracery of winding jungle rivers. The most fertile parts of the lowlands are being opened up by settlers and transmigration schemes. Other than a few loggers, only wild animals dwell in the remote northeast; the area has been turned into the **Way Kambas Wildlife Reserve**. Elephants, in particular, seem to thrive in this marshland, and Way Kambas is said to be the best place in Sumatra to see them.

Lampung as a whole is, nevertheless, the most domesticated province of Sumatra. There is even a passenger railway running from South Sumatra into Lampung. Started in 1911, it is the only one in Sumatra which still carries passengers. All of the roads and railways converge on the twin cities of **Tanjungkarang** and **Telukbetung**. These two cities, sometimes known collectively as **Bandar Lampung**, have the teeming, tacky, half-modern atmosphere of a Javanese port; even the *war-teg* food stalls are here, with their absurdly cheap fried *tahu* and *tempe*. Beyond Telukbetung are **Panjang** and **Bakauheni**, embarkation points for Java and Jakarta.

BENGKULU (Area Code 0736)
LUXURY: **Horison**, Jl. Pantai Nala 142, tel: 21722. *MODERATE:* **Cempaka Raya**, Jl. Mayjan. Sutoyo 135, tel: 21661. **Wisma Balai Buntar**, Jl. Khadijah 122, tel: 21254. **Nala Seaside Cottage**, Jl. Pantai Nala 133, tel: 21855. *BUDGET:* **Ragli Kuning**, Jl. Kenanga 99, tel: 22682.

Tourist Information
Dinas Pariwisata, Jl. Pembangunan 14, tel: 21272.

Post / Telecommunications
Post office, Jl. S. Parman 111. **Telecom**, Jl. Kol. Barlian 51, open 24-hours.

Museum
Jl. Pembangunan, Tue-Thu & Sun 8 am-1 pm, Fri 8-11, Sat 8-12, closed Mon.

Arrival / Transportation
AIR: Daily flights to Jakarta, 3 times a week to Palembang. *Airline offices:* **Merpati:** in Hotel Samudera Dwinka, Jl. J. Sudirman 246, tel: 42337. **SEA:** Ships call at harbor **Pulau Baai**. **Pelni**, Jl. Siti Khadijah 10, tel: 21013. **BUS:** Most buses on trans-Sumatra route run via Lubuklinggau, Curup & Bengkulu. Main bus station is **Terminal Air Sebakul**, 9 km from town.

TELUKBETUNG / TANJUNGKARANG
(Area Code 0721)
LUXURY: **Indra Palace**, Jl. W. Monginsidi 70, Tanjungkarang, tel: 262766. **Sahid Krakatau**, Jl. Yos Sudarso 294, Telukbetung, 488888. *MODERATE:* **Kurnia City**, Jl. Raden Intan 114, Tanjungkarang, tel: 262030. **Hartono**, Jl. Juanda, Telukbetung, tel: 262525. *BUDGET:* **Rarem**, Jl. W. Rarem 23, Telukbetung, tel: 261241. **Lusy**, Jl. Diponegoro 186, Telukbetung, tel: 48595.

Tourist Information / Post
Tourist office, **Dinas Pariwitasa**, Jl. W. R. Supratman 39, Telukbetung, tel: 482565. **Post office**, Jl. K. H. A. Dahlan 21, Tanjungkarang. **Telecom**, Jl. Majapahit 1, Tanjungkarang, open 24-hours.

Museum
Jl. Tenku Umar, 7 km N of Tanjungkarang in Rajabasa. Tue-Thu 9 am-2 pm, Fri 9-11 am & 1-3 pm, Sat & Sun 9 am-3 pm, closed Mon.

Arrival / Transportation
AIR: Branti Airport, 22 km N of Tanjungkarang, with taxi. **Merpati**, Jl. Jen. A. Yani 88B, tel: 258046. **SEA:** Ferries to Java (Merak) from **Bakauheni**. **RAIL:** Train to **Palembang** & **Lubuklinggau** (for Bengkulu and western route to N) terminates in **Panjang**; you can also board at station in center of Tanjungkarang. 2 trains daily. **BUS:** Long-distance buses await ferry passengers at **Bakauheni**, or leave from **Terminal Rajabasa**, 7 km N of Tanjungkarang. **LOCAL: Taxi 333**, Jl. Ikan Manyung 2, Telukbetung, tel: 485579. **Trans Bandar Taxi**, Jl. Kartini 69, Tanjungkarang, tel: 263068.

INDONESIAN CUISINE

Several different styles of cooking have been combined to create the gastronomic arts that are traditional Indonesian cuisine. These culinary triumphs can make gourmets giddy and greatly expand the horizons of those who simply enjoy a good meal.

One cannot fully appreciate Indonesia until experiencing its savory authentic cuisine, or at least one of the popular dishes that can be found throughout the archipelago, such as *Opor Ayam*; chicken in a mild cream sauce. It is made from chicken, coconut milk and a mixture of candle nuts, green ginger, *laos* root, coriander, cumin, garlic and onions, which are finely ground and fried in oil. Salam leaves, lemon juice, tamarind juice and a touch of salt round out this tasty dish. The practical know-how of an experi-

Preceding pages: A Javanese wedding. Above: Selling fish in Denpasar. Right: Hot peppers and sambal paste.

224

enced chef can turn this aromatic mix of simple ingredients and freshly ground spices into an unforgetable dining experience, full of magnificent flavors and an aroma you never dreamt existed. *Opor Ayam* is usually accompanied by a vegetable dish such as *Sambal Goreng Buncis* (stir-fried green beans in coconut milk), *Pergedel Kentang Dengan Daging* (meat served with potato croquettes), *Kerupuk* (crackers) and *Serundeng* (roasted coconut with peanuts). Every dish compliments the last, adding to the pleasure.

Indonesian meals are not served as separate courses and all of the dishes mentioned above are eaten with boiled white rice. The rice supplies the bulk of the meal, and its simple blandness is ideal for absorbing and combining the complex flavors of the meat and vegetable dishes, and acting as the background against which to savor the contrasting tastes and textures.

People often think that dishes from Minangkabau are hot and spicy, but they are only half right. They don't realize that slow cooking reduces the pungency of chilies, and that chilies mixed with other spices and ingredients in the right proportions, can blend beautifully, making it wonderfully appealing. If the measurements are right, no individual ingredient should dominate the flavor of any particular dish.

There are hundreds of dishes from Indonesia: hot ones, mild ones, sweet ones, sour ones, tangy and creamy ones, salty and bland ones. There are also hundreds of ethnic groups in Indonesia and they all have numerous dishes of their own. One could eat for weeks witout seeing the same dish served twice.

Many people's favorite, *Sate*, is made from pieces of beef, chicken, lamb or goat that are placed on bamboo skewers, marinaded in spices and grilled over a bed of charcoal, then served with a sauce made from ground peanuts mixed with chilies, garlic, onions, sugar, soy sauce, vinegar, salt and water; or a sauce made from soy sauce, sliced shallots, sliced chilies, crushed garlic and lime juice. *Sate* is an excellent dish to eat in- or outdoors, at informal gatherings or at cocktail parties, and foreigners usually take to it like ducks to water. In Jakarta, Jl. Jen. Sudirman is a good place to find a number of excellent *Sate* restaurants. It is usually served with *Lontong*, compressed, cooked rice that is steamed in a banana leaf, or *Ketupat*, another form of compressed rice, that is boiled in square bags (or other shapes) that have been plaited from young coconut palm leaves.

Vegetarians and those who prefer vegetables to meat, should ask for a dish called *Gado-gado*, a kind of vegetable salad served with peanut sauce. It consists of lettuce, boiled shredded cabbage, boiled carrots (cut into matchstick-size strips), boiled and sliced green beans, scalded bean sprouts, quartered ripe tomatoes, and quartered hard-boiled eggs. All of these ingredients are attractively arranged on a platter, and the whole cre-

ation is topped with peanut sauce and fried onion flakes. The peanut sauce is simply made from ground garlic and onion and chilies which are all stir-fried in a small amount of oil. Some water and ground peanuts are added, and the entire mixture is brought to the boil. Sugar and vinegar are then added, as well as a pinch of salt to taste.

Tempe is an Indonesian food, much sought after by vegetarians, which is both nutritious and tasty. It is prepared from boiled soybeans which are then fermented, a process that takes three days. The finished product is firm and compact like a cake, the beans being tightly bound together and covered evenly with a light coating of white mold, with an aroma something like that of fresh mushrooms. *Tempe* is firm enough not to crumble when sliced thinly and is a source of high-quality protein.

Because of its high nutritional value and low price, *Tempe* is popular among Indonesia's lower income groups. Unlike fish, chicken or beef, a pound of *Tempe* is a pound of *Tempe*. There are no bones, gristle or fat; in other words nothing that goes to waste. Today, with increasing numbers of the well-educated upper-class turning towards more vegetarian dishes, they, too, often prefer *Tempe* to meat.

Fried *Tempe* is served with rice for breakfast, lunch and dinner in most homes in Indonesia, and in a variety of dishes at many restaurants. To try it, ask for *Tempe Goreng* (fried *Tempe*) or *Sambal Goreng Kering Tempe* (crisp, deep-fried *Tempe* with seasoning), which consists of thin slices of crisp, deep-fried *Tempe* with a sweet and spicy coating. The latter is also available in the market or in food shops, wrapped in shiny banana leaves or cellophane.

Yet another vegetarian favorite, also high in protein and entirely free of cholesterol, is *Tahu*, known in the West as soybean curd. Like *Tempe*, it is prepared from fermented soybean paste.

It originated in China about two thousand years ago, and is now an important part of the daily diet throughout East Asia, and is widely available in Western countries. It was first brought to Indonesia by Chinese travelers so many years ago that Indonesians regard it as belonging to their own cuisine, for they have their own ways of preparing it. For example they serve it as *Tahu Goreng* with *Gado-gado*. *Tahu* is available, fresh daily, in most parts of Indonesia.

Nasi Gudeg, which is best sampled in Yogyakarta, is a dish that is specific to Central Java. It consists of pieces of chicken and chopped, young jack-fruit, that are cooked in coconut milk, on low heat for several hours, with spices like coriander and cumin, as well as shrimp paste, onions, garlic, candle nuts ground into a paste, *laos*, brown sugar, lemon grass, and a pinch of salt added for flavor. It is served with white rice.

Right: Delicious gifts from a bountiful sea.

Nasi Campur consists of a portion of white rice scooped onto a plate, topped with either fish, beef, chicken or goat, together with a mixture of vegetables, sprinkled with *Serundeng*, and, finally, topped with a piece or two of *Krupuk*. This makes a tasty, substantial and reasonably priced meal.

Nasi Padang is so called because it is named after, and indeed characteristic of, the cuisine of Padang, a port and the capital city of West Sumatra. There are a number of Padang restaurants in Yogya. Indeed, there is hardly a city in Indonesia without its quota of Padang restaurants. Such restaurants are best known for their variety of curries and hot, spicy dishes prepared from beef, chicken, goat, liver, tripe, kidneys, eggs and fish, and numerous vegetable dishes. Watch especially for dishes called *Kalio Ayam* (creamy chicken curry), and *Rendang*, a wonderfully flavored beef dish. And don't forget to try *Dendeng Balado*, fried, seasoned, sun-dried meat with a spicy coating. These three dishes alone make Minangkabau cuisine stand well above any other.

In Indonesia food is not only served and eaten to satisfy hunger. It is also a means of communication. There are special dishes to mark critical points in the life-cycle. In Java, for example, a dish called *Nasi Tumpeng* is prepared when a woman has reached the seventh month of pregnancy. It consists of boiled rice pressed and shaped into a cone, 30 to 40 centimeters high, set in the center of a large, round bamboo platter that is lined with banana leaves; the cone shape symbolizes ascent and progress. It is surrounded by seven miniature cones of rice with a variety of dishes, vegetable, beef and chicken, interspersed with brightly colored sweatmeats. Relatives and neighbors are invited to join in the celebrations. The serving of this dish announces to the community the happy news that the seventh month has been reached safely; it is at the same time, an act of thanksgiving

and a prayer for future blessings in which all are invited to share. *Nasi Tumpeng* is also prepared to mark other occasions, such as birthdays, weddings and wedding anniversaries. The basic shape and pattern remain the same, but the meat and vegetable dishes that surround it differ according to the nature and importance of the occasion.

Nasi Tumpeng is also prepared when a death has occurred. In this case, the cone is cut neatly from tip to base, and the two halves are placed back to back, indicating that life, and with it any onward or upward movement, has come to an end.

In Bali, known as Pulau Dewata, the Isle of the Gods, food also plays a major role, not least in religious ceremonies. Bali is home to thousands of temples, and an important part of Balinese religious devotion is expressed by taking food to these temples as offerings. The act of presenting these offerings has a deep symbolic meaning. It is above all, an expression of thanks from the worshippers to *Sang Hyang Widhi*, the paramount

God, for all his gifts to mankind. Everything offered to him, or any of the lesser deities, must be as beautiful and perfect as possible.

As soon as the morning cooking is done, before anything is eaten, small offerings consisting of a tiny mound of freshly cooked rice, a smidgin of ground chili with salt, and a stem or two of flowers are set on a small piece of banana leaf and put in one of a variety of places deemed important; in the household shrine, next to the hearth, by the well and at the gate, to protect the dwelling from evil spirits who are thought to be everywhere.

Everyday meals are cooked by women. Only men, however, may prepare the ceremonial meals and banquets which include such specialities as *Babi Guling*, roast suckling pig. Bali is also known for its turtle steak and turtle *Sate*, delicacies that are not readily available anywhere else in Indonesia. (These delicacies should, however, be avoided because the turtles are now an endangered species.)

227

TRADITIONAL ARTS AND CRAFTS

Batik is undoubtedly the art form for which Indonesia is best known, although this technique of patterning textiles with wax-resist dye is almost exclusive to Java. *Batik* cloth, however, is immensely popular throughout Indonesia and in many other parts of Southeast Asia. In fact *batik* is the term used throughout the world for the wax-resist technique of patterning fabric, an acknowledgement of the Javanese supremacy at this art. Although widely used elsewhere, this method has reached its most refined state in Java, where the hot molten wax is applied to the surface of fine cotton fabric with a *canting* (pen-like instrument) that permits the application of intricate patterns of very fine dots and lines.

In addition to these elaborate *batik* techniques, during the 19th century a *cap*

Above: Well-earned reward for skill and patience.

(copper stamp) was also invented in Java, to provide a speedier means of applying the molten wax and enabling local textile producers to counter the flood of printed cottons coming from the factories of industrial Europe. The *batik* textiles that are produced by this method (*batik cap*) are considerably cheaper than the painstaking, hand-drawn and labor intensive *batik tulis*. In recent years, textile factories in Java have mass-produced printed cloth in batik-like patterns, which is known fallaciously as "*batik*" print, although no wax is ever applied to these fabrics.

Batik still exhibits great regional variations in color and design, although the largest *batik* companies are now able to sell these under the one roof. The *batik* cloths of central Java (*kain panjang*) are probably the most familiar. The designs are usually based on geometric all-over patterns, and the typical colors of these cloths are blue-black and brown against a cream ground (in Solo) or a white ground (in Yogyakarta). The sombre elegance of the *batiks* of these old central Javanese principalities is in sharp contrast to the vibrant colors of the floral and bird designs from north-coast centers such as Pekalongan.

The art of coastal Java has been strongly influenced by trade: European, Chinese and Arab influences can be identified in the *batik* designs of these areas. North-coast *batik* cloth usually displays the tubular *kain sarong* design structure featuring a contrasting head-panel section, or the *pagi soré* ("morning and evening") style, with different designs at each end of one cloth. Another variation of particular interest is the *batik* of the Cirebon region on the border between West and Central Java, where large frieze-like patterns or rocks, shrines, clouds and mythical monsters appear against pale, plain grounds. These *batiks* are still produced in workshops in Trusmi and Plered on the outskirts of the city. Meanwhile, from the other end of Java, in the Tuban area, simple but charming village *batik* textiles are still produced on hand-spun cotton.

More Batik

The export of *batik* cloth to regions outside Java, especially Bali and Sumatra, has been taking place for centuries and old *batiks* are still an important part of ceremonial costume on those islands. Blue and white *batiks* from north-coast Java are especially favored in Bali, and these are often embellished with gold leaf *perada* (gluework) to enhance their appearance as costumes for dance-dramas and royal ceremonies. Gold leaf (or gold dust) is also applied to plain fabric by painting or stamping glue patterns onto the cloth surface to which the costly gold substance adheres. The crisp rustling of these lustrous garments complements their dazzling impression, although many of these cloths are now made by stenciling the lotus and other floral designs in

gold paint. While such textiles continue to achieve spectacular effects at theatrical performances, close scrutiny reveals them to be far less subtle than the genuine, older and more expensive *kain perada*.

The Balinese have produced many types of textiles using a multitude of decorative techniques, including tie-dye, tapestry weave, twill weave, weft *ikat* and supplementary weft brocade. At textile craft centers such as Gianyar and Batuan such textiles are made in considerable quantities for local and tourist markets. Usually in silk, the weft *ikat* (*endek*) is produced by tying and dyeing the weft threads into patterns before weaving them into a plain warp. The technique is sometimes combined with gold thread brocade weaving (*songket*) in which supplementary wefts of gold-wrapped thread are added to provide floating patterns, especially in borders and elaborate triangular ends. The effect is a sumptuous textile that is suitable for ceremonial use by the traditional aristocracy. Such fabrics, displaying designs derived from imported, luxury textile heirlooms, or shadow-puppet-style motifs taken from the great Hindu epics were, in the past, only woven for the fastidious Balinese elite.

One justly famous textile – the double *ikat geringsing* – is made only in Bali and on that island, exclusively in the small village of Tenganan, near Karangasem in the east. According to this complicated technique, both the warp threads and the weft threads are separately tied and dyed into patterns which the weaver combines during the weaving process to reveal the complex designs. These masterpieces of textile art are worked on the simplest of backstrap tension looms, yet they are sacred objects and the support of the gods is sought through offerings that are made at the various stages that are required to create them. Like many other traditional textiles, the *geringsing* are used in the various ceremonies of the religious

calendar and life-cycle. The central role of the *geringsing* in rituals and ceremonies explains the great care that is taken to produce these beautiful traditional cloths.

The Sasak people, who inhabit the isolated slopes of Mt. Rinjani, on the island of Lombok, also make sacred textiles which fulfill similar important functions. Although some of the most ritually potent Sasak textiles are decorated only with simple stripes and rich natural dyes, such fabrics are often embellished with vast quantities of old Chinese coins that are threaded through the fringes to add to their spiritual presence.

Textiles are widely used as ceremonial gifts among the Batak peoples of northern Sumatra. At a wedding, for instance, each guest wraps the seated bridal couple in a traditional *ulos* of appropriate design and complexity, according to the giver's age, social standing and family relation-

Above: Wayang golek puppets. Right: A Balinese basket-weaver.

230

ship to the bride or groom. Toba Batak textiles are distinct from those of the Karo, the Simalungun and the Angkola Batak groups. In addition, within each of these Batak regions, different villages specialize in producing one or two of the district's characteristic textiles. The finest of these include the *ulos ragidup* ("Cloth of Life"), with intricately woven black and white supplementary weft inserts of male and female symbols, made around Tarutung, Porsea and Muara, on the shores of Lake Toba as well as the *ulos ragi hotang*, in simple stripes, but with striking, wide twined end-braid made around Baligé, and the dark-blue warp *ikat ulos sibolang* from the island of Samosir, in the center of Lake Toba.

Batak textiles are always woven from cotton, and with the exception of the Angkola Batak *abit* and *parompa*, which display bright tapestry-weave bands and glossy beads, the cloths are worked in sombre earth or indigo tones appropriate to the misty atmosphere of the Batak highlands. The textiles of the various

Malay peoples of Sumatra, however, are bright and colorful, like those of the Balinese. Intricate examples of Minangkabau gold- and silver-thread weaving from Pandai Sikat, and Malay silk and gold brocade from Palembang are made in traditional styles using time-tested apparatus and techniques. Only the quality of the gold thread has changed, and unlike other types of more robust traditional textiles, these splendid textiles must be rolled and not folded during storage and transportation to avoid permanent creasing and damage.

As social and religious changes have occurred, other textile traditions have steadily become less important. In Aceh it is not weaving, but gold-thread embroidery that has survived, and ceremonial hangings, cushions and food covers, items of regalia – even such items as mosquito-net clasps – carry decorative designs stitched to an expensive basecloth such as luxurious velvet. Sadly, one of the greatest textile-producing cultures in all of Southeast Asia, the Paminggir of southern Sumatra, no longer weave their famous ship-cloths. The National Museum in Jakarta has a fine collection of these supplementary weft hangings and splendidly embroidered women's skirts that display fanciful ships with mythical creatures and human riders. A few 19th-century examples are available at high prices in antique shops, and an enterprising weaver in Java is reproducing the Sumatran ship-cloths in considerable numbers for the tourist trade.

Other Crafts

Similar regional variations are evident in the other arts of western Indonesia. In the past, particular styles of sculpture, metalwork, basketry, leatherwork and pottery, could be identified with specific ethnic groups, and even with certain villages. Historically, the peoples of Indonesia depended upon imported glazed

ceramics from China and mainland Southeast Asia. Although their own traditional low-fired pottery, for water and cooking vessels, is still used, it is rapidly being replaced by plastic and metal containers, and although the traditional utensils are still found throughout Indonesia, they remain most prominent in Bali and West Lombok where clay vessels are an integral part of the paraphernalia required for religious offerings. Matting and plaiting skills are also under threat from cheap plastic manufacturers, although fine durable cane and palm-leaf objects are widely available. Lombok basketry in traditional forms is particularly attractive, and the Tasikmalaya area of West Java produces some of the best plaited objects in all of Indonesia.

Metalwork has received an enormous boost from the tourist industry, and in Bali and Java, traditional metal-smithing villages have maintained and expanded their repertoire, offering well-made products in an elaborate traditional form or simple modern style. Metal workers continue to make *kris* (ceremonial swords) and the musical instruments that form part of the *gamelan* (traditional percussion orchestras) of Java and Bali. The smiths of Kota Gede, near Yogyakarta, display high quality silver-working skill. Celuk in Bali and Kota Gadang in West Sumatra are other long-standing silver-smithing centers where regional styles of jewelry are still produced. Gold has long been regarded as a safe investment against inflation, and is widely available in every Indonesian town and city. Judged largely by weight, gold jewelry is usually made in a contemporary style, although in regional centers such as Banda Aceh it is still possible to seek out gold worked with particular traditional regional designs.

The art of wooden sculpture is also region-specific. Javanese centers such as Jepara, on the north coast, and Balinese villages such as Ubud and Mas continue to produce wood-carvings in various styles for both domestic consumption and foreign tourists. Objects as large as doors, room-dividers and furniture, and as minute as buttons and bangles are produced by these craftsmen. Unfortunately, sculptural mastery is now less apparent in Sumatra and it seems that the great traditional carving skills that once embellished the grand ancestral dwellings, meeting houses and rice barns of the Toba and Karo Batak, the Minangkabau and the inhabitants of the island of Nias, have steadily disappeared. Replicas of smaller, traditional objects carved from small buffalo horns, wood and bamboo are available, but the spiritual qualities that imbued the magic wands, charm containers and sacred book covers of the village shaman, and great stone sarcophagi for the bones of the ancestors are difficult to achieve in a more secular age.

Pigment painting on cloth has traditionally been of less significance in

Southeast Asia than in the West, and in Indonesia it is only in Bali that traditional painting is still practiced. These paintings take a variety of forms, and include Balinese traditional calendars, scenes from the great Hindu epics and romances, and stylized panoramas of village life and ritual which flourished in the 20th century. Painting, however, is still important in the production of the dance masks and leather shadow-puppets required for the vital theater arts of Java and Bali. Village artisans specialize in the working of buffalo leather to produce the *wayang kulit* puppets. An intricate patterning of bright pigments and the gilding of clothing and jewelry identify the various characters. Balinese shadow-puppets are more rounded and less attenuated than those used in Central Java. In West Java the puppets (known there as *wayang golek*) take on a three-dimensional form and the performances take place in the round without a shadow screen.

While the most famous instances of Indonesian art are the massive stone monuments of great antiquity that dot the landscape, many of the finest objects in other less permanent media – textiles, wooden sculpture, paintings and *wayang* puppets – can still be examined in the collections on display in the national, regional and palace museums in most of the provinces of western Indonesia. These institutions are often housed in fine old buildings and are imposing examples of regional traditional architecture. With many of these art forms, the skills have been maintained over the centuries by the demands of ritual and the need to continually replace artifacts consumed by time and ceremonial use. Some of these no longer hold a place in modern Indonesia. In Bali, however, the ceremonial cycle is still of paramount importance. Yet much of that island's art is of the most transitory nature. The splendor of the great rituals is often achieved with the most temporary and fragile materials – offerings of flowers

Right: A Madurese leti-leti canoe.

and colored rice cakes, banners of plaited palm leaves, cremation towers and coffins of soft woods and paper – which quickly deteriorate or are destroyed after the ceremony.

Sailing Boats and Outrigger Canoes

Nowhere in the world is there such a variety of colorful fishing villages and maritime cultures as in Indonesia; thriving, busy and open for all to see, but often a little more isolated than the average tourist prefers. Hunting after the traditional sailing *prahu* (boat) and haunting rural fishing villages, usually involves discomfort for a rewarding collection of memories and photographs. To find fishing villages, one must search for the *kampong nelayan*; there is often one at the edge of the coastal towns, but those on stretches of isolated coast are cleaner and more beautiful.

Prahu harbors are often located away from the port areas for powered ships, for example at Kali Baru, beyond Tanjung

Priok to the east of Jakarta, and at Gresik just to the north of Surabaya, on the straits of Madura. These are the places to see concentrations of sailing *prahu*. Ports along the north coast of Java and almost every town among the eastern islands, usually have a corner reserved for traditional sailing vessels.

Traditionally, communication depended on the sea, and a great variety of local boat-styles have developed over the centuries. Today many have vanished forever, but the persistent traveler can still find a rewarding variety.

Indonesia is not only a nation of islands, with few roads in pre-colonial days, but also a place that is kind to ships. The winds blow steadily from the southeast from May to October, then reverse and blow the other way from November to April, allowing for annual return trips from one end of the archipelago to the other. Rot-resistant timbers and material for sails, strings and floats are readily available, and sheltered harbors are abundant (except on the shores of the open oceans). And durable trade goods such as rice, cloth, metal, spices and luxury goods, not naturally available on many of the archipelago's islands, can easily be distributed by ship.

Boat building is traditionally done by specialist craftsmen. These holders of ancient trade secrets have a spiritual commitment to the preservation of tradition; ceremonies performed at every stage of a boat's construction reinforce the importance of the supernatural world. Any deviation from the ways of the ancestors is likely to be punished by the spirits.

Like any other object that is made by a skilled craftsman, a boat has a spirit of its own which is derived from the life-force of its creator and locked into the hull with a ceremony. The days to fell the trees, lay the keel, start a new section or launch the boat, are fixed by a priest or soothsayer. Offerings are made at each stage; in Bali, offerings are made every 210 days, at the feast of Galungan, to the spirits of every outrigger canoe, each of which is decorated with a *sarong*. Knots in the tree have to be considered, insects in the wood are a disaster, timber must not be used twice, women may not stand on the partly constructed boat, the top and bottom of the timber may be significant, but above all, every measurement is a ratio between simple numbers carried in the master builder's head. The size of each boat is fixed by a unit length, which in an outrigger canoe is the inside length of a hull, and on a planked boat is the length of the keel. The large unit length is always divided into twelve parts (equal to the number of ribs in the human body) and every dimension of the boat is a multiple or fraction of this unit.

Houses in Bali are also built on the principle of ratios, taken from the physical dimensions of the master builder.

Right: A friendly jungle-guide at Bohorok's Orangutan Rehabilitation Center (Gunung Leuser National Park).

The basic boat is the dug-out canoe, which, in Indonesia, has an outrigger on each side, and is almost always specialized for fishing. The double outrigger provides a stable platform, so that the occupants (often only one) can turn their attention to the fishing. Nets, lines and trawling are the usual methods. Single outrigger canoes are specialized for use with the throwing net.

A wonderful place to see double outrigger canoes is the Lombok Straits, where hundreds of Balinese *jukung* trawl for tuna.

The dug-out hull was originally built by lashing and sewing planks together, but about a thousand years ago the technique of connecting the planks edge-to-edge with dowels was introduced. Ribs were lashed into place and the whole structure could easily be dismantled. Ships weighing several hundred tons were built for trade with China and India. Western designs have been introduced slowly and patchily over the centuries, and the process is still not complete.

The principal modern boats are the Bugis' *prahu*, now almost entirely motorized; the Madurese *leti leti*, of which several hundred still operate, with a large triangular sail fixed between two booms; Madurese *janggolan*, a few of which are still trading along the north coast of Java, with a complicated rig that is supported by beams pushed out on each side; and the Western-style *lambo*, which looks something like a modern yacht, often with gunter-lug rig and one or two jibs. Older designs have lateral rudders; modern ones, often sailed by Butungese, have a center rudder and a tiller. These boats are all well adapted to Indonesian waters, where they can easily run for shelter, but they are not designed for the high stresses of the fore-and-aft rig; the planks are often short, and the deckhouse is easily swept away; they are not, then, suitable for Western yachtsmen looking for a cheap hull.

WILDLIFE AND ENVIRONMENT

Western Indonesia used to abound with wildlife of every kind, mostly rain forest dwellers, but some specialized to life in open woodland, mountain moorland or limestone hills. Unfortunately, the human population explosion, combined with the depradations caused by unrestrained logging, have seen to it that most wildlife is confined to reserves and national parks, except for those birds, rats, frogs and fish that can live in ricefields. To see the more spectacular wildlife, visitors must travel to more remote areas.

National parks are relatively new to Indonesia; since about 1980 more and more have been set up, based on an already existing system of *cagar alam* (nature reserves) and *suaka margasatwa* (wildlife reserves). Many of these reserves have areas, *taman wisata*, where visitors are permitted to look around without restrictions, but to go into the reserve itself, a permit is necessary. These permits are easily obtained from the offices of the Perlindungan Hutan dan Pelestaroan Alam or PHPA (Directorate of Forest Conservation and Nature Protection) in Bogor.

JAVA: The most famous of Indonesia's reserves is probably **Ujung Kulon** (now a national park), on the western tip of Java. Here lives what may be the world's only remaining viable population of a once widespread and abundant species: the Javan rhinoceros. Rhinos are still actively, and illegally, hunted for the supposed medicinal properties of their horns; Western mythology has it that rhino horn is "used as an aphrodisiac in China," but actually it is used as a reputedly powerful fever-reducing drug – in 1988 the horns of Asian rhinos were worth over US$ 40,000 in Taiwan.

It says a great deal about the devotion of the staff, and the abilities of successive conservationists, that since the mid-1960s the number of rhinos in Ujung Kulon has risen from a couple of dozen to over 60 and that, despite numerous attempts, only one or two rhinos have been killed by poachers in a quarter of a century. Besides possibly seeing a rhino, visitors may also see deer, wild pigs, peacocks, hornbills, two or three species of monkey, and the rare *banteng* (*Bos javanicus*), a species of wild cattle. Visitors to Ujung Kulon who have already been to Bali will notice that *banteng* resemble a larger, leaner, longer-horned version of typical Balinese domestic cattle, with the same white legs and white rump; the bulls are usually black, the cows and calves golden-brown. Balinese cattle are also bred in eastern Java, Madura, Lampung and Sumatra Selatan, but the true wild *banteng* are confined now to a very few areas in Java.

There are leopards in Ujung Kulon, but tigers became extinct there in the 1950s; indeed they are probably gone from the whole of Java. A reserve, **Meru Betiri**, was set up to protect the last remaining population of the distinctive Javan tiger, but it was poorly guarded and they are almost certainly gone forever.

Other reserves in Java, which are worth visiting, include: **Cibodas**, a montane forest national park between Bogor and Bandung; **Pangandaran**, on the south coast of West Java, where the *banteng* and the rare *lutung* or Javan leaf-monkey live; and **Baluran**, in the far east (accessible from Surabaya), which is much more open than the more westerly reserves, and has a large population of *banteng*.

BALI: Just across the straits from Baluran lies the **Bali Barat National Park**, the last known home of the beautiful white starling or Rothschild's grackle, which is much sought after (and still sometimes illegally obtained) by aviarists. Crab-eating or long-tailed macaque monkeys are still common in Bali (in Java aud Sumatra, too), and live around Hindu temples; a race of the *lutung*, different from the Javanese one, survives in the forests on the volcano Mt. Batukau.

SUMATRA: Sumatra has fewer human residents than Java, and correspondingly, has more wildlife. In the **Gunung Leuser National Park**, in Aceh, lives the Sumatran rhinoceros, smaller than the Javan and with two horns instead of only one; though there are 130 to 200 there, they live in thick forest, mainly in the remote mountain valleys, and visitors are very lucky if they see one. (Despite all this, they are still occasionally killed by poachers.) Visitors are usually able to see orangutans, locally known as *mawas*, perhaps in the wild, but certainly at the **Bohorok** and **Ketambe Rehabilitation Centers**, on the edges of the park, where orangutans confiscated from illegal captivity are taught forest skills and eventually persuaded to return to the wild. Gunung Leuser National park is also inhabited by elephants, wild pig, *serow,*

Right: Baby Sumatran crocodiles.

tigers, sun bears, gibbons and other monkeys. The Bohorok center is easily accessible from Medan; Ketambe is north of Kutacane, on the Alas River, further inland.

Mt. Kerinci, Sumatras's highest mountain, is partly covered by a national park (**Kerinci Seblat**); here, too, live some 200 Sumatran rhinoceros, as well as its smaller relative, the curious black-and-white Malay tapir. **Bukit Barisan Selatan** is another national park, in far southwestern Sumatra, which has both rhinos and tapirs, as well as the bizarre bearded pig, and among the many birds is the beautiful argus pheasant. Tigers live, if sparsely, in all these reserves; the Sumatran tiger is slightly different from the Javan, but seems to be headed for the same fate unless it can be better protected than at present. Oddly, there are no leopards in Sumatra; but there is the slightly smaller clouded leopard, which can sometimes be seen up in the trees. Finally, the **Way Kambas Reserve** should be mentioned; the Javan rhinoceros once lived here, but was apparently sent into extinction in the 1930s, by a single Dutch hunter.

The Mentawai Islands, west of Sumatra, have very unusual fauna, including a species of gibbon and three species of monkeys, that are found only here, and are best seen in the **Tettei Batti Reserve**.

The Environment

Tropical rain forests, in a variety of guises, are typical of the western half of Indonesia. Along the Barisan Range in Sumatra, and the central mountain spine of Java, one mostly finds lowland forests known as montane and moss forests. The east coast of Sumatra is covered by wide areas of swamp forests; mangroves grow along the tidal zones themselves; and patches of specialized forest are found elsewhere, such as those distinct to limestone hills, as well as peat forests. What makes

these unusual among the world's rain forests is the dominance of a single plant family: *Dipterocarpaceae*, a valuable timber tree. Many of the lowland forests of Sumatra have now been clear-cut; only in mountainous regions are there still substantial stands of the original, old-growth rain forest.

As one travels east through Java, the climate becomes drier, and the flora changes from rain forest to monsoon forest and open country. As the flora changes, so does the fauna; gibbons, for example, are not found east of Gunung Slamet in Central Java nor (in the days of their abundance) were rhinos, whereas ecologically tougher species like wild pigs and *banteng* lived all over the island.

Bali, small though it is, is as diverse as Java in its environment. The whole of the western side is dry, almost scrubby forest. The wetter, hence more fertile, eastern side is densely populated and thus denuded of its natural vegetation.

In the past, forest clearance – especially rain forest logging – was almost unregulated; government control over logging and other forms of clearance is now much tighter, but illegal activities continue. Control of illegal settlements and wood-cutting in wildlife reserves is also less than perfect, although restrictive laws have been passed. Forest destruction used to be attributed to slash-and-burn agriculture, and the notion that planned commercial activities could be the real culprit has taken some time to be accepted.

Indonesia's laws regulating the killing and exploitation of wildlife are tough; they are, however, difficult to police, and many people aren't even aware they exist. One species these laws try to protect is the Sumatran rhinoceros. Its habitat is dense and difficult to control, but poachers, if caught by competent and honest authorities are dealt with severely. Yet, the Torgamba forest, where the species was known to live was scheduled for clear-cutting in the early 1980s, which seems to make a mockery of the strict preservation laws.

ISLAM

Few sounds are more evocative than the *azan,* the Islamic call to prayer which drifts over Indonesia's ricefields and rooftops five times daily, from the first glimmer of dawn to the evening dark. For the Indonesian Muslim, it is the sound of certainty and continuity which much of the West has lost forever. He knows that it has echoed through 13 centuries, and that the same Arabic chants can be heard from Morocco to the Philippines.

The timelessness, however, is deceptive. The *azan* now comes from an amplified cassette, and celebrates a fragmented and fast-changing faith. Change is nothing new to Islam; intrinsically the most puritanical of the great religions, it seems to have spent most of its history in a constant state of reformation. Yet in Indonesia the current changes are crucial. They

Above: Modern Islam in Jakarta's Istiqlal mosque, one of the world's largest. Right: Giggling Muslim girls in Banten, West Java.

are determining the relationship between ancient Islam and the new gods of progress, development and modernity.

Not that Indonesian Islam is under threat; quite the reverse. In a country already 87 percent Muslim on paper, it gains ground daily as ever more "identity card Muslims" (*Muslim KTP*) are persuaded to take the tenets and duties of their faith more seriously. Men whose Islam went no deeper than their excised foreskins, now answer the call of every *azan;* pagan and Hindu beliefs, which for centuries dove-tailed perfectly with Muslim practice, are being challenged. In the cities, signs of the revival are everywhere: Islamic bookshops and publishing houses are booming; new mosques and religious schools are opening; government offices, stations and airports now have special prayer rooms for the devout.

Why the new-found zeal? It is partly a conservative reaction against rapid social change and the urban immorality perceived as an import from the godless West. At another level, it may be seen as

a symptom of progress itself, as a developing people trades its rural superstition and hocus-pocus for a more consistent, analytic faith that is valid outside the insular society of the village, and is strong enough to sustain its adherents through the shocks of urban life. There is, however, another important element in this sudden upsurge in Islam's popularity: opposition to the political order. Suharto's government rode the Islamic tide where it could, funding schools and mosques, and trying to attract religious politicians into its fold. However, it could not direct the current, beneath which ran a strong undertow of criticism and protest.

In more than a thousand Islamic discussion groups, earnest young men and women debate not only the interpretation of the Koran, but also inequality, public morality, corruption, the relationship between Islam and politics, and the idea of an Islamic state. Since the slaughter of the opposition left in 1965, the social and moral prescriptions of Islam have attracted many discontented young people

who, in a different time or place, would probably have been socialists. And lurking somewhere in the murky wings, there are also a few men of religious violence. Muslim terrorists hijacked a Garuda airliner in 1984, and the Indonesian army exterminated an extremist group in Lampung in 1989. Suharto and other powerful figures wanted Javanese mysticism to be recognized and sponsored as an approved religion, to challenge the growing momentum of Islam, but were unable even to get such a bill passed by even their own tame parliament. There was bitter opposition to the 1985 law obliging all political organizations to accept the principle of religious tolerance that is embodied in the official state philosophy.

The New Order hoped to forge the traditional religious tolerance and theological vagueness of Java into a sort of pseudo-secularism that was appropriate to a modern industrial society. Instead, the economic crisis of 1998/99 resulted in the election of a Muslim president — Abdurrahman Wahid.

METRIC CONVERSION

Metric Unit	US Equivalent
Meter (m)	39.37 in.
Kilometer (km)	0.6241 mi.
Square Meter (sq m)	10.76 sq. ft.
Hectare (ha)	2.471 acres
Square Kilometer (sq km)	0.386 sq. mi.
Kilogram (kg)	2.2 lbs.
Liter (l)	1.05 qt.

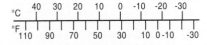

TRAVEL PREPARATIONS

Climate

Indonesia has a very hot, wet climate. In coastal cities the daytime temperature hovers around 28°C, and air humidity often hovers around 80 percent throughout the year. During the wet season, usually November till April, it will rain hard every afternoon. Wear light, loose, quick-drying cotton clothes. Take hints from the way the locals behave: walk slowly, without tension; seek shade at all times; nap indoors during the early afternoon if you can; take a cooling *mandi* three times a day.

Temperatures fall rapidly with altitude, however, and a windy mountain pass in Java can be downright cold, especially at night, so pack a sweater.

Wear sandals unless visiting someone or hiking – but remember to bring them with you if you have big feet, because Indonesians will laugh if you ask to buy a pair of size elevens.

Health

Always remember that Indonesia has a tropical climate that Western bodies need to get accustomed to, and in part be inoculated against. There are standard vaccinations against: typhoid, hepatitis A and B (both should be administered at least six months before traveling), and cholera.

At least two weeks before your trip, an experienced, up-to-date doctor should be consultd about prevention of malaria, the tropics' most dangerous disease. Using an effective insect repellent is a helpful additional precaution.

Water should always be boiled for at least ten minutes before drinking, which is why you might ask the street vendors not to cool drinks with crushed ice. Raw fruit and foods, cold cooked meats, even ice cream, possibly made with unpasteurized milk, should be avoided. Try to peel fruit yourself.

In the course of tasting and experiencing the local culture, your body may react to unaccustomed foods, even safe ones, by contracting diarrhea. This is normal and any commercial anti-diarrhoeal will take care of the problem; try *Immodium* if the case is especially bad.(Note: Product names in italics are the local Indonesian name.)

Fungal infections can be battled with *Canesten* – keep applying it long after the battle is apparently won. Use antiseptic soap (*Sapoderm*, for example) to help prevent skin infections. Avoid walking barefoot as some parasites (such as ringworm) enter the body through the sole of the foot.

Antiseptics can also be useful, especially if you aim to travel far from any urban center. For example, *Betadine* is excellent for treating small cuts. *Cicatrin* is a topical antibiotic. You may also want have an oral antibiotic, such as *Bactrin*, available for treating more serious infections.

Most of these products are readily available in Indonesia, but it helps to know exactly what you are looking for. Watch out for dangerous fakes!

Remember to use SPF 15+ sun screen and to drink beyond your thirst to prevent heat stroke and dehydration.

Indonesia has a fair number of provincial hospitals and doctors with varying competence. If you need major treatment try to get to a big city, preferably Jakarta. Ask your consulate, embassy or expatriate residents to recommend a doctor. The Pertamina Hospital (Jl. Kyai Maja, Kebayoran Baru, Tel. 021 / 7200289) is most often used by foreigners in Jakarta. In case of an emergency, you may want to fly to Singapore or even return home; make sure that your travel or medical insurance covers such things as air ambulance.

Money

US dollars are the most useful foreign currency in Indonesia, and traveler's checks (preferably American Express) should always be in dollars. Take proof of purchase with you. Change money and checks at banks if you can, not in airports or hotels. Exchange rates are by far the best in Jakarta. There is no black market in foreign currencies. Credit cards are accepted in most of the better hotels and restaurants.

There is a chronic shortage of change, though not as chronic as pocket-groping taxi-drivers would have you believe. Get bills in small denominations and save coins for bus fares, telephone calls, etc.

Although travel tickets, prepared food and some of the more expensive urban shops have fixed prices, bargaining is the norm in many everyday transactions. Indonesian participants usually have a rather accurate idea of the outcome before they start, but insist on reaching it through a protracted struggle in which both exorbitantly high and insultingly low figures are named. This conflict, necessary and even enjoyable for the local, may be highly stressful for the uninitiated foreigner. Shop around first, ask advice and take along an Indonesian friend if you can. Be patient, smile, play down your interest, but never make a bid you do not mean. As a last resort, try the old walk-away trick – but be warned, even the grubbiest stallholder can be an excellent judge of intent.

Visas

Citizens of Australia, New Zealand, Canada, the USA, and all western European nations except Portugal, are not required to obtain tourist visas prior to their arrival. Provided they carry a passport that is valid for at least six months after entry, and have onward or return tickets or proof they have purchased such, they are issued a **Short Visit Pass** (valid for 60 days) upon arrival. Other nationalities must apply at an Indonesian embassy or consulate abroad. With the two-month Short Visit Pass, no extensions whatsoever are possible – you must leave Indonesia when your pass expires. If you want to stay longer you must leave the country, normally for Singapore, and re-enter.

Other types of visa, available only by prior application to an Indonesian embassy, include the **Visitor Visa**, which is initially valid for five weeks, but is extendable by increments to six months at Imigrasi offices, and the **Business Visa**, which is initially valid for 30 days and is also extendable to six months. Both of these visas require letters of sponsorship.

GETTING TO INDONESIA

By air: Indonesia's main international air gateways are **Soekarno-Hatta Airport** in Jakarta, and **Ngurah Rai Airport** in Denpasar. Many airlines serve these increasingly important termini from the major cities of Southeast and East Asia, Western Europe, and the USA's west coast, with less frequent flights from some South Asian and Middle Eastern airports.

Medan's **Polonia Airport** is also a long-standing international air destination, with cheap connections to Penang and Singapore. The air travel situation is becoming more complex and less rigid all the time, with **Padang**, **Palembang**, **Surabaya** and **Solo** now receiving direct international flights from Singapore. For through travelers, there are also a few international flights in and out of eastern Indonesia: Pontianak to Singapore and Kuching, Tarakan to Tawau, and Kupang to Darwin. For the typical, long-distance, short-stay, non-Asian visitor, the choice is usually Jakarta, Denpasar or the short connections from Singapore and west Malaysia. When purchasing tickets, keep in mind that it is more informative and often cheaper to go to a reputable agent than to deal directly with an airline.

By ship: Ironically, it is difficult to enter this island nation by sea. The only regular international passenger services are ferries between Singapore (**Finger Pier**) and Batam island (with onward connections to Pekanbaru, Jakarta and elsewhere once inside Indonesian territory), and between Penang and Medan.

TRAVELING IN INDONESIA

The **domestic passenger shipping** network which once tied the archipelago together is in a skeletal state today, but what there is is safer and more reliable than it was a decade ago. Since they upgraded their fleet to modern, German-built liners, the state-owned shipping concern **Pelni** has become a competitive alternative for those with more flexible timetables.

Several Pelni ships ply the ports of East Sumatra and North Java on long, scheduled circuits; one, the *Kerinci*, also serves the west coast of Sumatra as far north as Sibolga. Pelni tickets can be bought only at Pelni offices – see the local *Guidepost* sections. Many smaller shipping operations exist; one to avoid if possible is the "pioneer" line **Perintis**, which is active in the Riau archipelago and whose ships are as bad as Pelni's used to be. On smaller vessels, enterprising members of the crew will probably offer to rent you the upper-deck cabin, which can dramatically increase the price of your ticket.

Domestic air travel in Indonesia is highly developed. Thanks to the squadrons of Fokker Fellowships, DC-9s and Airbuses on its internal routes, **Garuda**, the national carrier, has the largest air fleet in the southern hemisphere. If you have your ticket in your hand, you should have no problems flying with Garuda. Indonesia's second airline is **Merpati**, a Garuda subsidiary, which flies mainly turboprop machines and serves a more complete network, including airstrips that are too small for Garuda's jets. Where Merpati duplicates Garuda routes, it is slightly cheaper, but Merpati is not as professionally polished as Westererns have come to expect, and you should check-in early. Also cheaper are the private airlines, the biggest are **Bouraq** and **Mandala**, both of which operate mostly on outer island routes. Luckily, their ageing British turboprops were sturdily built. Locations of airline offices and headquarters in Jakarta, are listed in the local *Guidepost* sections. Passengers flying Garuda into Indonesia can often claim discounts on pre-booked internal flights, so be sure to ask in advance.

Only Java and Sumatra have **railways**, and of the three unconnected networks in Sumatra, only the southern one (Tanjungkarang to Palembang and Lubuklinggau) carries passengers. Java, which once had perhaps the most comprehensive rail network in the colonial world, still boasts quite an impressive system despite closures. All of the major cities are served, as are the ferry terminals at Merak and Banyuwangi. Exhaustive class gradations both between and within trains cater to every budget, and you get what you pay for. The cheapest (*Langsam, Cepat, Gaya Baru, Senja*) are like traveling Javanese villages, complete with livestock, hawkers and thieves.

At the other end of the spectrum are the *Bima* and *Mutiara Utara* air-conditioned express sleepers, which link Jakarta to Surabaya via Yogya and Semarang respectively. Somewhere in between the two extremes are the Jakarta to Bandung *Parahyangan* express and the Jakarta to Yogya *Senja Utama* night train. On long overland journies, trains can be far safer and more comfortable than buses, even if they are sometimes slower. They also take you to the city center, whereas long-distance bus terminals are usually peripheral. However, just buying tickets can be a problem. In Jakarta there are travel agents who can book them in advance, but in most places you must turn up and wait in line on the day of departure, the earlier the better. Trains generally leave on time, but more often than not they arrive late.

The length of paved **roads** in Indonesia has quadrupled since 1970, and many are now as good as, if not better than, rural roads in the US or Europe. Unfortunately, driving standards and practices are still rather primitive. Many drivers literally race down every good stretch, making traffic more lethal than before. You may even be thankful for the ever-increasing congestion which tends to cramp the style of the more suicidal drivers.

At least the express *bis* (**buses**) which are now displacing the trains as standard long-distance people-carriers in Java have the advantage of size in any violent encounter. The best new-generation of *bis malam* (night buses) have reservable, airline-type seats, air conditioning, on-board toilets, videos (providing the mixed blessing of blaring midnight melodramas), and meals included in the ticket price. Daytime and local buses, and the full-size *bis kota* ("town buses") found in some of the larger cities, are less salubrious, but still more comfortable than the tiny **colts** (pronounced "kol") and *bemo* which now dominate short-haul and intra-urban routes. A colt is a Japanese minibus, a *bemo* a covered pickup truck fitted with plank seats. Pick the seat you want – always try to get an aisle seat in a

colt – and keep it, by whatever means you find necessary. Have the appropriate coins ready, plus an extra one for knocking on the coachwork to signal when you want to get off. Marvel at the casual, gritty efficiency of the driver/conductor team. Such vehicles are always plentiful and cheap, but seldom leave a terminal until they are full; don't get on an empty one if you can avoid it!

Immense distances and poor roads make overland travel in **Sumatra** a far rougher option than in Java or Bali. The euphemistically-named "Trans-Sumatran Highway," which runs the entire length of the island, from Lampung to Medan and Aceh, is always passable with patience, but you might need a lot of it, as well as an iron constitution, especially in the wet season (any time from October to April). The short wheelbase Mercedes and high-chassis, wide-tired Japanese buses now used are up to the job, but they have not abolished the misery of regular break-downs, window leaks and blaring Indonesian pop-music. Under ideal conditions, the Tanjungkarang to Medan trip takes 4 days, but few foreigners have the stomach for such a sustained assault. Away from the highway, things can be even worse.

If you are brave enough and have an international driving licence, you can rent motorcycles and cars in Bali, and sometimes in Java. One rental-car office in Java is in front of Adisucipto Airport, Yogya. In Bali you will need to get a special local licence, available from Denpasar police after you pass a simple test and pay a hefty fee. Indonesians drive on the left – more or less.

Most so-called **taxis** in Indonesia are actually chauffeur-driven rental cars, Available by the hour for a minimum of one hour, they are usually expensive. Metered taxis exist on a large scale only in Jakarta, where there are plenty. However, you should ever use one whose driver says his meter is *mati* ("dead").

The most primative form of motorised passenger transportation is the *bajaj* (pronounced "bajai"), an Indian-designed, motorised tricycle-like contraption. Found mainly in Jakarta, the nimble *bajaj* can sometimes reach areas other vehicles can't reach, but unless you are a good bargainer it may well cost as much as a metered taxi.

Muscle power is not yet obsolete, even in urban Indonesia. **Horsecarts** (*andong, bendi, dokar*) are found in the smaller towns; they have an old-world charm, but animal lovers might prefer not watch the underfed, cowed beasts who are terrified by screaming *bemo*. And, while some enlightened Westerners may see the *becak*, (tricycle rickshaw), as a symbol of human oppression, they are in fact a normal means of conveyance which provides employment for many people. Though excluded from certain arterial roads, scores of these pretty, practical vehicles wait with their human engines at stations and junctions to ferry haughty passengers through the maze of back-streets and alleys. Foreigners usually overpay *becak* drivers, but then, they probably should.

Guided Tours

Do not be too quick to spurn local guided tours; some of these can show and teach you things you may not be able to discover on your own, or at least they will help you do it faster and cheaper. Mainstream internal tour organisers include **Vayatours** and **Natrabu**, but there are hundreds of small and off-beat operators; see most large hotels and local tourist offices for details.

National Parks

A permit from an office of the Directorate of Forest Protection and Nature Conservation (**PHPA**) is required to enter any national park or reserve, except for the pass-free enclaves called **Taman Wisata** (Tourist Parks). The PHPA headquarters is located in Bogor. For local branch offices, see the local *Guidepost* sections.

PRACTICAL TIPS FROM A TO Z

Accommodation

There is a huge range of accommodation types and standards available, and the cheap end tends to offer the more unusual and rewarding experiences, if you are up to its challenges. Prices vary geographically, being lowest in Bali and small-town Java and highest in urban Sumatra. In general, rooms in the **budget** category, which in this book means less than Rp 15,000 (about US$ 2) per night, are found in *losmen*. In some areas, particularly in Sumatra, these are known by the Malay term *penginapan*. Dormitories are rare in Indonesia and most rooms are individual, but in other respects the *losmen* is hostel-like, with thin walls, short beds, dicey wiring, very possibly no fans and certainly no air conditioning. Bring a 100 W lightbulb if you want to read; those supplied are usually impossibly dim. Toilets are of the squat type – you soon get used to them, but they are no place to read the paper. You *mandi* (bathe) by means of an open concrete *bak* (water tank) and a *gayung* (plastic scoop). Whatever you do, DO NOT climb into the tank! And don't scream for the manager if there are fish in it – they eat the larvae of dangerous mosquitos. Hygiene standards in *losmen* vary widely, but few are cockroach-free. Noise can also be a problem, especially from the TV set which is usually left on at full volume all evening; the only mercy is that transmission ceases at midnight.

After this catalogue of potential woes, it must be said that many *losmen* have a major redeeming feature in addition to their low cost: they are perfect places to learn about Indonesian lives, loves and languages. In some places, however, foreigners are beginning to expropriate and transform *losmen* culture. On Bali and in Yogyakarta, many *losmen* cater to European foibles, providing breakfasts and a higher than usual standard of toilet hygiene. Some are even explicitly closed to Indonesians!

A step above the ordinary *losmen*, both in price and comfort, **moderate** (Rp 15,000-60,000 or US$ 2-8) accommodation in Indonesia includes a motley variety of dowdy old colonial hotels, spartan new business hotels, and souped-up *losmen* and guesthouses, often wishfully calling themselves *wisma*. All three can be very good value, but shop around. Moderate range places may afford greater cleanliness, security and privacy than budget ones; many have western toilets, air conditioning and their own restaurants.

Above Rp 60,000 (US$ 8), are **luxury** rooms with all modern conveniences and often exceptional (they are certainly extensively staffed) service. Luxury-class hotels often offer programs of cultural events, folklore and videos.

Business Hours

The work week is a prime example of Indonesian flexibility. Sunday is a day of rest; and work stops at noon on Friday, in time for the Muslim midday prayer. Saturday afternoon is also free. Government offices are open Monday through Thursday from 8 a.m. to 3 p.m., Friday 8 to 11 a.m., Saturday 8 a.m. to 2 p.m. In practice, though, nothing much gets done on Friday or Saturday.

Commercial offices and banks, on the other hand, are open Monday to Friday, usually from 8 a.m. to between 3 and 5 p.m., with a half-day on Saturday. Retail stores often stay open as late as 10 p.m., including Saturday, although they may close for an afternoon siesta.

The phrase *jam karet* ("rubber time") is used, with a grin, whenever something is not finished on time or does not occur when it was supposed to.

Crime

Indonesia's violent crime rates are probably lower than in most western countries, but **theft** – from rooms, vehicles, bags and pockets – is a constant danger, especially for the foreigner, considered rich by definition. Leave as little as possible unattended, be alert and avoid crowds. Where hotels are concerned, security generally correlates with the price.

Drugs use is fairly widespread among local urban youth. **Warning**: Possession and purchase, even of cannabis, is prohibited for Indonesians and foreigners alike.

Customs

Customs can confiscate pornographic and 'subversive' literature – definitions of which may not correspond with yours. Video tapes are subject to lengthy inspection and are best avoided. Any writing in Chinese characters is forbidden. One liter of alcohol and 200 cigarets are duty-free.

Eating and Drinking

Eating is a major part of the magic of Indonesia. Not just the food itself, which is always an adventure and can be superlatively good, but also the experience of its public eating places, especially the ramshackle *warung* or canvas food stalls which line so many city streets. Often the most persistent memory of Indonesia is not a great work of nature or man, but one of eating simple food amid gaslight and *kretek* smoke, and unfamiliar cooking smells on a hot tropical night.

Restaurants, despite their often spartan appearance and blaring TVs, also have a special atmosphere of their own. Jot down your order on the pad provided, but do not set too much store by the printed menu, which except in very expensive places is probably very hypothetical. The bill is a *rekening*; tips are not customary.

Chinese food is rare in Indonesia, but you generally won't be disappointed if you can find it.

Electricity

Both 110 V/50 Hz and 220 V/50 Hz electricity supplies are in use, the intent being to convert entirely to the latter in the long term. Check the voltage before plugging in any foreign appliance.

Blackouts occur occasionally, even in big cities, and wild current fluctuations are commonplace – a hi-fi or computer will need a surge protector. Poor or remote villages have electricity only from dusk to midnight, or not at all.

Etiquette

Keep in mind that Western visitors are immediately obvious in Indonesia, and that historically they haven't always been well behaved.

Indonesians don't expect you to know and follow all the rules of every-day life, but following a few simple guidelines can make your life, communication and your entire trip much more pleasant.

Politeness is directly related to the relationship between two people. This means that the same people who act aggressively and chaotic in traffic, happily entertain guests and show respect to those of a higher status. Relationships between people emphasize their differences in age, family and social heirarchy. Keep in mind that as a guest, you are expected to always remain reserverd and friendly.

Symbols always play a key role in communication between people, but can be difficult to read, especially in a foreign country. In Asian cultures it is very important that no one is shamed or made to "lose face," especially in front of others. Conflicts are usually resolved through subtle hints; paraphrasing, euphamisims and indirect answers, almost to the point of being what Westerners would call outright lies, are key. Even the language itself is very indirect.

Associating with members of the opposite sex is also very reserverd. Although public physical contact between men and women is taboo, you will often see two people of the same sex holding hands; this is a common sign of friendship, not homōsexuality.

Clothes should be modest and clean. Shorts, sleeveless shirts and strapless tops are suitable only for the beach. The demands of 'formality' are not high – jackets and ties, for instance, are almost never worn – so there is little excuse for not meeting them. Talk quietly and with good humour, even in disputes, and try not to show anger, which is regarded as a weakness.

Certain gestures are also taboo. Never stand with hands on hips, which is viewed as being aggressive. To beckon or point with the forefinger is insulting; point instead with the thumb or pursed lips, beckon with the whole hand, palm downwards. Never give or receive with the left hand; it is used to clean yourself after using an Indonesian toilet.

Never eat a meal until your host explicitly invites you to start. If you empty your plate completely, it is usually taken to mean you are still hungry. Second helpings are customary, so do not overload first time round. Always eat something to avoid insulting the host. Small gifts, such as flowers or sweets are regularly given to hosts, but do not offer to share the cost of anything done for you. Indonesians will sometimes honor you by stooping as they pass your chair, keeping their head below yours; if you take this practice up yourself, you will impress traditionalists. Keep in mind, however, that some Indonesians, especially Christians, are actively against what they see as a "feudal" practice.

The guidelines above refer to more traditonal Indonesian households, which are still the majority, but students and urban families may think differently.

Holidays

One spin-off of Indonesia's religious diversity is a unique array of **national holidays**, including no less than three

New Year's Days – Islamic, Christian and Hindu. Islam contributes the most, but the dates of the Moslem holidays are not predictable without reference to the special lunar calendar. Avoid travelling during *Idul Fitri,* at the end of the Moslem fasting month, when millions of Indonesians hit the road to visit relatives.

Liquor

Alcohol does not play an important part in this mainly Islamic society, but for inflated prices you can buy imported liquor and beer at larger hotels and supermarkets. *Bintang* is the best of the many local beers.

Photography

There are only the usual restrictions such as defense installations and bridges. It is important to respect the privacy of individuals, especially in temples. If you buy film there, always check expiry date.

Post and Telecommunications

Indonesia's country code is +62.

Indonesian **postal service** can be fast and efficient when everything works, but theft is a huge problem; anything vaguely appealing usually disappears.

Inside the post office there are often lots of people, but no real lines. Anything short of assault is acceptable manners, but keep things impersonal by never catching the eyes of the people you elbow and jostle. Out of necessity, Indonesians re-glue their stamps, from vile pots provided, to ensure that they stay affixed. Also, try to watch the stamps being canceled yourself, so some lucky sub-postmaster can't supplement his meagre earnings by re-selling them, leaving your letter without any. Always use the *Kilat* or *Kilat Khusus* express services, and register anything valuable. Poste restante services are widely available. Only larger post offices can send parcels.

Although it is still under tremendous pressure, the **telephone system** is now remarkably good by third world standards. Even public booths usually work. Most cities of western Indonesia now have international direct dialing, but it is much cheaper to use the local telephone office than your hotel phone.

Time

Indonesia spans no less than three time zones; most of the areas covered in this book, however, fall within the western zone, which is 7 hours ahead of Greenwich Mean Time. The exceptions are Lombok, Bali, and Sulawesi, which are 8 hours ahead of GMT.

Weights and Measures

Indonesia uses the metric system in both weights and measures (see p. 240).

ADDRESSES

Embassies / Consulates

Australia: *Jakarta:* Jl. M. H. Thamrin 15, tel: 5227034. *Denpasar:* Jl. Raya Sanur 146, P.O. Box 243, Tanjung Bungkak, tel: 25997/8. **Canada:** *Jakarta:* Wisma Metropolitan I, 5th floor, Jl. Jen. Sudirman Kav 29, P.O. Box 52 JKT, tel: 510709. **Ireland:** *Jakarta:* Jl. Gedung Hijau I 11, Pondok Indah, tel: 7690070. **New Zealand:** *Jakarta:* Jl. Diponegoro 41, tel: 330680. **United Kingdom:** *Jakarta:* Jl. M. H. Thamrin 75, tel: 330904. *Medan:* P.O. Box 163, tel: 518699. *Surabaya:* Jl. Janur Sari 150, P.O. Box 310. **USA:** *Jakarta:* Jl. Merdeka Selatan 5, tel: 360360. *Medan:* Jl. Imam Bonjol 13, tel: 322200. *Surabaya:* Jl. Raya Sutomo 33, tel: 69287.

Tourist Offices Outside Indonesia

Australia: Garuda Indonesia Office, 4 Bligh Street, P.O. Box 3836, Sydney 2000. **Europe:** Wiesenhüttenplatz 17, 60329 Frankfurt/Main., Germany tel: +(49) 69/233677. **N. America:** 3457 Wilshire Blvd., Los Angeles, CA 90010, tel: +(1) 231-387-2078.

LANGUAGE GUIDE

Hello	*salam*
Good morning	*selamat pagi*
Good day	*selamat siang*
Good evening	*selamat sore*
Good-bye	*sampai bertemu lagi*
What's your name (he)?	*apa nama tuan?*
What's your name (she)?	*apa nama nyonya?*
My name is...	*nama saya...*
I live in...	*saya tinggal di...*
Where is the...?	*(di)mana...?*
How far is it from...to...?	*berapa jauh?*
How do I get to...?	*bagamaina saya ke...?*
How much is it ?	*berapa harga?*
May I have the menu?	*saya mau lihat daftar makanan*
I'd like something to drink	*saya mau minum*
The bill, please!	*saya mau bayar*
I will stay here...days	*saya tinggal disini...hari*
What's this?	*apa ini?*
What's that?	*apa itu?*
What time is it?	*jam berapa?*
I	*saya*
you	*kamu*
we	*kami / kita*
okay	*baik*
yes	*ya*
no	*tidak*
big	*besar*
small	*kecil*
today	*sekarang*
afternoon	*siang*
evening	*sore*
night	*malam*
week	*minggu*
month	*bulan*
year	*tahun*
clean	*bersih*
dirty	*kotor*
hot	*panas*
cold	*dingin*
please	*silahkan*
thank you	*terima kasih*
less	*kurang*
more	*lebih banyak*
to come	*datang*
to go	*pergi*
price	*harga*
shop	*toko*
medicine	*obat*
market	*pasar*
room	*kamar*
vegetable	*sayuran*
water	*air*
tea	*teh*
milk	*susu*
rice (cooked)	*nasi*
rice (uncooked)	*beras*
sugar	*gula*
salt	*garam*
butter	*mentega*
meal	*makanan*
breakfast	*makanan pagi*
one	*satu*
two	*dua*
three	*tiga*
four	*empat*
five	*lima*
six	*enam*
seven	*tujuh*
eight	*delapan*
nine	*sembilan*
ten	*sepuluh*
eleven	*sebelas*
twelve	*duabelas*
twenty	*duapuluh*
thirty	*tigapuluh*
forty	*empatpuluh*
fifty	*limapuluh*
sixty	*enampuluh*
seventy	*tujuhpuluh*
eighty	*delapanpuluh*
ninety	*sembilanpuluh*
one hundred	*seratus*
one thousand	*seribu*
ten thousand	*sepuluhribu*

Pronunciation:

j	as j (jet-set)
y	y as in yes
c	pronounced as tj or ts
h	pronounced even at the end of a word

AUTHORS

David E. F. Henley is a geographer, and was the project editor and the main author of *Nelles Guide Indonesia*. His love of Indonesia led ultimately to a doctoral thesis on the country's colonial past and to this travel guide ("Traveling in Indonesia," "Islam").

James J. Fox is a noted anthropologist who has written extensively on several Indonesian regional cultures and is now fascinated above all by Java, where his involvement in development projects takes him regularly ("The Culture of Java").

Putu Davies is a historian who combines her academic knowledge with the practical insights of more than a decade spent living in her beloved Bali ("Beyond the Myth of Bali").

Anthony J. S. Reid is professor of southeast Asian history at the Australian National University. His work includes classic books on the Indonesian national revolution and the history of northern Sumatra ("A Portrait of Sumatra").

Yohanni Johns is a lecturer in Indonesian language and literature and is also an expert cook who has produced a number of books on the cuisine of her native Indonesia ("Indonesian Cuisine").

Robyn Maxwell is an acknowledged expert on Indonesian arts and handicrafts. She has traveled to the most remote corners of the archipelago collecting textiles for the Australian National Gallery ("Traditional Arts and Crafts").

G. Adrian Horridge is a leading authority on Indonesian sailing craft, which he pursues indefatigably during breaks from his work as a research biologist ("Traditional Arts and Crafts").

Colin P. Groves is a naturalist whose research on southeast Asian mammals has led him to a deep interest in ecological and conservation issues in Indonesia ("Wildlife and the Environment").

Berthold Schwarz, Managing Editor, was "bitten by the Indonesia bug" in 1981, on a research grant to Sumatra. Since then he's photographed many areas and led study groups there. He's also written travel books, including *Nelles Guide Indonesia*, *Bali* and *Morocco* ("Sulawesi").

Werner Mlyneck is a globe-trotter who's been traveling around the world since the 1970s. As an Indonesia specialist, he's a *Nelles Guide* correspondent.

PHOTOGRAPHERS

Gunderson, Nick	45, 159
Höbel, Robert	8/9, 10/11, 35, 38, 40, 59, 80, 141 L, 155, 160, 194, 227, 228
Kohl, Günter	73, 90, 224, 235
Kunert, Rainer E.	12, 14, 16, 44, 50, 52, 54, 58, 74/75, 94, 116, 130, 135, 139, 164, 178
Maeritz, Kai	110, 152, 191, 238
Müller, Kai Ulrich	62, 184, 213
Muller, Kal	15, 18, 19 R, 21, 24, 26, 27, 28, 31, 32, 36, 42, 48, 53, 60, 63, 65, 66, 67, 69, 70, 71, 82, 86, 91, 96, 97, 106, 111, 122, 127, 129, 132, 137, 138, 141 R, 144, 174, 177, 183, 185, 187, 188, 189, 203, 206, 210, 216, 220, 222/223, 225, 230, 231, 233, 237, 239
Oey, Eric	202
Rex, Peter	Cover
Schwarz, Berthold	154, 170, 171, 172, 186
Steinhardt, Jochen	19 L, 23, 41, 46, 56, 76/77, 100, 105, 107, 131, 140, 149, 150, 156, 157
Vestner, Rainer	199.

Explore the World

NELLES MAPS

AVAILABLE TITELS

Afghanistan 1 : 1 500 000
Argentina *(Northern)*, **Uruguay**
  1 : 2 500 000
Argentina *(Southern)*, **Uruguay**
  1 : 2 500 000
Australia 1 : 4 000 000
Bangkok - *and Greater Bangkok*
  1 : 75 000 / 1 : 15 000
Burma → *Myanmar*
Caribbean - **Bermuda, Bahamas,**
  Greater Antilles 1 : 2 500 000
Caribbean - **Lesser Antilles**
  1 : 2 500 000
Central America 1 : 1 750 000
Central Asia 1 : 1 750 000
China - *Northeastern*
  1 : 1 500 000
China - *Northern* 1 : 1 500 000
China - *Central* 1 : 1 500 000
China - *Southern* 1 : 1 500 000
Colombia - **Ecuador** 1 : 2 500 000
Crete - Kreta 1 : 200 000
Dominican Republic - **Haiti**
  1 : 600 000
Egypt 1 : 2 500 000 / 1 : 750 000
Hawaiian Islands
  1 : 330 000 / 1 : 125 000
Hawaiian Islands – **Kaua'i**
  1 : 150 000 / 1 : 35 000

Hawaiian Islands – **Honolulu**
 - **O'ahu** 1 : 35 000 / 1 : 150 000
Hawaiian Islands – **Maui - Moloka'i**
 - **Lāna'i** 1 : 150 000 / 1 : 35 000
Hawaiian Islands – **Hawai'i, The Big**
 Island 1 : 330 000 / 1 : 125 000
Himalaya 1 : 1 500 000
Hong Kong 1 : 22 500
Indian Subcontinent 1 : 4 000 000
India - *Northern* 1 : 1 500 000
India - *Western* 1 : 1 500 000
India - *Eastern* 1 : 1 500 000
India - *Southern* 1 : 1 500 000
India - *Northeastern* - **Bangladesh**
  1 : 1 500 000
Indonesia 1 : 4 000 000
Indonesia **Sumatra** 1 : 1 500 000
Indonesia **Java - Nusa Tenggara**
  1 : 1 500 000
Indonesia **Bali - Lombok**
  1 : 180 000
Indonesia **Kalimantan**
  1 : 1 500 000
Indonesia **Java - Bali** 1 : 650 000
Indonesia **Sulawesi** 1 : 1 500 000
Indonesia **Irian Jaya - Maluku**
  1 : 1 500 000
Jakarta 1 : 22 500
Japan 1 : 1 500 000
Kenya 1 : 1 100 000
Korea 1 : 1 500 000

Malaysia 1 : 1 500 000
West Malaysia 1 : 650 000
Manila 1 : 17 500
Mexico 1 : 2 500 000
Myanmar *(Burma)* 1 : 1 500 000
Nepal 1 : 500 000 / 1 : 1 500 000
Nepal Trekking **Khumbu Himal -**
 Solu Khumbu 1 : 75 000
New Zealand 1 : 1 250 000
Pakistan 1 : 1 500 000
Peru - **Ecuador** 1 : 2 500 000
Philippines 1 : 1 500 000
Singapore 1 : 22 500
Southeast Asia 1 : 4 000 000
South Pacific Islands 1 : 13 000 000
Sri Lanka 1 : 450 000
Taiwan 1 : 400 000
Tanzania - Rwanda, Burundi
  1 : 1 500 000
Thailand 1 : 1 500 000
Uganda 1 : 700 000
Venezuela - Guyana, Suriname,
  French Guiana 1 : 2 500 000
Vietnam, Laos, Cambodia
  1 : 1 500 000

FORTHCOMING

Bolivia, Paraguay 1 : 2 500 000
Chile 1 : 2 500 000
Cuba 1 : 775 000

Nelles Maps are top quality cartography!
Relief mapping, kilometer charts and tourist attractions.
Always up-to-date!

Explore the World

NELLES GUIDES

AVAILABLE TITLES

Australia
Bali / Lombok
Berlin and Potsdam
Brazil
Brittany
Burma → Myanmar
California
  Las Vegas, Reno,
  Baja California
Cambodia / Laos
Canada
  Ontario, Québec,
  Atlantic Provinces
Canada
  Pacific Coast, the Rockies,
  Prairie Provinces, and
  the Territories
Canary Islands
Caribbean
  The Greater Antilles,
  Bermuda, Bahamas
Caribbean
  The Lesser Antilles
China – Hong Kong
Corsica
Costa Rica
Crete
Croatia – Adriatic Coast
Cyprus
Egypt
Florida

Greece – The Mainland
Greek Islands
Hawai'i
Hungary
India
  Northern, Northeastern
  and Central India
India – Southern India
Indonesia
  Sumatra, Java, Bali,
  Lombok, Sulawesi
Ireland
Israel - with Excursions
  to Jordan
Kenya
London, England and
  Wales
Malaysia - Singapore
  - Brunei
Maldives
Mexico
Morocco
Moscow / St. Petersburg
Munich
  Excursions to Castles,
  Lakes & Mountains
Myanmar (Burma)
Nepal
New York – City and State
New Zealand
Norway
Paris
Philippines

Portugal
Prague / Czech Republic
Provence
Rome
Scotland
South Africa
South Pacific Islands
Spain – Pyrenees, Atlantic
  Coast, Central Spain
Spain
  Mediterranean Coast,
  Southern Spain,
  Balearic Islands
Sri Lanka
Sweden
Syria – Lebanon
Tanzania
Thailand
Turkey
Tuscany
U.S.A.
  The East, Midwest and South
U.S.A.
  The West, Rockies and Texas
Vietnam

FORTHCOMING

Cuba
Dominican Republic
Peru
Poland

Nelles Guides – authoritative, informed and informative.
Always up-to-date, extensively illustrated, and with first-rate relief maps.
256 pages, approx. 150 color photos, approx. 25 maps.